# Since we are Justified by Faith

## Justification in the Theologies of the Protestant Reformations

T0385274

A full listing of titles in this series
appears at the end of this book

# Since we are Justified by Faith

## Justification in the Theologies of the Protestant Reformations

Edited by Michael Parsons

Foreword by Keith G. Jones

**Paternoster:**
*thinking faith*

Paternoster is an imprint of Authentic Media
52 Presley Way, Crownhill, Milton Keynes, Bucks, MK8 0ES

www.authenticmedia.co.uk
Authentic Media is a division of Koorong UK, a company limited by guarantee

09 08 07 06 05 04 03  8 7 6 5 4 3 2 1

**British Library Cataloguing in Publication Data** A catalogue record for this
book is available from the British Library

ISBN 978–1–84227–777–5

Typeset by Michael Parsons
Printed and bound in Great Britain for Paternoster

*To Peter Parkinson*

*with gratitude for introducing me to the grace of God
in the writings of John Calvin*

'Faith alone, without works, justifies, frees, and saves'—Martin Luther

'If, in short, we partake of Christ, we shall in him possess all heavenly
treasures . . . that lead us into life and salvation'—John Calvin

# Series Preface

This series complements the specialist series of Studies in Evangelical History and Thought and Studies in Baptist History and Thought for which Paternoster is becoming increasingly well known by offering works that cover the wider field of Christian history and thought. It encompasses accounts of Christian witness at various periods, studies of individual Christians and movements, and works which concern the relations of church and society through history, and the history of Christian thought.

The series includes monographs, revised dissertations and theses, and collections of papers by individuals and groups. As well as 'free standing' volumes, works on particular running themes are being commissioned; authors will be engaged for these from around the world and from a variety of Christian traditions.

A high academic standard combined with lively writing will commend the volumes in this series both to scholars and to a wider readership

# Series Editors

# CONTENTS

# PREFACE

We used to speak of the Reformation as though it was a monolithic, uniform phenomenon that spread through Europe from a central point during the sixteenth century. Not so, now, though. We have come slowly to understand that the theologies that made an impact during these tumultuous years were diverse and often in conflict with one another. It is better to speak of reformations as a plural term. And the plurality of ideas was never more clear, nor divisive, perhaps, than over the doctrine of justification by faith. This present volume is, in part, an attempt to recognize that diversity. It also recognizes the central significance of the doctrine of justification to Christian theology, to life, to witness and to worship, and the watershed that the sixteenth century was for this biblical teaching.

We recognize, too, the present academic and ecclesial debate about the true meaning of the Apostle Paul's doctrine of justification by faith, and its inevitable application and ramifications in church life, its preaching and, perhaps, even its mission. This volume seeks to be a peripheral part of that argument and to add to our understanding; not because the reformers always got things right, but because we cannot afford to ignore the strenuous efforts of these men to think biblically. They certainly have something to teach us today—their faithful reading of Scripture, their humility when faced with God's Word, their centralizing of Jesus Christ, their oftentimes over-enthusiasm, and their deep commitment to what they thought to be right, all speak to us of people who were energized by the Holy Spirit in their day and in their culture as we should be today.

I am very grateful to the contributors to this project. The chapters were all originally papers given at the Evangelical Theological Society's Annual Conference, held in Atlanta in 2010—a conference I was privileged to attend. The papers have been reworked, enhanced and enlarged to fit better into an academic book such as the present one. They demonstrate attention to detail, a profound understanding and a commitment to the subject. I am grateful, too, to Keith Jones for taking the time and trouble to read the whole manuscript and in writing the Foreword.

Thank you, too, to Rob Bootes of Koorong and Authentic Media for allowing me to attend the Evangelical Theological Society's conference. It is a particular privilege to speak to authors, publishers and potential writers at such an austere gathering.

Particular thanks go, as always, to my wife, Becky, and to my children, Chris and Katy, for their love and support. They know how much sixteenth century theology means to me. And they share in the Lord's grace found in Jesus Christ, 'through whom we have gained access by faith into this grace in which we now stand' (Rom. 5.2).

But, mostly, may this short volume add to our understanding of Paul's great doctrine of justification by faith and may it, in some small way, motivate us, first, to glorify the Lord who gives us salvation freely in Christ and, second, to be robustly missional in our own time.

*Michael Parsons*
*Didcot, Oxfordshire, 2012*

# FOREWORD

There are great themes of evangelical faith which believers regularly refer to in an almost shorthand way, sometimes reducing an important and vital area of theological exposition to the equivalent of an advertising strap-line and some might judge 'justification by faith' to be such a phrase.[1]

It might be argued that the great theme of justification can be subject to a relative minimalisation on the grounds that all women and men of faith immediately claim to understand both the full biblical dimension and subsequent theological discourse of the phrase across two millennia and that this is done in the twinkling of an eye.

This is to make a grievous error. For the theology of justification has a long history of discussion and of being expounded amongst some of the greatest of Christian thinkers down through the ages and like a great mountain emerging from the plain, merits observation and reflection from more than one vista, or fixed position. This volume seeks to do that, even if focusing on a particular era in the narrative of Christian history and life.

The biblical expression of justification is closely related to the concept of rightousness and both have their roots in the New Testament Greek word *dikaiosunē*, 'to be made righteous,' as applied to human beings. The theology of being in the right, or righteous, when tested, examined or judged by the one true God, is a deep and abiding concept at the heart of the covenantal relationship between God and the Hebrew people. This was explored and re-evaluated by the Apostle Paul, who declared in Romans 3.23-24 that 'all have sinned and fall short of the Glory of God; they are now justified by his grace as a gift' (NRSV). This Pauline imagery and adjustment of the Old Testament covenantal concept of justification[2] has been central to much theological discourse down through the Christian centuries, with key people such as Augustine[3] having great influence, even through the Reformation era on such theologians as Tyndale and Cranmer. However, perhaps, for many, the theme of Justification reaches its zenith of discussion in Reformation times and in the subsequent lives of the magisterial and radical reformation churches. Today it is a central plank of belief amongst those who claim the name 'evangelical.'[4]

---

[1] Alister E McGrath, *Christian Theology: An Introduction* (Oxford: Blackwell, 1994), 437ff; James W. McClendon Jr., *Systematic Theology :Doctrine* (Nashville, TN: Abingdon Press, 1994), 2.111ff.

[2] Ralph P Martin, 'Justification', in Bruce M. Metzger and Michael D. Coogan (eds), *The Oxford Companion to the Bible* (Oxford: Oxford University Press, 1993), 405.

[3] See Peter Brown, *Augustine of Hippo* (Berkley, CA: University of California Press, 2000).

[4] Derek J. Tidball, *Who are the Evangelicals ?*(London: Marshall Pickering, 1994), 105.

xi

Within western Catholic theology and interpretation justification has been seen as faith furnished with love. Major Catholic theologians such as Hans Küng have sought to explore the theology expressed in the Pauline notion.[5] For the Protestant and Gathering church communities[6] justification by faith alone or *sola fide* has been a stance which has been important, if not foundational to the theology and life of the churches.

This present work seeks to explore 'justification' as it came to be understood by these diverse communities of Christian believers which arose out of the theological ferment of Europe in the critical years of the development of systems of theology amongst Luther and his followers; with the radical reformers; amongst those who emerged out of the reform occurring within the Swiss Cantons of Zürich, Berne, Basle and Geneva and those who drew from various wells of theology to develop the first theological ideas of the community we today call Anglican.

Within this book we are treated to an exploration of the theme of 'justification' from that crucial era and not only as initially understood and expounded by Luther, but in the dialogue between Luther and his younger colleague, Melanchthon. Here we can explore in a fresh way insights of two key thinkers. Yet, though we might suppose Lutheranism sets the ground rules of the exploration of the theme, this does not happen in isolation and so we realise other reformers such as Oecolampadius in Basle or, later, Bullinger in Zürich[7] also engage with justification by faith. Certainly, as this volume demonstrates, justification was a theme worthy of exploration and exposition by radical reformers such as Pilgram Marpeck. He takes an interesting and divergent view from the Lutheran norm proposing that justification restores the *imago Dei* in the baptized believer. Then, of course, we cannot ignore the fact that biblical and theological exploration of the theme is central to the work of Jean Calvin and the Reformed church in Geneva. Finally, amongst the English reformers such as Tyndale, Cranmer and Hooker, the topic receives notable

---

[5] Hans Küng, *Justification* (London: Thomas Nelson, 1964).

[6] Whilst many regard all Christian traditions arising in the sixteenth century as being simply Protestant, there is a growing body of scholarly opinion which divides the streams of Christianity emerging from Europe at this time into two larger families. The Magisterial Protestants—Lutheran, Reformed and possibly Anglican—and the Radical Reformers, the Anabaptists, the Spiritualists, Mennonites and Baptists. For this second group various names have been used including 'Believer's Church,' 'baptistic churches,' 'Pneumatic churches'. My preference is 'Gathering churches'. See John H.Y. Briggs (ed), *A Dictionary of European Baptist Life and Thought* (Milton Keynes: Paternoster, 2009), 219.

[7] Henrich Bullinger and his writing *Decades* was prescribed as essential reading after the Bible for would-be preachers by Archbishop Whitgift during Elizabethan times in England. See G.W. Bromiley, *Zwingli and Bullinger* (Philadelphia: Westminster Press, 1953), 283.

attention, drawing on the theology of Augustine as well as the newer continental insights.

Hopefully, as we imbibe the scholarly reflections within these pages, like the reformers and radical reformers of old, our understanding of 'justification' will be enhanced and enriched and we will see more than one vista of this particular theological mountain and, in so doing, readers will gain a greater perception of the depth of the activity of God in and through the Lord Jesus Christ.

*Keith G. Jones*
*Prague*
*Epiphany 2012*

# CONTRIBUTORS
## (IN ALPHABETICAL ORDER)

**Mary Patton Baker** is Deacon at All Souls Anglican Church in Wheaton, and a PhD candidate at Wheaton College, Illinois.

**Jeff Fisher** is a Ph.D. candidate at Trinity Evangelical Divinity School in Deerfield, Illinois, USA.

**André Gazal** is Professor of Historical Theology, Northland International University, Dunbar, WI, USA.

**David W. Hall** is Senior Pastor at Midway Presbyterian Church, Powder Springs, GA, USA.

**Keith G. Jones** is Rector and Course Leader in Baptist and Anabaptist Studies at the International Baptist Theological Seminary, Prague, Czech Republic.

**Kirk R. MacGregor** is Adjunct Professor of Theology at Trinity Christian College and Adjunct Professor of Religion at Carthage College, USA.

**Cameron A. MacKenzie** is Forrest E. and Francis H. Ellis Professor of Historical Theology, Concordia Theological Seminary, Fort Wayne, Indiana, USA.

**Aaron O'Kelly** is Instructor of Bible/Theology and Latin at Augustine School in Jackson, Tennessee, USA.

**Michael Parsons** is the Commissioning Editor for Paternoster, and an Associate Research Fellow at Spurgeon's College, London, UK.

**Bonnie L. Pattison** has taught Theology at Wheaton College, North Park University in Chicago, and the Cameroon Baptist Theological Seminary in West Africa.

**Timothy Shaun Price** is a PhD student in Practical Theology, Aberdeen University, Scotland.

**H. Chris Ross** teaches Humanities for Brazos Christian School in Bryan, Texas.

**Karin Spiecker Stetina** is Adjunct Professor at Wheaton College, USA, and an Associate Editor for Luther Digest.

# ABBREVIATIONS

| | |
|---|---|
| CNTC | *Calvin's New Testament Commentaries*, 12 vols (ed. David W. Torrance and Thomas F. Torrance. (Grand Rapids: Eerdmans, 1960). |
| CO | *Ioannis Calvini Opera Quae Supersunt Omnia.*, 59 vols., *Corpus Reformatorum* (ed. Guilielmus Baum, August Eduard Cunitz, and Eduard Reuss: Bad Feilnbach, Germany: Schmidt Periodicals, 1990). |
| CR | Corpus Reformatorum (Halle: C. A. Schwetschke, 1834-1900; reprint, New York: Johnston Reprint, 1964). |
| CTS | *Calvin's Commentaries* from the Calvin Translation Society, 1843-55. |
| DB | *Deutsche Bibel*, that part of the Weimar edition devoted to Luther's German Bible. |
| 1536 *Inst.* | *Institutes of the Christian Religion, 1536* (ed. and trans., Ford Lewis Battles; H.H. Meeter Center for Calvin Studies; Grand Rapids: Eerdmans, 1986). |
| 1541 *Inst.* | *Institutes of the Christian Religion: 1541 French Edition*, (trans. Elsie Anne McKee: Grand Rapids: Eerdmans, 2009). |
| 1559 *Inst.* | *Institutes of the Christian Religion, 1559* (ed. John T. McNeill, trans. Ford Lewis Battles: Philadelphia: Westminster Press, 1960). |
| LW | Jaroslav Pelikan and Helmut T. Lehmann (eds), *Luther's Works* (55 vols; St. Louis: Concordia, and Philadelphia: Fortress Press, 1955-86). |
| T & T | *Calvin's Tracts and Treatises*. Selected Works of John Calvin. Volume 2 (trans. Henry Beveridge: Edinburgh: Calvin Translation Society, 1858). |
| WA | *D. Martin Luthers Werke, kritische Gesamtausgabe* (Weimar: Hermann Böhlaus Nachfolger, 1883-). |

# CHAPTER 1

## 'Everything is forgiven by grace.'[1] Justification in the Reformation—a brief introduction

### Michael Parsons

Martin Luther, John Calvin and the other sixteenth century magisterial reformers and Anabaptist dissenters appear to have gleaned their understanding of what it is to be justified before God primarily from the Scriptures, the Word of God. Some reformers filtered their understanding through theological works such as those of Augustine, Bernard of Clairvaux, and other important voices, towards the diversely nuanced shapes it took amongst them.[2] Generally, then, the doctrine of justification by grace through faith became central to the reform movement in almost all its guises and crucial to preaching and to social change in the period.

In this short introductory essay I propose to move from a comment or two about Paul's doctrine of justification, as I understand it, to the importance of that teaching in the Reformation movements of the sixteenth century. Whilst touching on the current debate about justification in the Pauline corpus, the purpose of the essay is not to enter that controversy, but rather to devote space to that doctrine in the reformers' teaching. It was so central and foundational to reform—reform of theology, of preaching, of ecclesiastical, political, social and familial life and piety—that it deserves to be taken seriously. It seems to me that as the so-called 'traditional' understanding of justification comes under fire, the Reformation as a watershed moment in that understanding has by some been exposed to critical caricature and false judgment. This should not be al-

---

[1] Martin Luther, *LW* 32.227.

[2] See Else M.W. Pedersen, 'Justification and Grace. Did Luther Discover a New Theology or Did He Discover Anew Theology of Justification and Grace?' *Studia Theologica* 57 (2003), 143-61. Some of that nuanced diversity is clear in the present volume. Also, J. David Lawrence, 'Medieval Refinements in Augustinian Theology. Scholastic Foundations for the Reformation,' *Fides et Historia* 33.2 (2001), 53-62; A.N.S. Lane, 'The Role of Scripture in Calvin's Doctrine of Justification', in C. Raynal (ed.), *John Calvin and the Interpretation of Scripture* (Grand Rapids: Calvin Studies Society, 2006), 368-84.

lowed to continue without a very much closer reading of justification by grace through faith in this marvelous, yet troubled and volatile, period of history.[3]

## The Pauline doctrine

The Old and New Testaments both delineate the foundational issue that prevails for humanity as the question of how guilty sinners can be acquitted and restored to a relationship with an infinitely righteous and just God. And, fundamentally, justification by grace through faith is the Pauline answer to this troubling question. This is stated clearly in the following apostolic conclusion.

> Therefore, since we are justified by faith we have peace with God through our Lord Jesus Christ through whom we have gained access by faith into this grace in which we now stand (Rom. 5.1).

Justification, then, is a fairly nuanced Pauline image that seeks to convey a thoroughly complex situation in the salvific and eschatological relationship between the human and the divine. It is, therefore, a metaphor that carries an enormous weight.[4] Its broad characteristics (seen in the brief quotation from Romans, above) are the centrality and significance of Jesus Christ, the importance of faith and the resultant peace and grace, together with a positional assurance ('this grace in which we now stand').

The Apostle Paul's terms for 'justification' are concentrated in his epistles to the Romans and to the Galatians. Indeed, 'to justify' is found only outside of Galatians and Romans at 1 Corinthians 6.11, 'You were washed, you were sanctified, you were justified in the name of the Lord Jesus Christ and by the Spirit of our Lord,' and at Titus 3.7, 'having been justified by his grace'. However, though justification appears as a word primarily in the Pauline corpus, it has its important antecedents in the Old Testament terms for righteousness (Hebrew, *tsedeq* and *tsedeqah*), the root idea of which is conformity to a norm.[5] Religiously, righteousness (right behavior) is the standard God has set—this norm is both determined by God's character and is entirely consistent with it. The righteous person is the one who in God's estimation meets his standard, and thus is in the right with God (Ps. 9.4-8; 50.4-6; Isa. 59.17-19; cf., Hab. 1.13.)

---

[3] We should remember, of course, that the diverse understandings of the doctrine of justification were, in themselves, somewhat divisive in this period.

[4] Geoffrey Wainwright, *Doxology. A Systematic Theology* (London: Epworth Press, 1980), 410, is right to assert that justification 'is part of a complex of images which includes also redemption and liberation'. See, also, the short, incisive treatment in Peter Lewis, *The Glory of Christ* (Chicago: Moody Press, 1997), 321-34.

[5] The righteous man is the one who fulfills the demands of a relationship in which he stands, e.g., Tamar is more righteous than Judah because she was more faithful to family relationships than he was (Gen. 38.26); David was said to be righteous because he didn't slay Saul, with whom he stood in a special relationship (1 Sam. 24.17, 26.23).

If righteousness is conformity to God's standards, then justification will be the process in which conformity is either attained, or declared to be attained. It is important to remember that current scholarship has noted that Old Testament texts on righteousness emphasize the context as being God's covenant relationship with his people. That is, righteousness is appropriate *covenant* behavior—behavior suitable to the relationship he has graciously established; for instance, being loyal, steadfast, merciful and faithful (see Deut. 32.4-5). In other words, righteousness is not simply to be right with God, but to be related to God's own righteousness, and so to be righteous.

Paul's use of 'justification' is, of course, seminal to our own thinking and that of the Reformation theologies. In the largely forensic metaphor, the Apostle employs the picture of a courtroom in which God is the Judge. That is to say, to declare that someone is justified is to say that they are acquitted at the bench of God's justice.[6] Justification amounts to God's declaration that a person is right with God. It is the normal word to use when the accused is declared to be 'Not guilty.' This is confirmed by the phrase that Paul uses—'in the sight of God' (significantly, in reformational parlance, *coram Deo*—humanity before an all-seeing and judging God). At Romans 2.13, for instance, he states that 'it is not those who hear the law who are righteous in God's sight, but it is those who obey the law who are declared righteous' and, again, at Romans 3.20, where he repeats the negative side of the comment, 'Therefore, no one will be declared righteous in God's sight by observing the law.' It is, also, strikingly seen in the Apostle's use of the word in the following eschatologically-laden remark, 'Who will bring any charge against those whom God has chosen? It is God who justifies. Who is he that condemns?' (Rom. 8.33-34).

The characteristics of Paul's use of 'justification' appear to be as follows:
(a) justification presupposes God's anger against sin;
(b) the objects of justification are those who are termed the 'ungodly' or 'sinners' (Rom. 4.5);
(c) justification is intrinsically and specifically a metaphor with a forensic aspect to it (Rom. 5.9-10, 8.33-34), though it has other facets, too—redemptive-historical ('in Christ'),[7] and imputative, for example;
(d) justification is clearly initiated by God (Rom. 3.24);

---

[6] The Hebrew word *sādēq* and the Greek, *dikaioō* bear forensic meaning: pronounce, accept, treat as righteous. Herman Ridderbos, *Paul. An Outline of his Theology* (London: SPCK, 1977), 174, is adamant, 'It is . . . out of the question that by "to justify" here [Rom. 4.5] anything other or more is intended than what it means for Paul over and over again: acquittal in the judgment of God.' Gordon J. Spykman, *Reformational Theology. A New Paradigm for Doing Dogmatics* (Grand Rapids: Eerdmans, 1992), 496, speaks of justification as 'the reassuring declaration of God's gracious act of reinstatement'.

[7] Wainwright, *Doxology*, 411, 'Out of sheer grace God has declared us righteous in our faith-union with Christ.'

(e) justification is eschatological (Rom. 2.13, 5.19, 8.33f.; Gal. 4.4-5)—righteousness is something 'for which we hope' (Gal. 5.5). That is, it appears to have a future referent as well as having to do with the beginning of the Christian life;

(f) we receive the fruit of justification—for example, we are saved from divine anger and condemnation, we are given forgiveness, reconciliation, eternal life, and so on (Rom. 5.9; 8.1);

(g) in the Apostle's Christ-centered theology, the ground for our justification is firmly in the death of Christ (Rom. 3.24-25; 5.9; Gal. 3.13, 4.4-5). That is, importantly, God's justifying work is outside of us (*extra nos*)—in Christ. Also, as Simon Gathercole puts it, 'Being "in Christ" means participating in the sphere of righteousness that he has opened up and that he defines';[8]

(h) the means of our justification is faith; that is, faith enabled by the Holy Spirit (Rom. 3.24-25, 28, 4.5; Gal. 2.16). It is worth noting, though, as Alister McGrath points out, that 'not all Paul's statements regarding justification are specifically linked with the theme of faith';[9]

(i) justification is a matter of covenant relationship—that is, justification is concerned with covenant membership and identity;

(j) justification is not to be detached from the whole of salvation—including forgiveness, restoration of fellowship, adoption, eternal life, sanctification,[10] glorification, hope, and so on. Mark Seifrid, understandably, in this context, speaks of the traditional order of salvation (*ordo salutis*) as not so much a series as a comprehensive act of God in Christ;[11]

(k) importantly, there can be no justification of the sinner which is not simultaneously a justification of God in his wrath against the sinner.[12]

A key Pauline passage is Romans 3.21-26 in which we can see many of these characteristics.

[21]But now apart from the law the righteousness of God has been made known, to which the law and the prophets testify. [22]This righteousness is given through faith

---

8  Simon Gathercole, 'The Doctrine of Justification in Paul and Beyond: Some Proposals', in Bruce L. McCormack (ed.), *Justification in Perspective. Historical Developments and Contemporary Challenges* (Grand Rapids: Baker Academic / Edinburgh: Rutherford House, 2006), 222.

9  See Alister McGrath, 'Justification', in Gerald F. Hawthorne, Ralph P. Martin and Daniel G. Reid (eds), *Dictionary of Paul and his Letters* (Leicester: InterVarsity Press, 1993), 517[b]-523[b], specifically 518[b].

10  We might say that justification is the divine indicative and that sanctification is the divine imperative. See Michael Parsons, 'Being Precedes Act: Indicative and Imperative in Paul's Writing', in Brian S. Rosner (ed.), *Understanding Paul's Ethics: Twentieth Century Approaches* (Grand Rapids: Eerdmans / Carlisle: Paternoster, 1995), 217–47.

11  Mark A. Seifrid, *Christ, Our Righteousness. Paul's Theology of Justification* (Downers Grove: InterVarsity Press, 2000), 173.

12  Seifrid, *Christ*, 171.

in Jesus Christ to all who believe. There is no difference between Jew and gentile, [23]for all have sinned and fall short of the glory of God, [24]and all are justified freely by his grace through the redemption that came by Christ Jesus. [25]God presented Christ as a sacrifice of atonement, through the shedding of his blood—to be received by faith. He did this to demonstrate his justice, because in his forbearance he had left the sins committed beforehand unpunished—[26]he did it to demonstrate his justice at the present time, so as to be just and the one who justifies those who have faith in Jesus.

Many of these characteristics will be embedded in the reformers' understanding and teaching on justification: notably, the extreme predicament in which fallen men and women reside outside of Christ, the divine justice, the centrality of Jesus Christ and our union with him, the grace of the triune God towards us, the forensic nature of justification, the importance of faith, and so on.

The so-called 'new perspective' on Paul[13] argues that the traditional reading of the Apostle has been mistaken. It is said to be mistaken on the basis of four arguments. First, because of the Old Testament stress on covenant-relationship, it argues that Second Temple Judaism was gracious, not legalistic, as has previously been thought. Second, it argues that the model of Christianity in which one moves from the failure of the law to the grace of God does not faithfully represent Paul's own experience—particularly that on the Damascus road, which appears to be all about grace. Third, it claims that the Apostle is actually using boundary markers between Jewish Christians and gentile Christians rather than the law *per se*. And, finally, it asserts that Paul has been read through Luther's interpretation and that of the Reformation, and that this reading appears to be somewhat anti-Semitic.

Paul Zahl criticized the 'new perspective' in an article in 2001 and concluded—rather optimistically, as it turns out—that the 'new perspective' would come to nothing.[14] Six years later Karl Donfried asked, 'Did Luther really get it

---

[13]  See the following early seminal works: J.D.G. Dunn, 'The New Perspective on Paul,' *Bulletin of the John Rylands University Library of Manchester* 65 (1983), 95-122; E.P. Sanders, *Paul and Palestinian Judaism* (Philadelphia: SCM, 1977); idem, *Paul, the Law, and the Jewish People* (Philadelphia: Fortress Press, 1983); K. Stendahl, *Paul Among Jews and Gentiles* (Philadelphia: Fortress Press, 1976); N.T. Wright, 'The Paul of History and the Apostle of Faith,' *Tyndale Bulletin* 29 (1978), 61-88. See, also, the later works by N.T. Wright, *The Climax of the Covenant: Christ and the Law in Pauline Theology* (Minneapolis: Fortress Press, 1991); 'New Perspectives on Paul', in McCormack (ed.), *Justification in Perspective*, 243-264; *Justification: God's Plan and Paul's Vision* (Downers Grove, IL: InterVarsity Press Academic, 2009).

[14]  The summary in the preceding paragraph is largely an abridgement of Paul F.M. Zahl, 'Mistakes of the New Perspective on Paul,' *Themelios* 27.1 (2001), 5-11. McGrath, 'Justification,' 523[a], sees it differently, stating that 'It is likely that the years ahead will witness still further wrestling with this aspect of Pauline thought.'

all wrong?'[15] He concludes that the diverse manifestations of the 'new perspective' are characterized by a minimalist view of justification, a redefinition of the function of the law, an alternative translation of *pistis christou* and a reductionist reinterpretation of the death of Christ. Following a thorough discussion of the reformer's exegesis of the salient passages in Romans, he concludes—rightly, I think—that Luther got the essence of Paul's teaching correct.

Other writers want to argue against the traditional reading of Paul on different grounds altogether. For example, Clark Pinnock and Robert Brow argue on more generalized reasons in their book, *Unbounded Love*.[16] They claim, rather surprisingly, I think, that the biblical notions of justice and judgment are *not* so much law-court categories, but more words of salvation.[17] They contrast the law-court image with a family model.

> In the family model, the love of God is viewed like that of a loving parent encouraging children to become loving. Any judging of such a parent is part of loving. This is in contrast to the judicial model, where wrath flows against sinners in a courtroom setting as people are condemned before an awesome judge. In that picture God starts loving only when his justice has been satisfied. Is there any doubt which picture fits the biblical revelation?[18]

Briefly, in response to this, we would have to ask, though, whether this caricature of the traditional reading is even close to that which was being taught, say, by the reformers in sixteenth century Europe. Does God not initiate the whole scene through his love and grace? Is it not God who sends his Son, Jesus Christ? Does he not justify sinners (the ungodly, the unrighteous) in his mercy? Is it not God the heavenly Father who responds to sinners in fatherly love? The conclusion is difficult to avoid that maybe a distortion of the traditional view makes an alternative image easier to construct.

### Reformation and justification

Whether Luther discovered a new theology or discovered one which had been all but lost in past ecclesiastical generations,[19] it is clear that Luther, and other reformers following,[20] found in the Apostle Paul's image a crucial element of

---

[15] Karl P. Donfried, 'Paul and the Revisionists: Did Luther Really Get it All Wrong?' *Dialog* 46.1 (2007), 31-39.

[16] Clark H. Pinnock and Robert C. Brow, *Unbounded Love* (Downers Grove: InterVarsity Press, 1994).

[17] Pinnock and Brow, *Unbounded Love*, 75.

[18] Pinnock and Brow, *Unbounded Love*, 74.

[19] See the discussion in Pedersen, 'Justification and Grace,' 143-61. See, also, Heiko Oberman, *The Dawn of the Reformation* (Edinburgh: T. & T. Clark, 1992), 104-25.

[20] Other reformers followed Luther, but not all. For example, some Anabaptists, including Hans Denck and Hans Hut, rejected the Reformation doctrines of *sola scriptura* and justification by faith. See, Rudolph Heinze, *Reform and Conflict. From the Medieval World to the Wars of Religion* (Grand Rapids: Baker, 2005), 147.

the Gospel of Christ.[21] Within the diverse nuances that existed in Reformation definitions of the doctrine, justification had a central core that remained the same. Luther places justification squarely in the post-fallen divine-human relationship, speaking of the 'proper subject of theology' as being humanity 'guilty of sin and condemned, and God the Justifier and Savior'.[22] In the following longer quotation he spells this out in the context of the oppression that comes from the application of the law to our own self-righteousness.

> To consciences so oppressed, terrified, miserable, anxious and afflicted, there was no need to inculcate the law. The great necessity then was to present the other part of the teaching of Christ in which he commands us to preach the remission of sin in his name, so that those who are already sufficiently terrified might learn not to despair but to take refuge in the grace and mercy offered by Christ.[23]

In his preface to his *Lectures on Galatians* (1535) the Reformer states that the doctrine of justification teaches 'that we are redeemed from sin, death, and the devil and endowed with eternal life, not through ourselves and certainly not through our works . . . but through the help of another, the only Son of God, Jesus Christ'.[24] Luther's emphasis is clear: 'God *alone*,' he says, 'justifies us *solely* by his grace through Christ.'[25]

Similarly, Luther's close friend and colleague, Philip Melanchthon, comments that 'we teach that a man is justified when, with his conscience terrified by the preaching of penitence, he takes heart and believes that he has a gracious God for Christ's sake'.[26] According to Melanchthon—as with Luther—God clothes the sinner with the alien righteousness of Christ:

> [T]he Mediator's entire obedience, from his incarnation until resurrection, is the true justification which is pleasing to God, and is the merit for us. God forgives our sins and accepts us, in that he imputes righteousness to us for the sake of the Son, although we are still weak and fearful. We must, however, accept this imputed righteousness with faith.[27]

---

[21] Philip Melanchthon characterized the Reformation as the age 'in which God recalled the church to its origins (*in qua Deus Ecclesiam iterum ad fonts revocavit*)'—quoted by W.K. Ferguson, *The Renaissance in Historical Thought. Five Centuries of Interpretation* (Cambridge, MA: Houghton Mifflin, 1948), 52. Going back to Paul's writing was part of the search for the church's origins.

[22] *WA* $40^2$.328.

[23] *WA* $39^1$.571, translated and quoted by James A. Nestingen, 'Challenges and Responses in the Reformation,' *Interpretation* 46.3 (1992), 251.

[24] *LW* 27.145.

[25] *LW* 26.99, emphasis original.

[26] Quoted by Brian A. Gerrish, 'The Chief Article—Then and *Now*,' *Journal of Religion* 63 (1983), 359.

[27] *Loci Communes* (1555) (ed. Clyde Manschrenk: Grand Rapids: Baker, 1982), 161.

John Calvin, a second generation reformer, gives two definitions in his major work, *The Institutes of the Christian Religion* (1556).[28] First, he has a brief definition in which he asserts that justification is 'the acceptance with which God receives us into his favor as righteous men'.[29] His longer definition, coming a little later, states,

> We define justification as follows: the sinner, received into communion with Christ, is reconciled to God by his grace, which cleansed by Christ's blood, he obtains forgiveness of sins, and clothed with Christ's righteousness as if it were his own, he stands confident before the heavenly judgment seat.[30]

To be justified, for Calvin, is to be 'accepted, cleansed in him [Christ], to be forgiven, to be clothed with the righteousness of Christ' and to receive 'peace and quiet joy' and a clear conscience.[31]

A brief and cursory glance at these quotations from Luther, Melanchthon and Calvin reveals clearly that justification was not *merely* a forensic category to them, not *simply* a technical term or metaphor. Captured within this image is an existential reality, the receiving of a Gospel gift, even of Jesus Christ himself. What is evident is that each theologian stresses the grace of God in Christ and the sinner's union with him in reception of his blessing—forgiveness of sin; true freedom[32] from sin, guilt, death, the devil; the gift of eternal life; imputed righteousness (the alien righteousness of Christ, *aliena iustitia Christi*), and above all, perhaps, acceptance in the sight of God—all through the selfless life and death of Jesus Christ.[33]

So, two brief comments, at least, are pertinent at this point. First, the context for the reformational doctrine of justification (as with the Pauline usage) is not entirely forensic. Indeed, the forensic image appears to be secondary to what it seeks to convey—this, after all, is the nature of metaphors. It is at its core relational. It has to do intrinsically with our union with Jesus Christ and his gracious union with us. Second, the experience of acceptance was crucially im-

---

[28] It is worth noting that the section on justification is one of the longest in the *Institutes*—chapters 11 to 29.

[29] *Inst* 3.11.2 (*OS* 4.183).

[30] *Inst* 3.17.8 (*OS* 4.260).

[31] *Inst* 3.13.5 (*OS* 4.220). Other reformers held to the doctrine of justification by faith, too—Guillaume Farel, Ulrich Zwingli, Martin Chemnitz, John Oecolampadius, Peter Martyr Vermigli, Katharina Schütz Zell, Martin Bucer, Andreas Bodenstein Karlstadt, Pilgram Marpeck, Richard Hooker, Thomas Cranmer, and others, though it does not appear to be central in the writings of Argula von Grumbach. See Peter Matheson, *Argula von Grumbach. A Woman's Voice in the Reformation* (Edinburgh: T. & T. Clark, 1995), 56-195.

[32] *Inst* 3.19.1 (*OS* 4.282), 'Freedom is especially an appendage [*appendix*] of justification and is of no little avail in understanding its power.'

[33] 'It is impossible for one to be a Christian unless he possesses Christ. If he possesses Christ, he possesses all the benefits of Christ'—*LW* 31.189-90 (*WA* 1.593). See, also, *LW* 26.130 (*WA* 40¹.229).

portant to believers receiving this doctrine. It was here that it all made sense; it was here where assurance of faith was discovered and certainty grasped. In this context, Philip Melanchthon, for example, says that 'justification is not the approval of a particular act but of the total person';[34] and, likewise, Luther in characteristic fashion, comments that 'A man is truly justified by faith in the sight of God, even if he finds only disgrace before man and in his own self.'[35] So faith (*fiducia*) becomes 'a daring confidence in God,' not a trust in one's self or one's works. In this context, David Steinmetz comments that 'Believers were not justified because they assented to saving truth; they were justified because they placed themselves unreservedly in the hands of a merciful God.'[36] The believer grasps hold of Christ, trusting that he is for them (*Christus pro Me*), for that is the only place they have to turn.

No wonder, then, that justification became so important to the reforming churches of the sixteenth century. Luther termed it 'the chief doctrine' of the faith.[37] 'Of this article nothing can be yielded, or surrendered,' he asserted, 'even though heaven and earth, and whatever else will not remain, should sink to ruin.'[38] Elsewhere, the Reformer speaks of justification as

> The master and prince, the lord, the ruler and the judge over all kinds of doctrines; it preserves and governs all church doctrine and raises up our conscience before God. Without this article the world is utter death and darkness.[39]

John Calvin articulates a similar thought, stating that the doctrine of justification is 'the main hinge on which religion turns (*praecipuum esse sustinendae religionis cardinem*)'.[40] T.H.L. Parker summarizes the Reformer's position: 'If we want the Christian religion to survive and flourish, Calvin is saying, we must put justification by faith alone at the heart of it: "For unless first of all you grasp where you stand with God and what his judgment on you is, you have no foundation on which your salvation may be established or on which *pietas* towards God may be raised" (*Inst* 3.9.1).'[41] Significantly, the doctrine becomes so important to the reforming process that the reformers claim central ground for it.

I would suggest that there are at least two reasons why the (re)discovery of the doctrine of justification by grace through faith was central to the Refor-

---

[34] Quoted in Gerrish, 'The Chief Article,' 367.
[35] Quoted by George Forell, 'Justification and Eschatology in Luther's Thought,' *Church History* 38.2 (1969), 173.
[36] The phrase 'a daring confidence in God' comes from David C. Steinmetz, 'The Intellectual Appeal of the Reformation,' *Theology Today* 57.4 (2001), 467.
[37] *LW* 23.129.
[38] *Book of Concord* (St Louis: Concordia Publishing House, 1950), 137.
[39] *WA* 39$^1$.205.
[40] *Inst* 3.11.1 (*OS* 4.182).
[41] T.H.L. Parker, *Calvin. An Introduction to His Thought* (London: Geoffrey Chapman, 1995), 96.

mation. The first is that the reformers discovered the doctrine in the Pauline corpus and then in other parts of Scripture, reading the Apostle's teaching retrospectively, as it were. The second is that justification by faith appeared to answer the gaping problem of the medieval penitential system. The former is a question of exegesis, the latter a question of pastoral integrity.

*Justification by grace through faith was discovered in Scripture*

It is worth remembering that the Reformation came about largely through a vigorous reading of the Scriptures, often accompanied by the careful and faithful preaching and lecturing on each book in turn. Primarily, then, the reformers were exegetes of the Scriptures. In Peter Matheson's words regarding the Wittenberg Reformer, 'Luther's supreme achievement was seen as letting the Word run free. . . . Perhaps the most pervasive image of the Reformation is that of the liberated Word of God.'[42] The reformers struggled to open up the Gospel to a new age and made themselves vulnerable in doing so. Many of them preached through Romans and Galatians (as well as other Old and New Testament books, of course). In them they found the Apostle's teaching on justification by faith and realized for themselves and their congregations the power of the Gospel of Jesus Christ—power to save and to liberate, power to clear consciences and to transform lives. In Romans, for example, Luther discovered an emphasis on the utter passivity of human beings in their justification, a stress on God's righteousness as *iustitia aliena*; abandoning the idea that by doing one's best (*facere quod in se est*) a person could somehow prepare for grace.[43] Whatever the difficulties regarding dates and the situation, it is fairly certain that Luther's breakthrough came from an examination of the meaning of Romans 1.17, 'For in the gospel the righteousness of God is revealed—a righteousness that is by faith from first to last, just as it is written: "The righteous will live by faith."' Philip Melanchthon also saw justification as the main theme of Paul's letter to the Romans. Indeed, as David Steinmetz points out, the Protestant pattern for justification by faith became the figure of Abraham, interpreted by Paul in Romans 4. He was justified solely by his faith—not his works, his circumcision, nor his obedience to the Mosaic Law (which had not at that time been given).[44]

Justification, for the reformers, was absolutely central to their understanding of what the Gospel is. It is worth noting, in the context of the Protestant elevation of the Gospel, that the phrase 'justification by faith' became for the re-

---

[42] Peter Matheson, *The Imaginative World of the Reformation* (Edinburgh: T. & T. Clark, 2000), 38. At its deepest level, this was an attempt to reroot the faith, to re-Christianize Europe. According to Scott Hendrix, 'Rerooting the Faith: The Reformation as Re-Christianization,' *Church History* 69.3 (2000), 561, 'They went about their task with zeal, planting a new and truer religion and denouncing the obstacles that stood in their way.'

[43] See Timothy George, 'Martin Luther', in J. P. Greenman and T. Larsen (eds), *Reading Romans Through the Centuries* (Grand Rapids: Brazos, 2005), 101-119.

[44] See Steinmetz, 'The Intellectual Appeal,' 467.

formers a phrase that conjured up the whole of the Gospel. Indeed, Brian Gerrish goes so far as to say that justification was identified with the Gospel and that other salvific themes tended to be subordinated to the doctrine of justification.[45] Scott Hendrix concurs, stating that the rerooting of Christianity 'required the recovery of the teaching and work of Jesus, which was often abbreviated in phrases like "preaching the gospel" or "justification by faith". For Luther and his followers, "justification by faith" was biblical code-language for "salvation for the sake of Christ alone".'[46]

For Luther, the Gospel is simply 'the message concerning Christ'.[47] 'The gospel,' he says, 'is a preaching of the incarnate Son of God, given to us without any merit on our part for salvation and peace. It is a word of salvation, a word of grace, a word of comfort, a word of joy.'[48] Little wonder, then, that in his *Lectures on Galatians* (1535) the Reformer defines the Gospel in terms that remind us of his definition of justification: 'The proper definition of the gospel is that it is the promise of Christ, which frees us from the terrors of the law, sin, death, and brings grace, forgiveness of sins, righteousness, and eternal life.'[49] The Gospel is God's proper work. It is the free and gracious gift of God to those who are without Christ and without hope. It is significant that Luther speaks here of the Gospel as 'a message,' 'preaching,' 'a word,' and 'a promise,' for there is only one true means of grace, for Luther—the voice of the living God. Again, the insights of Brian Gerrish are helpful. He says that grace 'comes as a message, a promise, a story, a word of God—in short, precisely as gospel'. If we are to be justified by faith (*fiducia*), faith needs to receive the divine communication of a gracious Father who cares for us in Jesus Christ. 'There has to be listening, understanding, behaving, trusting, obeying—in short, a faith that counts on the Word of God.'[50]

For Melanchthon, similarly, the Gospel of free forgiveness is the promise of justification to the unrighteous. He understood the Gospel as righteousness by faith and consolation of consciences.[51] Similarly, Calvin, argues that because Paul calls the Gospel 'the doctrine of faith' (1 Tim. 4.6) the Gospel must in-

---

[45] Gerrish, 'The Chief Article,' 355. Elvin W. Janetzki, 'The Place of the Historic Confessions in Christendom Today', in H.P. Hermann (ed.), *Theologia Crucis. Studies in Honour of Hermann Sasse* (Adelaide: Lutheran Publishing House, 1975), 101, asserts as much today: 'There is *no doctrine of the church apart from the doctrine of the Gospel*, for the church is the people of God created and sustained by the preaching of the Gospel and the administration of the sacraments,' emphasis added.
[46] Hendrix, 'Rerooting the Faith,' 566.
[47] *LW* 25.148.
[48] *LW* 31.231.
[49] *LW* 27.184.
[50] Gerrish, 'The Chief Article,' 367.
[51] See Heinz Scheible, 'Philip Melanchthon', in Carter Lindberg (ed.), *The Reformation Theologians* (Oxford: Blackwell, 2002), 67-82.

clude all the 'promises of free remission of sins'.[52] In it Christ offers us 'a present fullness of spiritual benefits'.[53] Preaching on Micah 2.6-7, particularly on the statement, 'the Word of God is good to those who walk uprightly,' Calvin asks what would happen if we were deprived of God's Word. He concludes that to be deprived of the Gospel is 'to be severed from salvation and all that is good'. It is to inherit hell itself.[54] The Reformer then elaborates on the Gospel and the divine intention.

[I]n ourselves we are already condemned. In what can our nature boast? We are already dead, being cursed of God in Adam. Yet God calls us to himself through his Word. He proclaims his desire to receive us in mercy. He longs to be our Father, though we are miserable creatures and are unworthy of the earth even sustaining us. Nevertheless, God wants to turn us into companions for his angels. Indeed, he wants to unite us so closely to our Lord Jesus Christ, his Son, as to make us members of his body.[55]

Calvin largely emphasizes the transforming nature of the Gospel, underlining and contrasting the state in which sinners are before they come to God (condemned, dead, cursed, miserable, unworthy) with the position in which they find themselves having been drawn by God through the Gospel (called, recipients of mercy, children of God, companions of angels, united to Christ, members of his body). The Reformer then explains how God accomplishes this:

To achieve this, he opens the way by granting us the forgiveness of our sins, by no longer imputing them to us, but by covering them with his infinite steadfast love.[56]

Calvin explains this last idea later as God covering sins 'by means of the righteousness and innocence of our Lord Jesus Christ, his Son'.[57] We see here clearly demonstrated that justification, for Calvin, though forensic at one level, predominantly demonstrates God's love and mercy in Christ. Indeed, Calvin seems here almost to identify 'infinite steadfast love' with 'the righteousness and innocence' of Christ—words that in the context exude the thought of justification, union with Christ and imputed righteousness.

---

[52] *Inst* 2.9.2 (*OS* 3.399).
[53] *Inst* 2.9.3 (*OS* 3.401).
[54] *Sermons on the Book of Micah* (trans. B.W. Farley: Phillipsburg: P&R, 2003), 105. On the Gospel and mission in Calvin's sermons, see Michael Parsons, *Calvin's Preaching on the Prophet Micah. The 1550-1551 Sermons in Geneva* (Lewiston: Edwin Mellen, 2006), 181-225.
[55] *Sermons*, 105-106. See, also, *Comm Matt.* 28.18, *CO* 45.821 (*CNTC* 3.250): '[God] opens heaven to admit to a blessed immortality with angels those who had formerly not only crawled on the earth but been plunged in the abyss of death.'
[56] *Sermons*, 106.
[57] *Sermons*, 106.

### *Justification by grace through faith answered penitential failure*

According to Alister McGrath the central question that was forced upon the church by the rise of humanism was, 'What must I, *as an individual*, do to be saved?' He concludes that this 'could not be answered with a great deal of confidence by the late medieval church'.[58] So, therefore, the crucial matter to be resolved in the sixteenth century church was the matter of the forgiveness of sins, the pardon of eternal guilt, and, more immediately, the alleviation of troubled consciences. The major theological and pastoral concern was, therefore, the true nature of penance. Anne Thayer, in her excellent work on penitence and the coming of the Reformation, underlines the fact that all the major reformers 'detested the late medieval sacrament of penance'.[59] Having examined the pervasiveness of penance in the period, and the characteristics of the medieval sermon collections, she summarizes in the following manner.

> While Protestants held a range of opinions concerning the alternatives to be set in place, they all identified two interrelated issues as the fatal flaws in the late medieval penitential system. The overriding pastoral issue was the lack of certainty of forgiveness for troubled consciences. . . . [Second] to ask the individual to make a personal contribution to his or her own salvation was to overestimate human abilities, underestimate the depth of sin and fail to recognize divine forgiveness.[60]

In contradiction to this, Thayer argues, the reformers contended that Christ had accomplished everything that was needed, and that this was to be personally appropriated by faith.[61] In other words, given the ecclesial situation, 'the new mode of justification made attractive sense to those raised on rigorist penitential preaching'.[62]

Justification was now defined as God's liberating act. Centralizing this doctrine was to give stability, certainty and assurance to those who trusted the divine offer and gift of Christ.[63] The distinction and tension between being right-

---

[58] A.E. McGrath, *Reformation Thought. An Introduction* (Oxford: Blackwell, 1993), 91, emphasis original.

[59] Anne T. Thayer, *Penitence, Preaching and the Coming of the Reformation* (Aldershot: Ashgate, 2002), 142.

[60] Thayer, *Penitence*, 143.

[61] Thayer, *Penitence*, 143. Later, speaking with reference to Luther, she says that 'Pastorally, he finds the divine promise of forgiveness with no human requirements a great comfort to consciences troubled by sin' (181).

[62] Thayer, *Penitence*, 194. Similarly, D. Cornick, 'The Reformation Crisis in Pastoral Care', in G.R. Evans (ed.), *A History of Pastoral Care* (London: Cassell, 2000), 223-51, argues that the doctrine of justification by faith laid waste the penitential system.

[63] See, on this, Bo Kristian Holm, 'Zur Funktion der Lehre bei Luther. Die Lehre als rettendes Gedankenbild gegen Sünde, Tod und Teufel,' *Kerygma und Dogma* 51.1 (2005), 17-32.

eous in Christ (*in Christo*) and being righteous in ourselves (*in nobis*) related now to a single anthropological reality 'within a complex Christological eschatology' in which believers could be certain of their standing before God in Christ—a standing that had come not through works, not through merit, but through grace alone.[64] Importantly, in this context, Martin Luther (reflecting the depths of his own experience, perhaps) asserts that, before God, 'There is no such thing as merit' and, therefore, that 'Everything is forgiven by grace.'[65] With this new and liberating assertion of grace over against merit came freedom to please God in working hard in this world to help the neighbor. Carter Lindberg sums this up, 'The doctrine of justification by grace alone through faith alone released energy for this world that had hitherto been devoted to achieving the next world. . . . [W]hatever a person did in the world that served the neighbor and helped build up the human community was pleasing to God.'[66]

The profound relevance of the doctrine of justification by faith is seen in the rhetorical questioning of Brian Gerrish in an excellent essay on sovereign grace:

> The crucial question is this: Who are the ones who are touched by grace? Is it those who, because their resources are limited, can climb no higher but may count on the assistance of grace because they have done all they can? Or is it those who can slip no lower because they have hit the bottom of frustration and despair and expect only condemnation? Is grace aid for the weak, or is it the promise of new life for the dead?[67]

---

[64] See George Hunsinger, 'A Tale of Two Simultaneities: Justification and Sanctification in Calvin and Barth', in Raynal (ed.), *John Calvin*, 225.

[65] *LW* 33.267, *LW* 32.227, respectively.

[66] Carter Lindberg, *The European Reformations* (Oxford: Blackwell, 1996), 363. See, also, Samuel Torvend, *Luther and the Hungry Poor. Gathered Fragments* (Minneapolis: Fortress Press, 2008), 25-42. The chapter's subtitle is 'The Social Implications of Justification by Grace.'

[67] Brian A. Gerrish, 'Sovereign Grace: Is Reformed Theology Obsolete? *Interpretation* 57 (2003), 45-57, specifically, 53. For other notable essays on the contemporary relevance of the doctrine, see, Brian A. Gerrish, 'The Chief Article—Then and *Now*,' *Journal of Religion* 63 (1983), 355-75; Wilfred Härle, 'Luthers reformatorische Entdeckung—dmals und heute,' *Zeitschrift für Theologie und Kirche* 99 (2002), 278-95; Martin R. Noland, 'Luther's Reformation and Its Ongoing Relevance Today,' *Logia* 13.4 (2004), 19-26; Theodor Dieter, 'Why Does Luther's Doctrine of Justification Matter Today?' in C. Helmer (ed.), *The Global Luther* (Minneapolis: Fortress Press, 2009), 189-209; Marcus P. Johnson, 'The Genius of Luther's Theology. A Wittenberg Way of Thinking for the Contemporary Church,' *Calvin Theological Journal* 44.1 (2009), 189-91.

The new Protestant understanding of the doctrine of justification ('a genuine theological *nova*,' according to McGrath)[68] claimed an uncompromising answer to these questions: those who have hit the bottom of frustration and despair and expect only condemnation find eternal satisfaction and justification in Christ; those who are dead in sin find life in Christ; those who are unrighteous discover that they can stand before a righteous God (*coram Deo*) simply on the complete victory of Christ upon the cross; those who were aliens and strangers can enjoy all the benefits of Christ as members of the divine covenant; those who stood in the dark, now stand confidently in the light of the Gospel of Christ; those who experienced God as Judge now find him to be a gracious Father. Justification by grace alone crucially centers God in the salvation of his people in a way that gives him glory for who he is and for what he has done in Jesus Christ.[69] And, for his abounding goodness in justifying us we are acutely grateful.

[68] Alister E. McGrath, 'Forerunners of the Reformation? A Critical Examination of the Evidence for Precursors of the Reformation Doctrine of Justification,' *Harvard Theological Review* 75.2 (1982), 241.

[69] For an excellent introduction to the subject covered by this present volume see Carl R. Trueman, 'Justification' in David M. Whitford (ed.), *T&T Clark Companion to Reformation Theology* (London: T. & T. Clark, 2012), 57-71.

# CHAPTER 2

## Martin Luther preaches salvation to his friends: justification by faith in the mature reformer

*Cameron A. MacKenzie*

In any volume devoted to justification in the Reformation, some treatment of Martin Luther is almost inevitable. One might even say *necessary*. After all, Luther was the first of the sixteenth century Protestant reformers, and he identified justification as the cornerstone of his theology. Although historians still quibble about when precisely Luther came to his new evangelical understanding of the faith, already in 1518 at the Heidelberg Disputation, Luther was saying things like, 'He is not righteous who does much, but he who, without work, believes much in Christ,' a sentiment on which he elaborated with these words, 'The righteousness of God is not acquired by means of acts frequently repeated . . . but it is imparted by faith. . . . works contribute nothing to justification. . . . His justification by faith in Christ is sufficient to him. Christ is his wisdom, righteousness, etc.'[1]

Justification by faith was a conviction, once acquired, that Luther never yielded. The 'mature' churchman as well as the 'young' reformer maintained this doctrine. In 1537, in the Schmalkald Articles, aptly described as 'Luther's Theological Testament,'[2] he identified justification by faith as 'the first and chief article' of the Christian religion and insisted that 'nothing in this article can be given up or compromised, even if heaven and earth and things temporal should be destroyed'. In Luther's characteristic fashion, he went on to write, 'On this article rests all that we teach and practice against the pope, the devil, and the world. Therefore we must be quite certain and have no doubts about it. Otherwise all is lost, and the pope, the devil, and all our adversaries will gain the victory.'[3] Luther's commitment to justification by faith was absolute.[4]

---

[1] *LW* 31.55-56 (*WA* 1.364.1-5, 11, 14-15).
[2] Luther composed them for a possible church council at a time when he was seriously ill. See William R. Russell, *Luther's Theological Testament: The Schmalkald Articles* (Minneapolis: Fortress Press, 1995).
[3] Schmalkald Articles 2.1.1-5. These articles are a part of the Lutheran Confessions, *Die Bekenntnisschriften der evangelisch-lutherischen Kirche, herausgegeben im Gedenkjahr der Augsburgischen Konfession 1930*, 4th ed. (Göttingen: Vandenhoeck

However, it is one thing to say that something is important in a document intended for a church council and quite another actually to preach it. Doctrinal statements and homilies are very different things, and preachers routinely make choices about what they are going to include in their sermons. So it is useful to examine the sermons of Martin Luther in order to test the importance of justification by faith in his practical ministry. How and to what extent did the Reformer make use of this doctrine when he preached?[5]

For Martin Luther *was* a preacher. According to one estimate, Luther preached about 4,000 times during his career, and of his sermons, around 2,300 have survived in one form or another.[6] The Reformation did not initiate a homiletical revival in the church;[7] but the reformers, beginning with Luther, embraced preaching as necessary for true Christian worship and viewed it as essential to authentic Christian ministry.[8] In one of his earliest efforts to reform worship, Luther had this to say about preaching:

---

& Ruprecht, 1959). The English translation is from Theodore G. Tappert (ed.), *The Book of Concord: The Confessions of the Evangelical Lutheran Church* (Philadelphia: Fortress Press, 1959).

[4] The literature on Luther and justification is voluminous; but for a good, clear exposition, see Bernhard Lohse, *Martin Luther's Theology: Its Historical and Systematic Development* (Minneapolis: Fortress Press, 1999), 258-66.

[5] Of course, this question has been treated before. See Fred W. Meuser, *Luther the Preacher* (Minneapolis: Augsburg, 1983), 16-25; Detlef Lehmann, 'Luther als Prediger', in *Oberurseler Hefte*, Heft 17 (Oberursel: Fakultät der Luth. Theol. Hochschule Oberursel, 1983), 13-15; Gerhard Heintze, *Luthers Predigt von Gesetz und Evangelium* (München: Chr. Kaiser Verlag, 1958); Ulrich Asendorf, *Die Theologie Martin Luthers nach seinen Predigten* (Göttingen: Vandenhoeck & Ruprecht, 1988), 65-66, 116-32, 139-44, 373-76. In this essay, we are looking very narrowly at the question of justification in the house postils.

[6] Fred W. Meuser, 'Luther as Preacher of the Word of God', in Donald K. McKim (ed.), *The Cambridge Companion to Martin Luther* (Cambridge: Cambridge University Press, 2003), 136. See, also, John W. Doberstein, 'Introduction' to *Sermons* I, *LW* 51.xi-xiii; Martin Brecht, *Martin Luther* (Philadelphia: Fortress Press, 1985), 1.150-55.

[7] Andrew Pettegree, *Reformation and the Culture of Persuasion* (Cambridge: Cambridge University Press, 2005), 10-17; John M. Frymire, *The Primacy of the Postils: Catholics, Protestants, and the Dissemination of Ideas in Early Modern Germany* (Leiden: Brill, 2010), 10-25. Frymire argues convincingly that late medieval preaching was much more extensive—beyond the cities and towns—than many scholars have previously thought.

[8] Pettegree, *Reformation*, 10-11. See, also, Larissa Taylor (ed.), *Preachers and People in the Reformations and Early Modern Period* (Boston: Brill, 2003), especially the articles by Beth Kreitzer ('The Lutheran Sermon', 35-63) and James Thomas Ford ('Preaching in the Reformed Tradition', 65-88). For the evangelical character of early Reformation preaching in Germany, see Bernd Moeller, 'What Was Preached in German Towns in the Early Reformation?' in C. Scott Dixon (ed.), *The German Reformation: The Essential Readings* (Oxford: Blackwell, 1999), 36-55.

17

> Know first of all that a Christian congregation should never gather together with-
> out the preaching of God's Word and prayer, no matter how briefly as Psalm 102
> says, 'When the kings and the people assemble to serve the Lord, they shall de-
> clare the name and the praise of God.' And Paul in 1 Corinthians 14 says that
> when they come together, there should be prophesying, teaching, and admonition.
> Therefore, when God's Word is not preached, one had better neither sing nor read,
> or even come together.[9]

'When God's Word is not preached, one might as well not even come together
for worship.' That's how important preaching was for Martin Luther.[10]

In part, Luther's commitment to preaching resulted from his convictions regarding the *oral* character of the Gospel. In his preface to the New Testament,
first published in 1522 but regularly reprinted thereafter, Luther defined the
word 'gospel' as 'a good message, good tidings, good news, a good report,
which one sings and tells with gladness'[11] and then described the Christian
Gospel as 'a good story and report, sounded forth into all the world by the
apostles, telling of a true David who strove with sin, death, and the devil, and
overcame them'.[12] This message, Luther insisted, 'Christ...commanded and
ordained . . . be *preached* [*aus zuruffen*] after his death in all the world. . . . A
poor man, dead in sin and consigned to hell, can *hear* [*horen*] nothing more
comforting than this precious and tender message about Christ.'[13]

A few paragraphs later, Luther again summarized the Gospel as 'the preaching about Christ', i.e., the 'Son of God and of David, true God and man, who
by his death and resurrection has overcome for us the sin, death, and hell of all
men who believe in him'.[14] This alone is the message that deserves the title
'Gospel'. It is not enough, Luther insisted, just to be familiar with what Christ
did or what was done to him. Such information becomes Gospel only 'when the
voice [*die stymme*] comes that says, "Christ is your own, with his life, teaching,
works, death, resurrection, and all that he is, has, does, and can do."' That's
what true preaching is: 'The voice . . . that says, "Christ is your own."'[15]

For Luther, Christ, Gospel, and preaching all go together. So the challenge
of treating justification in Luther's preaching turns out to be an embarrassment
of riches rather than a lack of evidence.

---

[9] 'Concerning the Order of Public Worship' (1523), *LW* 53.11 (*WA* 12.35.19-25).
[10] See, also, Meuser, *Luther the Preacher*, 11-34.
[11] *LW* 35.358 (*WA DB* 6.2.23-25).
[12] *LW* 35.358 (*WA DB* 6.4.4-6).
[13] *LW* 35.359 (*WA DB* 6.4.15-22), emphasis added. For the oral character of the Gospel
in Luther, see Jaroslav Pelikan, *Luther the Expositor: Introduction to the Reformer's
Exegetical Writings* (St. Louis: Concordia, 1959), 63-70.
[14] LW 35.360 (*WA DB* 6.6.22-26).
[15] LW 35.360-61 (*WA DB* 6.8.17-19). For Luther, Christian preaching was the same as
God speaking. See Meuser, *Luther the Preacher*, 11-16.

One way, however, to narrow the focus constructively is to examine a subset of Luther's sermons, defined perhaps by theme, text, or context. Among other possibilities, Luther's house postils stand out especially on account of their provenance. In the early 1530s, Luther, in poor health and extremely over-worked, for the most part quit preaching in Wittenberg's parish church; but he did not quit preaching. Instead, he preached at home to his family and friends—often quite a group on account of relatives, friends, and boarders who stayed at Luther's home in addition to his own wife and children.[16]

These sermons, transcribed at the time by some of those present, were later published in a couple of different versions. The only one that appeared during Luther's lifetime was that of Veit Dietrich in 1544. Modern editors recognize that Dietrich often combined two or three of Luther's sermons into one and occasionally used materials that Luther had preached 'publicly' and not at home. Sometimes Dietrich even included a sermon by someone other than Lu-ther! Nonetheless, Dietrich based the *Hauspostille* on Luther's private preach-ing and Luther acknowledged as much in an introduction he wrote for his friend's work.[17] Thus, the Luther presented here is not simply Luther preaching to his friends but Luther as mediated by a friend for public consumption. Obvi-ously not a perfect source, Dietrich's house postils still provide insight into what the mature Luther thought people needed to hear from the Word of God. Not surprisingly, justification is a major theme.[18]

As biblical texts for his house postils, Luther used the traditional Gospel les-sons of the medieval church year. He often preached on these texts since the Wittenberg church continued to use them in its services. One obvious ad-vantage from our perspective is that this facilitates comparison over long peri-ods of time of Luther's various treatments of particular Bible passages.[19]

In addition to the house postils, we also have the church postils from much earlier in Luther's career. These are quite different from the house postils in terms of their origins, because Luther initially intended them as homiletical helps for preachers rather than as sermons themselves. When Luther was 'hid-

---

[16] Brecht, *Luther*, 2.204.

[17] *WA* 52.1.3-8.

[18] Andreas Poach produced a second version of the house postils in 1559, more than a decade after Luther's death. For background to both versions, see the introduction by Georg Buchwald in *WA* 52.vii-xii. The Weimar edition also provides data on the rela-tionship between Dietrich's edition and the manuscript notes of one of the copyists, Georg Rörer. See, also, Emanuel Hirsch's introductory comments to each version in *Luthers Werke in Auswahl: Predigten*, 3rd ed. (Berlin: Walter de Gruyter, 1962), 7.69, 84.

[19] Gerhard Ebeling, *Evangelische Evangelienauslegung: Eine Untersuchung zu Luthers Hermeneutik* (Darmstadt: Wissenschaftliche Buchgesellschaft, 1962), 21-25, explains how it is that Luther retained the pericopal system and indicates that Luther came to appreciate the advantages of yearly repetition of certain scriptural texts for the young and the simple.

ing' at the Wartburg (1521-1522), he prepared postils or commentaries on the traditional Scripture lessons for the church year from Advent through Epiphany.[20] Thus, some of Luther's earliest homiletical materials, prepared specifically for evangelical preaching, concern the same biblical texts as the house postils that Luther preached years later. Therefore, the church postils provide a base line from which we can measure continuity or change in Luther's treatment of justification in sermons delivered a decade later (and published a decade after that).

Another good reason for examining the earlier set of postils is the fact that Luther prepared an introduction for them, entitled, 'A Brief Instruction on What to Look for and Expect in the Gospels'; and in this work, he set some priorities for evangelical preaching. For example, regarding the definition of Gospel, Luther was concerned that preachers not limit themselves to the first four books of the New Testament. Instead, he insisted that there was really 'only one Gospel, but that it is described by many apostles'. Whether presented in long or short form, it had the same essential content, 'Gospel is and should be nothing else than a discourse or story about Christ,' and in its most basic form it consisted of these points, 'that he is the Son of God and became man for us, that he died and was raised, that he has been established as a Lord over all things'.[21]

Significantly, Luther's description included two little words that made the Gospel more than simply a recitation of facts, viz., 'for us'. 'He is the Son of God and became man *for us* [*fur unss*]' (emphasis added). Whether the Gospel is actually good news or not depends on why God became man, suffered and died, and how he exercises his Lordship. Therefore, Luther's next main point was to emphasize and explicate the 'for us' character of the Gospel by insisting that preachers present Christ as a 'gift' before they describe him as an 'example'.[22]

Both treatments were legitimate, but Luther warned against so emphasizing the exemplary character of Christ as to turn him into another Moses or lawgiver, 'as if Christ did nothing more than teach and provide examples as the other saints do, as if the Gospel were simply a textbook of teachings or laws'. For Luther, such preaching hardly deserved to be called the Gospel because it did not help the hearer with their sins. 'On this level,' Luther explained, 'Christ is no more help to you than some other saint. His life remains his own and does not as yet contribute anything to you. In short this mode [of preaching] . . . does

---

[20] The church postils have a long and complicated history that was still ongoing in 1544, the year that saw the first publication of the house postils. See Doberstein, 'Introduction', xiv-xv; Ebeling, *Evangelienauslegung*, 30–37; and Frymire, *Primacy*, 31-37.

[21] *LW* 35.117-18 (*WA* $10^{1,1}$.9.6-7, 11-12, 19-20).

[22] *LW* 35.119 (*WA* $10^{1,1}$.11.12-14).

not make Christians but only hypocrites.' Sinners need a Savior not just an example.[23]

So Luther went on to insist that 'the chief article and foundation of the Gospel is that before you take Christ as an example, you accept and recognize him as a gift'. By employing this formulation, Luther emphasized the vicarious nature of the work of Christ, 'This means that when you see or hear of Christ doing or suffering something, you do not doubt that Christ himself, with his deeds and suffering, belongs to you. On this you may depend as surely as if you had done it yourself; indeed as if you were Christ himself.' And therefore, by depending on Christ, one obtains what Christ has obtained by his saving work, 'When you lay hold of Christ as a gift which is given you for your very own and have no doubt about it, you are a Christian. Faith redeems you from sin, death, and hell and enables you to overcome all things.'[24]

In short, the Gospel is the story of Christ, God made man, who rescued sinners from death and hell by taking their place. This God grants to those who trust in him. We call this justification by faith, and Luther said that it must be preached.

But Luther also acknowledged that 'when you have Christ as the foundation and chief blessing of your salvation, then the other part follows: that you take him as your example'. This then introduces the topic of good works, 'giving yourself in service to your neighbor just as you see that Christ has given himself for you'.[25] With respect to such works, Luther insisted on two things—first of all, that they were not a part of saving faith, 'As widely as a gift differs from an example, so widely does faith differ from works, for faith possesses nothing of its own, only the deeds and life of Christ.' Christ alone is the Savior and our works add nothing to him. However, Luther's other point about good works was that they necessarily followed faith, 'These [works] do not make you a Christian. Actually, they come forth from you because you have already been made a Christian.'[26]

Clearly, Luther's 'Brief Instruction' offers criteria for evaluating his treatment of justification in his sermons. So let's consider his presentation of the Gospel in the house postils as compared with the first of the church postils—the Christmas postils of 1522.[27] Taking our cue from the 'Brief Instruction,' we need first of all to examine how Luther presented Jesus Christ in each set of homiletical materials. Is Christ the center of the Gospel and is he the same

---

[23] *LW* 35.119 (*WA* 10[1,1].10.20-11.1, 11.8-10).
[24] *LW* 35.119, 120 (*WA* 10[1,1].11.12-18, 12.7-10).
[25] *LW* 35.120 (*WA* 10[1,1].12.12-15).
[26] *LW* 35.120 (*WA* 10[1,1].12.19-13.1).
[27] Luther's first publication of postils included homiletical helps for Epistle lessons as well as Gospels, and lessons for New Years and Epiphany as well as the Christmas season. See Doberstein, 'Introduction', xiv-xv. For details, see W. Köhler, '*Einleitung zur Wartburgpostille*', *WA* 10[1,2].xli-lxxix. In the interest of space, we are restricting our comparison in this essay to the postils on the Gospels for Christmas.

Christ in the later sermons as well as the earlier ones? The answer to both questions is, Yes.

As one might expect, Luther dealt at length with the person of Christ in his sermons on Christmas. The subject is especially hard to avoid when your text is John 1.1-14, 'The Gospel for the Main Christmas Service,' and Luther addressed it at length in his church postil on this text. So, for example, Luther summarized the evangelist's intentions this way, 'He wanted to indicate what was to be written about Christ in the whole Gospel, namely that he is true God and man, who has created all things, and that he was given to men to be life and light.'[28] Luther also maintained the integrity of each nature as well as the unity of the person of Christ[29] and insisted on distinguishing the person of the Son from that of the Father.[30] In other words, he was operating within the parameters of Chalcedonian Christology.[31]

He continued to do so in the house postils. Unfortunately, this set of sermons does not include an exposition of John 1. But it does include four sermons, based on Luke 2, for Christmas day; and in the first two of these, Luther preached directly and extensively on the incarnation. Luther spoke as clearly here as he did in the earlier set of homiletical helps, 'God himself becomes true man, with the result that out of God and human nature there comes to be a single person. . . . Now God has become man and still remains God.'[32]

One noteworthy element in Luther's treatment of the person of Christ in these postils is that he found edifying material for believers in the simple fact of incarnation without considering the work of redemption. Apart from the 'use and benefit' of the incarnation, Luther contended that it was an 'honor' [die Ehre] for humanity that God became a man. He did not do it for the angels, and the devil cannot do it. But God can and has.

> We should learn well, first of all, the honor we have received in that Christ has become man. This is such an honor that if someone were an angel, he would wish to become man just so that he could boast, 'My flesh and my blood sit above the angels.' Therefore, the creature who is called human is indeed a blessed creature.[33]

---

[28] LW 52.65 (WA 10[1,1].213.20-24).
[29] LW 52.54 (WA 10[1,1].198.22-24, 199.6-8)
[30] LW 52.43-44 (WA 10[1,1].183.25-28, 184.13-18).
[31] See Lohse, Luther's Theology, 207-21, for Luther's traditional Trinitarian and Christological doctrines in view of his own Reformation emphases.
[32] WA 52.43.1-6. See, also, WA 52.47.38-39. The house postils were not translated for Luther's Works. There is a 19th century translation (Martin Luther, Sermons on the Gospels [2 vols; Rock Island, IL: Augustana Book Concern, 1871]) that is of some help, but the translation in the text is my own.
[33] WA 52.43.35-36, 40.31-35. In another place (WA 52.48.2-8) Luther comments on how men and angels share the same Lord and, therefore, are neighbors and members of the same civil society.

Obviously, the incarnation should cause people to rejoice. Luther exclaimed over 'unhappy people' who knew nothing about the 'honor' of the incarnation and even more so over those who had heard about it and yet had no joy in it. 'So how can it be,' he asked, 'that we too do not rejoice in this, that we do not want to take it to heart, nor do we thank and praise God that my God has become my flesh and blood and now sits above on the right hand of God, a Lord above all creatures?'[34]

Luther returned to this theme of honor several times in these sermons and developed it in two additional ways. One of them was connected to justification in that the incarnation brings comfort to poor sinners.

> Therefore, he who has in his heart this idea—that God's Son has become man—can expect nothing bad from the Lord Christ but instead everything good. . . . Such an idea—if it were truly in our hearts—would melt in an instant all horrible examples of God's wrath like the Flood and the punishment of Sodom and Gomorrah. Everything like this must disappear in a single moment when I think about the only man who is God and has so honored poor human nature that he has become a man.[35]

As we shall see, this is hardly the entirety of Luther's teaching about the comfort of the Gospel, but nonetheless it is significant that Luther asserted it on the basis of the person of Christ and not his work, since usually it is the work of Christ to which Luther points as the heart of the Gospel.[36]

A second application of the incarnation is the encouragement it provides for showing love toward others. After all, Luther argued, if God has so honored humanity as to become human, how can we who *are* human do anything less than follow his example and love others?

> If we truly took this to heart, then we could never be hostile to any of our fellow-men. For who would want to be hostile or to do something bad to the form [*dem bilde*] that has flesh and blood like my God and yours. Should we not therefore for the sake of the honor that God has shown us also love all men and do everything good to them?[37]

The 'honor' of the incarnation is a major motif in the first two house postils for Christmas; but it is not the only theme or really the main theme in Luther's treatment as a whole. For Luther, the person of Christ is always a precondition for his work. The ultimate purpose of God's *becoming* a man is God's *redeeming* humanity.[38] This is evident already in the church postils from 1522. They include separate treatments for Luke 2.1-14 (the birth and its announcement by

---

[34]  *WA* 52.44.19, 27-29. See, also, *WA* 52.45.12-16.
[35]  *WA* 52.44.37-39, 45.3-7.
[36]  See, for example, the Schmalkald Articles, 2.1-3.
[37]  *WA* 52.43.36-40.
[38]  Lohse, *Luther's Theology*, 223-25.

the angels) and 2.15-20 (the response of the shepherds). In these postils, Luther affirmed the incarnation, but he also emphasized the 'for you' character of the Gospel. He found it especially in the announcement of the angel which he identified with the Gospel itself:

> The angel demonstrates the Gospel most clearly with his words. . . . He does not say, 'I preach to you,' but 'I am speaking a Gospel to you.' . . . And whereof does the Gospel speak? . . . 'For you is born a Savior, Christ the Lord.' . . . See there what the Gospel is: a joyous sermon concerning Christ, our Savior. . . . Thus, the Gospel does not merely teach the story and accounts of Christ, but personalizes them and gives them to all who believe.[39]

But what did it mean to believe that Christ was 'our Savior'? Not just that he was God and man, but that what he did as God and man, he did for us: 'The Gospel teaches that Christ was born for our sake and that he did everything and suffered all things for our sake.'[40]

Besides the passive quality of faith that receives what Christ is and has done for sinners, Luther also described the transformative character of faith. On the one hand, he separated works from justification:

> That man (if he has faith) may boast of such treasure as that Mary is his real mother, Christ his brother, and God his father. For these things are, all of them, true and they come to pass, provided we believe them; this is the chief part and chief good in all the Gospels, before one derives from them teaching concerning good works. Christ . . . must become ours and we his before we undertake good works. That happens in no other way than through such faith.[41]

But on the other hand, Luther insisted that works flow from this saving faith:

> That [faith] makes for a right knowledge of Christ; from it the conscience becomes happy, free, and contented; from it grow love and praise of God. . . . Then there follows a mind right willing to do, to refrain from doing, and to suffer everything that is pleasing to God.[42]

Such faith does *not* require special 'religious' works like fasting or wearing unusual clothing. Instead, the true Christian continues as always but with a new attitude, 'For a Christian knows that it all depends upon faith; for this reason he walks, stands, eats, drinks, dresses, works, and lives as any ordinary person in his calling.'[43] Works that are good in God's sight come from a believing heart and are directed to others. In fact, now—but only now—a believer should look

---

[39] *LW* 52.20 (*WA* 10[1,1].78.20-79.13).
[40] *LW* 52.14 (*WA* 10[1,1].71.9-10).
[41] *LW* 52.15–16 (*WA* 10[1,1].72.20-73.6).
[42] *LW* 52.16 (*WA* 10[1,1].73.7-11).
[43] *LW* 52.38 (*WA* 10[1,1].137.22-138.2). For Luther's doctrine of vocation, see Paul Althaus, *The Ethics of Martin Luther* (Philadelphia: Fortress Press, 1972), 36-42.

upon Christ as his example, 'Now there follows the example of good works, that you also do to your neighbor as you see that Christ has done for you.'[44]

From person and work of Christ to faith and the fruits of faith in the Christian, Luther laid out the plan of salvation in the Christmas postils of 1522. Many years later in the house postils, he was still doing the same thing. As in the earlier work, Luther identified the news that Christ was the Savior as the most important part of the angel's message to the shepherds, 'But beyond this natural honor and joy [in the incarnation] is still this—that he, the man Jesus, is also a savior. This is first and foremost the chief part [*allererst das rechte stück*] and the greatest reason why a person should be happy.'[45] And again, 'That which was spoken of before, viz., that God has become man, is itself a glorious, great matter. But it is a far greater thing [*weyt drüber*] that he shall be our spiritual and eternal Savior.'[46]

But what did Christ do in order to save humanity? For one thing, he humbled himself. In his recounting of the Christmas narrative, Luther emphasized humility in the circumstances of Jesus' birth—'the birth so poor and miserable'.[47] In this way, Jesus joined himself to the humanity he came to save. '[Aside from sin] everything was natural with him as with other men. He ate, drank, became hungry, became thirsty, suffered from cold—just like other men. These and similar natural weaknesses he possessed just as we do.' Luther contrasted this past humiliation with our Lord's present state of exaltation, 'He could easily have made it happen that he would become a human being *as he is right now in heaven*. He has flesh and blood as we do, but does not do what we do.'[48]

Like the incarnation, Luther understood the humiliation as a presupposition for redemption,

> The Christmas story is preached every year for this reason: that every young person should keep it in his heart and be thankful to God and say, 'I have no want or need, because I have a brother who has become just like me. . . . For this has happened in order that he might deliver me from sin and eternal death.'[49]

Significantly, the 'me' in this statement is universal. Christ has redeemed not just 'every young person' but every person—all:

> The little phrase, 'for you' [in the words of the angel to the shepherds] should indeed make us happy. For with whom is he speaking? With wood? Or with stones?

---

44  *LW* 52.16 (*WA* 10[1.1].74.2-4). More than Christ, Luther uses the example of the shepherds to discuss the *response* of faith in works and attitudes like humility, love of neighbors, joy in sharing the Gospel, action, confession, vocation, and praising God (*LW* 52.33-38).
45  *WA* 52.45.23-25.
46  *WA* 52.46.28-30.
47  *WA* 52.38.5.
48  *WA* 52.39.28-31, 34-36, emphasis added.
49  *WA* 52.40.3-7.

No, but with men, not with one or two only but with all people [*mit allem volck*]. . . . Is it not a great thing that an angel from heaven brings such news to people? And therefore so many thousands of angels are so happy, wish for and preach that we human beings [*wir menschen*] should also be happy and accept such grace with thanks.[50]

But, now, how did the Son of God, humbled as well as incarnate, actually redeem all people? Theologians have answered this question in a variety of ways, and Luther himself offered more than one explanation.[51] In the house postils for Christmas, the Reformer explained the work of Christ principally but not exclusively as defeating the devil: the devil is our enemy and Christ has rescued humanity from him. In a couple of places, Luther indicated that the work of Christ also reconciled God with humanity, 'He [the Christ child] shall be our help and comfort so that henceforth all wrath between God and us is taken away while pure love and friendship remain.'[52] But that's about it. Luther did not describe redemption as assuaging the wrath of God against sin or as paying the penalty for sin as our substitute.

True enough, our problem is sin,[53] but the Reformer treated sin along with death as the devil's mechanism for enslaving humanity. He said:

> Through sin and death the devil has cast us down and placed us into a state of extraordinary misery. Not only are we stuck fast in original sin and liable to eternal death, but also must expect daily all sorts of misfortune in the world from him. Therefore virtually no one is secure for a single moment in either his body or property.[54]

Elsewhere Luther called the world 'a horrible hell' and explained that in it is nothing except

> lies, deceit, greed, gluttony, drunkenness, prostitution, violence, and murder, i.e., the abominable devil himself. . . . There is neither love nor faithfulness. No one is sure of anyone else. One must stay on guard against friends as much as against enemies, and sometimes even more. This is the kingdom of this world that the devil runs and rules.[55]

---

[50] *WA* 52.46.4-6, 19-22.

[51] Lohse, *Luther's Theology*, 223-28. The classic treatment of this question in Luther and others is Gustaf Aulén, *Christus Victor: An Historical Study of the Three Main Types of the Idea of the Atonement* (New York: Macmillan, 1986), but see, also, Paul Althaus, *The Theology of Martin Luther* (Philadelphia: Fortress Press, 1966), 218-23, who called Aulén's treatment 'a significant misinterpretation of Luther'.

[52] *WA* 52.48.36-37. See, also, *WA* 52.50.22-29.

[53] 'This birth belongs to you who are poor, depraved, and lost human beings,' *WA* 52.46.25-26.

[54] *WA* 52.42.10-14.

[55] *WA* 52.55.35-37, 56.1-4.

But Christ has come precisely to rescue humanity from Satan. Commenting on the angel's phrase, 'Christ the Lord,' Luther explained:

> From the fact that Christ is called 'a Lord,' we must understand . . . that he will claim you and me as his own and that he will demand his own from the devil and will tell him: 'Give me this person whom you are holding captive. He is not yours but mine—indeed, my creation which I did not only create but also have purchased with my body. Therefore, let him go and return him to me, for he belongs to me.'[56]

Aside from Christ's facing down the devil in this way, Luther did not otherwise describe how he defeated the devil[57] anymore than he explained how Christ removed God's wrath from sinners. Instead, Luther was content simply to affirm that Jesus was the only Savior of humanity: 'This child alone is our Savior, in whom alone we shall have all consolation and joy as in the greatest treasure.'[58] And this Savior 'shall accomplish everything that concerns [our] salvation'.[59]

The message of Christ's redemptive work was the only Gospel and God offered it in his word, especially by *preaching*. As we saw above, the young Reformer was insistent that the word be preached. This was still true in the house postils. Commenting on the situation of the papal church that retained baptism, the text of the Gospel, the Lord's Prayer, and the like, Luther lamented that the people did not know what they were singing or talking about. 'The problem,' he said, 'is with the preachers who are supposed to open up the ears of the people and to stir up the word so that they understand what they hear, read, or sing.' Instead, the preachers themselves were asleep, 'and a sleepy preacher can put to sleep even an eager hearer'.[60]

Presumably, evangelical preachers like Luther himself were presenting the word faithfully and effectively. But how should his hearers respond? In faith, of course. Luther indicated that appropriating the work of Christ was a matter of trusting the message rather than earning God's favor. Regarding the angel's announcement that 'to you is born a Savior,' Luther called it an 'excellent, dear word,' aimed at men and women to show them their Savior from sin and death. 'Whoever really perceived and believed that,' Luther said, 'would know what real joy was.'[61]

Luther recalled the tyranny of pre-reformation religion, 'when poor consciences were oppressed on every side and no one could find any real com-

---

[56] *WA* 52.47.24-25, 27-32. See, also, *WA* 52.48.4-6, 49.7-10, 55.8-9.
[57] He did connect it to the Incarnation, however, when he further imagined Christ saying to Satan, 'I am the Lord. It belongs to me *by nature* [*von natur*] and not to you that I should rule over men,' *WA* 52.47.35-36, emphasis added.
[58] *WA* 52.48.41-49.2. See, also, *WA* 52.52.23-30.
[59] *WA* 52.53.2. See, also, *WA* 52.48.35-37.
[60] *WA* 52.51.23-25, 27-28.
[61] *WA* 52.46.23, 30-31. See, also, *WA* 52.47.3-5.

fort'.[62] Too many, he complained, have forgotten those bad old days; and so, he summoned his hearers to follow Mary as 'an example of someone who rightly hears God's word'[63]—the word of the Gospel—'that her son was indeed the Son of God and the Savior of the whole world'.[64]

Luther did not always use the word 'faith' [*der Glaube*] but he did urge exclusive reliance upon Christ the Savior. 'The Law,' he maintained, 'could not help against sin and death; one's own works and piety also could not help. . . . The angels preach that Christ is the one who will do it and in him everyone will find everything that belongs to the forgiveness of sins and eternal life.' But if Christ was the exclusive Savior, then one must reject every alternative—'every kind of doctrine and religion, through which people want to direct humanity to eternal life apart from Christ'.[65] In that same passage, Luther rejected the cult of the saints and monasticism as false Christs.[66] In another place, he called the mass and the pomp surrounding it a form of idolatry because people depended on such works for salvation.[67] From Luther's perspective, therefore, to be a Christian meant to rely on Christ as Savior and on nothing and no one else.

However, just as in the 1522 treatment, Luther insisted that such faith would transform one's life. It began in the heart, since faith was not simply an intellectual assent to the truth of the Gospel but also involved a change of attitude toward God. Luther said, 'This is the real change for which Christ has come, viz., that a man becomes completely different within in his heart . . . so that it can say: "I know that God accepts me and truly loves me [*mich mit trewen meindt*], for he has sent his Son."'[68] But this was only the beginning, for faith also transformed one's attitude toward life. Luther continued, 'Our dear Lord Christ has worked it out so that the heart and the soul should have a completely new and different understanding, will, pleasure, and love.'[69]

As in 1522, however, the new attitude did not lead away from worldly responsibilities and into monasticism but instead to a new motivation for carrying out one's ordinary duties: 'The heart has a new desire and will, but a person remains in his calling and outer circumstances just as before.'[70]

> Man should maintain all estates . . . for they do not hinder the Christian faith and Christ does not ask what your external situation is—whether you are man or woman, emperor or stableboy, mayor or constable. He lets all such things remain

---

[62] *WA* 52.58.35-36.
[63] *WA* 52.59.18-19.
[64] *WA* 52.59.31-33.
[65] *WA* 52.50.33-39.
[66] *WA* 52.50.39-51.12.
[67] *WA* 52.52.23-28.
[68] *WA* 52.61.25-26, 35-37.
[69] *WA* 52.62.3-4.
[70] *WA* 52.62.15-17.

as they are and says: 'People should be obedient to God in every estate and way of life and should not refrain from it.'[71]

Serving God by carrying out your vocation; trusting in God's word that promises you forgiveness and eternal life for the sake of Christ; and recognizing that Christ, God and man, has rescued humanity from sin, death, and hell—the power of the devil—these principles were the essence of Luther's teaching regarding justification in 1522 and they remained the same more than a decade later, at least according to the evidence of the Christmas postils (both sets).

So what should we make of this? Just this, the first of the Protestant reformers not only articulated justification by faith in treatises and commentaries and not only recommended that others employ it in their sermons, he also preached it himself loud and clear. God had become a man in the person of Jesus Christ in order to save sinners. People needed to hear it, so Luther told them precisely that.

---

[71] *WA* 52.62.31-36.

# CHAPTER 3

## Luther and Melanchthon on justification: continuity or discontinuity?

*Aaron O'Kelley*

Is it possible that the theologian of justification *par excellence*, Martin Luther, has been misunderstood on the very question of justification, not only by the theological tradition that bears his name, but also by Protestantism as a whole? Moreover, is it possible that such a misunderstanding has arisen largely from an imposition of Philip Melanchthon's heavily forensic doctrine of justification onto Luther himself? Scholarly discussion surrounding Luther's theology in relation to that of Melanchthon sometimes suggests that Melanchthon departed radically from the teachings of his colleague and subsequently led Lutheranism as a whole down a faulty path, one that essentially buried Luther's rich, life-giving teaching under the dry soil of legal fiction. For example, after tying Luther's doctrine of justification to that of Osiander, Stephen Strehle writes, 'No matter how one might feel about this matter or other details of Osiander's system we must at least recognize that the church has become greatly impoverished in adopting Melanchthon's one-dimensional concepts to the exclusion of other tensions in Luther's thought—tensions that Osiander had hoped to bring forth.'[1] Mark Seifrid similarly argues, '[It] is clear that Melanchthon and Luther differ dramatically from one another on the question of justification because they proceed from radically different perspectives.'[2] This 'Luther against the Lutherans' thesis has gained a bit of traction in recent years with the rise of the so-called 'Finnish School' of Lutheran interpretation, representing an ecumenical agenda that ties Luther's doctrine of justification closely to Eastern Orthodox theology by proposing that Luther was concerned primarily with ontologi-

---

[1]  Stephen Strehle, *The Catholic Roots of the Protestant Gospel: Encounter Between the Middle Ages and the Reformation* (New York: Brill, 1995), 82-83.

[2]  Mark A. Seifrid, 'Luther, Melanchthon and Paul on the Question of Imputation: Recommendations on a Current Debate', in Mark Husbands and Daniel J. Treier (eds), *Justification: What's at Stake in the Current Debates* (Downers Grove, IL: InterVarsity Press, 2004), 143. It should be noted that Seifrid's concern is not to tie Luther to Osiander, as Strehle attempts to do.

cal, and not legal, categories.[3] Always a controversial figure among his Roman Catholic opponents, Luther continues to play the role today among his Protestant friends.

Does Luther stand against the Lutherans? More specifically, does a comparison between Luther and Melanchthon on the doctrine of justification suggest continuity or discontinuity? The answer to this question is not a simple affirmation of one or the other, for the evidence suggests elements of both. However, I propose that the elements of discontinuity between Luther and Melanchthon on justification can be subsumed within a larger context of more significant continuity. A close comparison of Luther and Melanchthon to each other in the context of late medieval Catholic theology indicates that Luther and Melanchthon hold much more in common on the question of justification than they hold in tension, thereby undercutting the 'Luther against the Lutherans' thesis. Specifically, this essay will argue that a divine demand for perfect obedience and its theological corollaries—a law-gospel distinction and alien righteousness—form the basis of continuity between the two reformers. While Melanchthon did come to depart from Luther on free will, the nature of faith, and the uses of the law, he remained faithful to the broad theological vision that separated Luther from Rome.

Luther's doctrine is one of unconditional justification based on the free grace of God through the creation of faith in the sinner who hears the Gospel and to whom Christ and his righteousness are made present in faith so that Christ's righteousness is imputed to the believer. This claim will be demonstrated by a chronological survey of some of Luther's works, beginning with the period 1513-1521. In his first lecture series through the Psalms (1513-1514), it is clear that Luther, who had studied the works of Gabriel Biel, was still an adherent to the theology of the *via moderna*, a late medieval theological development whose proponents argued that human works, of no intrinsic value before God, are nevertheless acceptable to God on the basis of a freely ordained covenant that God has made between himself and humanity. Thus, even though no one can ever please God by his works, God nevertheless gives grace, in accord with the terms of the covenant, to the one who does what is in him (*facienti quod in*

---

[3] See Tuomo Mannermaa, *Christ Present in Faith: Luther's View of Justification* (Minneapolis: Fortress Press, 2005); Carl E. Braaten and Robert W. Jenson (eds), *Union with Christ: The New Finnish Interpretation of Luther* (Grand Rapids: Eerdmans, 1998). Responses to the methodology of the Finnish School include Timothy J. Wengert, 'Review of *Union with Christ: The New Finnish Interpretation of Luther*, ed. Carl E. Braaten and Robert W. Jenson,' *Theology Today* 56 (1999), 432-34; Carl R. Trueman, 'Is the Finnish Line a New Beginning? A Critical Assessment of the Reading of Luther Offered by the Helsinki Circle,' *Westminster Theological Journal* 65.2 (2003), 231-44; R. Scott Clark, '*Iustitia Imputata Christi*: Alien or Proper to Luther's Doctrine of Justification?' *Catholic Theological Quarterly* 70 (2006), 307-10; Mark A. Seifrid, 'Paul, Luther, and Justification in Gal. 2.15-21,' *Westminster Theological Journal* 65.2 (2003), 215-30.

*se est*). Commenting on Psalm 115.1, the early Luther makes this very point. Speaking of the necessity of preparation to receive grace, Luther writes,

> Hence the teachers correctly say that to a man who does what is in him [*facienti quod in se est*] God gives grace without fail, and though he could not prepare himself for grace on the basis of worth [*de condigno*], because the grace is beyond compare, yet he may well prepare himself on the basis of fitness [*de congruo*] because of this promise of God and the covenant of His mercy.[4]

As Alister McGrath has argued, it is this theological context that best explains Luther's transforming encounter with 'the righteousness of God' in Romans 1.17, an experience Luther recounts in his 1545 preface to his Latin works.[5]

Given his theological context, it is likely that the early Luther understood God's righteousness to refer to his strict, impartial equity in the administration of the terms of the covenant: God is righteous precisely because he is no respecter of persons but rewards impartially with grace those who do what is in them and condemns those who do not fulfill this covenant stipulation. Thus, 'justification can only be based upon merit' as God, the impartial judge, allows human beings to distinguish themselves by their deeds.[6] As grace-based as the covenantal theology of the *via moderna* was, the decisive element in justification had to come from the human side of the equation. The young Luther would have struggled to understand how this notion of righteousness could be good news for the sinner (as stated in Rom. 1.17) when it was impossible to know whether one had truly done what is in him (*quod in se est*). McGrath observes,

> The 'righteousness of God' thus remains an unknown quality, the impersonal attribute of an utterly impartial and scrupulously just judge, which stands over and against man, and ultimately justifies or condemns him on the basis of a totally unknown quality—and is thus the cause of much *Anfechtungen*! To someone such as Luther, who appears to have become increasingly uncertain about his own moral qualities as the *Dictata* progress, it must have seemed inevitable that God, in his righteousness, would condemn him.[7]

And so the theology of the *via moderna* provides a plausible context within which to understand Luther's struggle over the righteousness of God.

McGrath further argues that a major breakthrough occurred in 1515 that set Luther on a trajectory toward a very different understanding of justification. Adducing evidence from Luther's 1515-1516 lectures on Romans, he argues

---

[4]   Martin Luther, *First Lectures on the Psalms II: Psalms 76-126*, *LW* 11.396-97.
[5]   Alister E. McGrath, *Luther's Theology of the Cross: Martin Luther's Theological Breakthrough* (Malden, MA: Blackwell, 1985).
[6]   McGrath, *Luther's Theology*, 109.
[7]   McGrath, *Luther's Theology*, 110-11.

that by this time Luther's theology has taken an Augustinian turn.[8] In these lectures Luther no longer urges his listeners to do what is in them in order to attain grace. Instead, he argues that one must receive the first grace passively,[9] and this is directly related to the fact that the will is enslaved to sin and cannot, apart from grace, will anything good.[10] Luther explicitly repudiates his earlier view that the human will is decisive in salvation.[11] He espouses instead an Augustinian doctrine of predestination.[12] Necessarily, this new understanding of the particularity of grace entails that God's righteousness can no longer consist in his impartial administration of a covenant that allows human beings to distinguish themselves by their deeds. God's righteousness, he notes in his comments on Romans 1.17, does not consist in his personal rectitude; it is, rather, that by which he makes us righteous.[13]

Even at this early stage Luther begins to move beyond Augustine by teaching a doctrine of alien righteousness. To take just one example, in his comments on Romans 4.7, Luther writes, 'Therefore, I was correct when I said that all our good is outside of us [*Extrinsecum nobis*], and this good is Christ, as the apostle says (1 Cor. 1.30)'.[14] Alien righteousness appears in other writings from this period. In his sermon 'Two Kinds of Righteousness' (1519), Luther articulates a distinction between the righteousness that comes from outside of us and that which is properly our own. Alien righteousness is 'instilled from without'.[15] That some notion of imputation is present here is evident from the context, for Luther goes on to argue that the person who has received this alien righteousness can justly claim, 'Mine are Christ's living, doing, and speaking, his suffering and dying, mine as much as if I had lived, done, spoken, suffered, and died as he did.'[16] It is impossible to account for this kind of transfer of Christ's obedient life to the believer without at least a nascent doctrine of imputation.

Luther does not, however, speak of alien righteousness as received all at once. He says that the righteousness of Christ is given in baptism as well as anytime a person is truly repentant. Furthermore, he speaks of a progression in this righteousness: 'Christ daily drives out the old Adam more and more in accordance with the extent to which faith and knowledge of Christ grow. For alien righteousness is not instilled all at once, but it begins, makes progress, and

---

8   The discussion that follows draws on the insights of McGrath, *Luther's Theology*, 128-36.
9   Martin Luther, *Lectures on Romans*, *LW* 25.368 (*WA* 56.378).
10  Luther, *Romans*, *LW* 25.375 (*WA* 56.385).
11  Luther, *Romans*, *LW* 25.372 (*WA* 56.382).
12  Luther, *Romans*, *LW* 25.373-78 (*WA* 56.383-88).
13  Luther, *Romans*, *LW* 25.151 (*WA* 56.172).
14  Luther, *Romans*, *LW* 25.267 (*WA* 56.279).
15  Martin Luther, 'Two Kinds of Righteousness,' *LW* 31.297, *Sermo de duplici iustitia* (*WA* 2.145).
16  Luther, 'Two Kinds of Righteousness,' *LW* 31.297 (*WA* 2.145).

is finally perfected at the end through death.'[17] Luther is not referring here to the believer's growth in personal righteousness, that is, the righteousness of good works. That is the second kind of righteousness, a subject that he has not yet addressed at this point in the sermon. What Luther is apparently referring to here as a growth in alien righteousness is progress in faith. In fact, only a few lines earlier Luther had virtually identified faith with Christ's righteousness.[18] As faith, which is God's work within the believer, continues to grow and progress, so does the believer's possession of alien righteousness. It is then from the root of alien righteousness that our own proper righteousness, that of good works, grows.[19]

Several quotations above indicate that Luther still conceived of righteousness as in some sense infused into the believer. How does this differ from the standard Catholic teaching of his day? Luther differs from Rome on this point by linking infused righteousness to Christ's obedience in such a way that what Christ has done is counted to the believer. Whereas Rome proclaimed a doctrine of a grace-empowered cultivation of a righteousness of works through the infusion of charity, Luther argued that the believer's righteousness is nothing other than Christ himself, who has been united to the believer like a husband is united to his wife. This righteousness is alien in that it belongs properly to Christ, and the believer has done nothing to warrant acceptance in God's sight. The believer's only hope is in the righteousness of another. Yet this righteousness is also infused through the divine work of faith, by which Christ himself is present within, as Paul Althaus explains,

> It is not enough, however, to say either that faith receives justification or that man receives justification *in* faith. Luther's thought must be expressed more definitely. Justification is received *with* faith, that is, in the form of faith. Faith is the work and gift of God. God justifies a man by giving him faith. Christ is the righteousness of men and to this extent this righteousness is outside of us. But Christ is my righteousness only if I appropriate him and make him my own.[20]

For Luther, justification by faith does not refer to faith as the instrument that receives righteousness, but rather as the righteousness itself that God gives to the believer through the Gospel.

In the 1519 lectures on Galatians, Luther speaks of two ways of being justified, and these two ways correspond to the law-gospel distinction that would become a hallmark of Lutheran theology. The first is the way of works, which

---

[17] Luther, 'Two Kinds of Righteousness,' *LW* 31.299 (*WA* 2.146).

[18] 'In many passages of the Psalter, faith is called "the work of the Lord," "confession," "power of God," "mercy," "truth," "righteousness". All these are names for faith in Christ, rather, for the righteousness which is in Christ'—Luther, 'Two Kinds of Righteousness,' *LW* 31.299 (*WA* 2.146).

[19] Luther, 'Two Kinds of Righteousness,' *LW* 31.300 (*WA* 2.147).

[20] Paul Althaus, *The Theology of Martin Luther* (Philadelphia: Fortress Press, 1966), 231. See, also, Seifrid, 'Luther, Melanchthon, and Paul,' 137-52.

leads to justification before men but is damnable in the sight of God. The second way is the way of faith, wherein a person views his or her own former righteousness as nothing and trusts only in the mercy of God in Christ.[21] Luther speaks of alien righteousness again in this context, arguing that Christ's righteousness and that of the Christian are one and the same. Just as all have become sinners by the sin of another, so do all become righteous because of the righteousness of another.[22]

Commenting on Galatians 3.10, Luther implicitly affirms the criterion of perfect obedience as necessary for divine approval. He acknowledges the tension between Paul's quotation of Deuteronomy 27.26, which pronounces a curse on all who *do not* do the works of the law, and Paul's explicit argument that those who *are* of the works of the law are, therefore, cursed.[23] At first the opposite conclusion might seem to follow: because the law curses those who do not fulfill its demands, therefore, we ought to perform the works of the law in order to avoid the curse. Yet Luther argues that Paul's logic moves in a different direction because of his presupposition that no one can fulfill the law. Perfect obedience is an impossible standard for sinful human beings to attain. For this reason, all who place themselves under the law are, *de facto*, cursed: 'The result is that with this word Moses has forced all men under the curse; and when he says: "Cursed be everyone, etc.," he means exactly what he would mean if he were to say: "No man will do these things that are written; therefore all will be cursed and in need of Christ as Redeemer."'[24] Thus, Luther draws a line in the sand to separate the law from the Gospel. The former can only condemn sinful humanity, and thus sinners must seek righteousness in the Gospel alone.

The same themes emerge in the 1520 treatise *The Freedom of a Christian*. Here Luther argues that only the Word of God can bring righteousness, and it must be received by faith, not works.[25] He then expounds three effects of faith. First, faith alone justifies.[26] This argument is dependent on the distinction between commands and promises, a distinction that would later be formulated in terms of law and Gospel. The law demands perfect obedience, an obedience that no human being can render, as Luther states:

> Now when a man has learned through the commandments to recognize his helplessness and is distressed about how he might satisfy the law—since the law must be fulfilled so that not a jot or tittle shall be lost, otherwise man will be condemned without hope—then, being truly humbled and reduced to nothing in his own eyes, he finds in himself nothing whereby he may be justified and saved.

---

[21] Martin Luther, *Lectures on Galatians 1519*, LW 27.219-22 (*WA* 2.489-90).
[22] Luther, *Galatians 1519*, LW 27.222 (*WA* 2.491).
[23] LW 27.255-56 (*WA* 2.513).
[24] Luther, *Galatians 1519*, LW 27.256.
[25] Luther, *The Freedom of a Christian*, LW 31.345 (*WA* 7.50).
[26] Luther, *Freedom*, LW 31.347 (*WA* 7.52).

Here the second part of Scripture comes to our aid, namely, the promises of God which declare the glory of God, saying, 'If you wish to fulfill the law and not covet, as the law demands, come, believe in Christ in whom grace, righteousness, peace, liberty, and all things are promised you. If you believe, you shall have all things; if you do not believe, you shall lack all things.'[27]

The law exposes the sinfulness of humanity, thereby revealing the emptiness of works and demonstrating that justification must be by faith alone.

The second effect of faith is that it truly fulfills the law of God. By ascribing to God truthfulness and reliability, faith fulfills every divine demand.[28] Unlike Calvin and the Reformed tradition, Luther does not speak of faith as something empty in and of itself. For Luther, faith is the righteousness of a Christian.[29] The third effect of faith 'is that it unites the soul with Christ as a bride is united with her bridegroom.'[30] Herein lies the doctrine of alien righteousness, for the sinner's wickedness and damnation now belong to Christ, and Christ's righteousness now belongs to the sinner. The doctrine of imputation flows from the faith-union that a believer shares with Christ.

In the years after his break from Rome (1522-1546), Luther apparently did not undergo any major theological shifts comparable to his discovery of the true meaning of the righteousness of God. The most notable development in his theology during this time is that the doctrine of justification became the center and organizing principle of his whole theology.[31] This fact is evident as early as 1522 where, in his 'Preface to the New Testament,' Luther clearly articulates a law-gospel distinction as a hermeneutical axiom. The command-promise dichotomy previously mentioned in *The Freedom of a Christian* now becomes the key to faithful interpretation of Scripture:

> Necessity demands . . . that there should be a notice or preface, by which the ordinary man can be rescued from his former delusions, set on the right track, and taught what he is to look for in this book, so that he may not seek laws and commandments where he ought to be seeking the gospel and promises of God.[32]

Justification by the free grace of God, given in the Gospel, determines his approach to Scripture as a whole.

---

[27]  Luther, *Freedom, LW* 31.348-49 (*WA* 7.52-53).

[28]  Luther, *Freedom, LW* 31.350 (*WA* 7.54).

[29]  'Therefore faith alone is the righteousness of a Christian and the fulfilling of all the commandments'—Luther, *Freedom, LW* 31.353 (*WA* 7.56).

[30]  Luther, *Freedom, LW* 31.351 (*WA* 7.54-55).

[31]  Alister E. McGrath, *Iustitia Dei: A History of the Christian Doctrine of Justification*, 3rd ed. (New York: Cambridge University Press, 2003), 223.

[32]  Martin Luther, 'Preface to the New Testament,' *LW* 35.357.

In 1525 Luther published what has widely been regarded as his greatest work, *The Bondage of the Will*,[33] a response to Erasmus of Rotterdam's *The Free Will*.[34] In the conclusion of this work, Luther commends Erasmus for being the only theological opponent to cut through extraneous matters and address the main issue of contention between Luther and Rome.[35] This comment indicates the importance of the doctrine of the bound will for Luther, a doctrine that requires in turn a monergistic work of grace to result in salvation. Although monergism and alien righteousness are not identical concepts, for Luther they necessarily go together, so that Luther's doctrine of the bound will becomes a succinct expression of his doctrine of unconditional justification.[36] Whereas the early Luther conceived of the righteousness of God as a personal attribute by which he upholds the terms of the covenant and so allows human beings to distinguish themselves by their own free will, the mature Luther regarded such a notion as antithetical to the Gospel and instead conceived of the righteousness of God as a divine gift given through the Gospel to the elect. There can be no human preparation for justification. It is the work of God, who creates faith by means of the Gospel. The act of creating faith in the hearer of the Gospel is the act of justification, for the faith that apprehends Christ thereby possesses him as righteousness.

Although the subject of imputation arises rarely in this work, Luther does speak of justification, in line with Romans 4.2-3, as a forensic reckoning of righteousness.[37] Because, according to Paul, righteousness is reckoned not to the one who works but to the one who does not work, justification cannot result from a synthesis of grace and merit. One must either work or not work in order to attain justification:

> In short, Paul sets the one who works and the one who does not work alongside each other, leaving no room for anyone between them; and he asserts that righteousness is not reckoned to the former, but that it is reckoned to the latter provided he has faith. There is no way of escape for free choice here, no chance for it to get away with its endeavoring and striving. It must be classed either with the one who works or with the one who does not work. If it is classed with the former, so you are told here, it does not have any righteousness reckoned to it, whereas if it is classed with the latter—the one who does not work but has faith in God—then it

---

[33] Martin Luther, *De servo arbitrio*, *WA* 18.551-787; Luther, *The Bondage of the Will*, *LW* 33.3-295.

[34] Desiderius Erasmus, *De libero arbitrio*, in *Desiderii Erasmi Opera Omnia* (New York: Georg Olms Verlag, 2001), 9.1215-47; idem, *The Free Will*, in *Discourse on Free Will* (New York: Frederick Ungar, 1961).

[35] Luther, *Bondage*, *LW* 33.294. Among the extraneous matters are the Papacy, purgatory, and indulgences.

[36] Luther, *Bondage*, *LW* 33.266-70.

[37] Luther, *Bondage*, *LW* 3327 (*WA* 18:772).

does have righteousness reckoned to it. But in that case it will no longer be a case of free choice at work, but of being created anew through faith.[38]

Luther's problem with Erasmus is not that the latter lacks any conception of grace.[39] It is, rather, that by failing to understand the true nature of justifying grace, Erasmus has sought a middle ground between grace and works. For Luther, this error entails the nullification of grace, replacing the Gospel with a kind of moralism comparable to the Pelagian error.

Luther's 1535 commentary on Galatians reiterates the centrality of justification. In his summary of the letter's argument, he asserts that the whole of true Christian doctrine hangs on this one article.[40] Justification does not occur through the active righteousness of works, the righteousness that operates on the earthly plane among human beings.[41] Rather, justification results from the passive righteousness of faith, the righteousness that is Christ himself, seated in heaven at the right hand of the Father: 'Sin cannot happen in this Christian righteousness; for where there is no Law, there cannot be any transgression (Rom. 4.15).'[42] Faith alone takes hold of Christ in heaven and his righteousness, in spite of the fact that the sinner remains on earth under the condemnation of the law.[43] The believer is, therefore, *simul iustus et peccator*, a sinner in this earthly sphere but righteous in Christ. It is, therefore, essential that these two kinds of righteousness (that of the law and that of the Gospel) be distinguished from one another.

A particularly striking contrast between Luther and Rome appears in his comments on Galatians 2.16. Whereas Rome attributes the formal righteousness of faith to the virtue of charity that animates it, Luther attributes the justifying power of faith to Christ himself.[44] Faith 'takes hold of Christ in such a way that Christ is the object of faith, or rather not the object but, so to speak, the One who is present in the faith itself.'[45] This contrast constitutes a succinct

---

[38] Luther, *Bondage*, *LW* 33.271.

[39] On Erasmus's doctrine of grace, see *The Free Will*, sections 20, 44, 48-50, 52, 56.

[40] 'For if the doctrine of justification is lost, the whole of Christian doctrine is lost'— Martin Luther, *Lectures on Galatians 1535*, *LW* 26.9 (*WA* 40[1].48).

[41] Luther, *Galatians 1535*, *LW* 26.4-6 (*WA* 40[1].40-42). Clark, '*Iustitia Imputata*', 294, oversteps the evidence when he argues that *iustitia activa* 'is that accomplished by Christ'. Luther does not mention Christ's own righteousness in this context.

[42] Luther, *Galatians 1535*, *LW* 26.8 (*WA* 40[1].47).

[43] Luther, *Galatians 1535*, *LW* 26.9 (*WA* 40[1].48).

[44] 'But where they [the scholastics] speak of love, we speak of faith. And while they say that faith is the mere outline but love is its living colors and completion, we say in opposition that faith takes hold of Christ and that He is the form that adorns and informs faith as color does the wall. Therefore Christian faith is not an idle quality or an empty husk in the heart, which may exist in a state of mortal sin until love comes along to make it alive. But if it is true faith, it is a sure trust and firm acceptance in the heart'—Luther, *Galatians 1535*, *LW* 26.129 (*WA* 40[1].228).

[45] Luther, *Galatians 1535*, *LW* 26.129 (*WA* 40[1].228-29).

expression of the major difference between Rome and Luther on the question of justification. For Rome, faith derives its significance from an infused virtue, and Christ's atoning work is relegated to a necessary precondition for the infusion of grace. For Luther, faith justifies because the crucified Christ is present in it, and *he* constitutes the believer's righteousness. The former locates the legal basis of right standing with God in a grace-wrought virtue intrinsic to the believer; the latter locates it outside of the believer, in Christ, who is possessed by faith.

To summarize, for Luther the article of justification is the cornerstone of Christian theology, for it alone expresses what is required for sinful humanity to be made right with God. In the particularity of his grace, God creates faith in his elect by means of the Gospel. Faith justifies because it takes hold of Christ, who is the righteousness of the sinner. God's act of justification is essentially his act of evoking faith through the effective power of his Word, so that faith is not so much the condition of justification as it is the means by which God justifies. Crucial to this doctrine is the distinction between law and Gospel, in contrast to the Roman Catholic synthesis of grace-wrought merit. The law demands perfect obedience, and without the hope of offering such to God, the sinner's only recourse is to the Gospel.

Having surveyed Luther's doctrine of justification, we may now proceed to Melanchthon, organizing the discussion first around elements of continuity between the two and then proceeding to elements of discontinuity. Regarding the continuity that exists between Luther and Melanchthon, it is worth noting first that the 1521 edition of Melanchthon's *Loci Communes* may best be described as an organized arrangement of Luther's theology. On point after point Melanchthon follows closely on the heels of his Wittenberg colleague. He affirms that all things happen by necessity and that, therefore, there is no such thing as free will.[46] He draws a clear distinction between law and Gospel, attributing justification solely to the mercy of God to the exclusion of all human merit.[47] He affirms that faith itself is righteousness and that it is not within the power of human nature.[48] He argues that the law's proper function is 'to reveal sin and especially to confound the conscience'.[49]

The main contours of Luther's doctrine of justification would remain in place throughout all of Melanchthon's subsequent works. In the 1521 *Loci* he

---

[46] Philip Melanchthon, *Loci Communes Theologici* [1521], LCC, 19.24 (CR 21.87-88).

[47] Melanchthon, *Loci* [1521], 70-71 (CR 21.139).

[48] Melanchthon, *Loci* [1521], 89 (CR 21.159-60).

[49] Melanchthon, *Loci* [1521], 118; see Philip Melanchthon, *Paul's Letter to the Colossians* (Sheffield: Almond, 1989), 64-66, for an exposition of a twofold use the law. The latter work was originally published in 1527. The third use of the law would not make its appearance in Melanchthon until 1534.

affirms repeatedly that the law demands the impossible,[50] a conviction that remained unchanged by the time he published his 1543 edition:

> There is no doubt that the law of God demands both inner and outward obedience, as it says, 'You shall love the Lord your God with all your heart,' Deut. 6.5. But since this corrupted nature of men cannot produce perfect obedience, as Paul so clearly testifies in Romans 7-8, and since this sin remains in us in this life in the form of doubt, lack of faith and insufficient fear and love of God, and countless desires which run counter to the law of God, it follows that men are not pronounced righteous, that is, accepted before God by reason of the Law.[51]

It is the theological reality of divine justice, a justice that cannot be compromised by an easing of the law's demand, combined with the anthropological reality of sin that drives Melanchthon to affirm that justification must be on account of Christ and not by law.[52] Human righteousness must be radically distinguished from the righteousness that avails before God.[53] Contrary to the Roman doctrine, the atoning work of Christ is not the prerequisite for a gift of grace that enables sinners to attain right standing with God by law.[54] On the contrary, for Melanchthon, Christ's righteousness is our righteousness, and the blessing of justification is given by God's free grace alone, apart from all works or merits.[55] Given the divine demand for perfection, it could be no other way. The law-gospel theology of Luther, a dividing line drawn between himself and Rome, remains intact for Melanchthon from beginning to end.

In the 1530s Melanchthon began to forge his own path on certain issues, although none of these theological developments threatened the central reality of alien righteousness or the law-gospel distinction. Three issues related to the doctrine of justification are worthy of mention.

First, Melanchthon eventually modified Luther's doctrine of the will. Whereas the first edition of the *Loci Communes* sounds virtually identical to Luther's later work, *The Bondage of the Will*, by 1535 Melanchthon had made some adjustments to his former view. In later editions of the *Loci Communes* he denies that all things happen by necessity and affirms that human beings have

---

[50] 'The law demands impossible, and the conscience, convicted of sin, is assailed in all directions'—Melanchthon, *Loci* [1521], 85 (CR 21.156).

[51] Philip Melanchthon, *Loci Communes 1543* (St. Louis: Concordia, 1992), 72; *Tertia Aetas Locorum Theologicorum ab Ipso Melanthone Editorum* 4, CR, 21.716.

[52] Melanchthon, *Tertia Aetas* 4, CR, 21.664.

[53] Melanchthon, *Colossians*, 38-42, 46-57.

[54] Melanchthon, *Prima Aetas* 58b.14-61b.4, CR 21.143-47; LCC, 74-77, criticizes the medieval teaching that the Gospel is the 'new law', a doctrine that conflates law and Gospel.

[55] Melanchthon, *Loci Communes* [1521], 89.

some measure of free will in relation to civic righteousness.[56] However, he continues to maintain that humanity's fallen condition renders the will incapable of pleasing God, and so the will remains bound in some sense.[57] There is no evidence that Luther opposed Melanchthon on this score, but it is important to note that the transition involved here constitutes an embrace of a form of synergism. This fact is evident from a passage in the 1543 *Loci*:

> The free choice in man is the ability to apply oneself toward grace, that is, our free choice hears the promise, tries to assent to it and rejects the sins which are contrary to conscience. . . . Further, these points become clearer when the promise is considered. Since the promise is universal and since in God there are not conflicting wills, it is necessary that there is some cause within us for the difference as to why Saul is rejected and David received, that is, there must be a different action on the part of the two men.[58]

The distinction between David and Saul finally owes, not to the divine will, but to David's assent to grace and Saul's obstinacy toward it. Such an idea is foreign to Luther's doctrine of unconditional justification. For the mature Melanchthon, the two issues of alien righteousness and monergism, necessarily joined together in Luther, became separated, as Melanchthon upheld the former but ultimately denied the latter.

Second, the mature Melanchthon modified his understanding of the nature of faith. Like Luther, the early Melanchthon did not hesitate to affirm that faith itself is righteousness. By 1543 Melanchthon no longer speaks with such terminology. Instead, he locates righteousness in Christ and affirms that faith is merely an instrument that grasps Christ, and, as such, is intrinsically unworthy in itself:

> [We] do not say that we are righteous by faith in the sense that this is a worthiness of such great power that it merits remission, but in the sense that there must be some instrument in us by which we lay hold upon our Mediator who intercedes for us, and on account of whom the eternal Father is favorable toward us.[59]

Whereas Luther spoke of Christ and faith as virtually indistinguishable, for the mature Melanchthon, Christ alone is the sinner's righteousness. Even faith cannot stand in his place.

---

[56] Philip Melancthon, *Secunda Aetas Locorum Theologicorum ab Ipso Melanthone Editorum* 18a (ed. Henry Ernest Bindseil), CR 21.271; Melanchthon, *Tertia Aetas* 4, CR 21.654; cf. Melanchthon, *Colossians*, 39–42.
[57] Melanchthon, *Tertia Aetas* 4, CR 21.663.
[58] Melanchthon, *Loci Communes 1543*, 44.
[59] Melanchthon, *Loci Communes 1543*, 109.

Third, contrary to Luther, the mature Melanchthon promoted a third use of the law.[60] Highly motivated to defend his theology against the charge of antinomianism, Melanchthon began to argue by 1534 that the law has an ongoing function in the lives of believers, namely, to aid them in the practice of obedience.[61] In the 1543 *Loci* Melanchthon argues that believers have been freed from the law's condemnation, but nevertheless the law must continue to be preached to the regenerate in order to point out the remnants of sin in them and to inform them of what God demands.[62] It is evident in his argument that his concern is to safeguard an objective standard of righteousness for believers so that they will not seek to worship God on the basis of their own imaginations but will adhere to what he has revealed.[63] Some have argued or implied, with some degree of plausibility, that the rise of the third use of the law in Melanchthon resulted from a truncated view of the effectiveness of justification.[64] While this may indeed be the case, it must be kept in mind that the mature Melanchthon explicitly and consistently separated the believer's obedience to the law from the ground of justification, thereby preserving the firm law-gospel distinction that separated Luther from Rome.

Luther continued to speak approvingly of Melanchthon's work, granting high praise to the 1535 edition of the *Loci Communes*, the first revision in which Melanchthon's independence had started to show:

> If anybody wishes to become a theologian, he has a great advantage, first of all, in having the Bible. . . . Afterward he should read Philip's *Loci Communes*. This he should read diligently and well until he has its contents fixed in his head. If he has these two he is a theologian, and neither the devil nor a heretic can shake him. . . . There's no book under the sun in which the whole of theology is so compactly presented as in the *Loci Communes*. . . . No better book has been written after the Holy Scriptures than Philip's.[65]

Clearly, Melanchthon was an independent thinker. But it is difficult to maintain the 'Luther against the Lutherans' thesis, with Melanchthon as the primary villain, in light of such statements on Luther's part.

---

[60] The historical context and origin of this doctrine in Melanchthon is explained in Timothy J. Wengert, *Law and Gospel: Philip Melanchthon's Debate with John Agricola of Eisleben over* Poenientia (Grand Rapids: Baker, 1997).

[61] Wengert, *Law and Gospel*, 195–96.

[62] Melanchthon, *Tertia Aetas* 6, CR, 21.719.

[63] Melanchthon, *Tertia Aetas* 6, CR, 21.719.

[64] Seifrid, 'Luther, Melanchthon, and Paul', 142, writes, 'Since "justification" no longer had an effective dimension, the Law (in its "third use") moved in to fill the vacuum left behind.' Wengert, *Law and Gospel*, 190-91, hints very strongly at a similar evaluation.

[65] Martin Luther, *Table Talk* (ed. and trans. Theodore G. Tappert), *LW* 54.439-40. This comment is dated in the winter of 1542-1543.

For both Luther and Melanchthon, the doctrine of justification is developed on the basis of a divine demand for perfect obedience, which no sinful human being can attain. For this reason, in contrast to medieval Catholic theology, right standing with God must come from an alien righteousness, namely, the righteousness of Jesus Christ imputed to the sinner. Unable to seek righteousness on the basis of the law, the sinner must look only to the Gospel, and thus the strong law-gospel distinction, a hallmark of Lutheran theology, stands firmly in place for both reformers. This shared theological outlook, in spite of Melanchthon's eventual independence on free will, the nature of faith, and the third use of the law, ties these two men close together in their common opposition to the law-gospel synthesis of medieval Catholic theology. Where they differ, they do so on matters of in-house debate within a shared Lutheran tradition.[66]

---

[66] An earlier form of this article appeared in *Global Journal of Classic Theology* 9.3 (2012).

# CHAPTER 4

# The doctrine of justification in the teaching of John Oecolampadius (1482–1531)

*Jeff Fisher*

The recent debates about justification have compelled scholars to reassess the traditional understanding of the doctrine, particularly considering whether the interpretation of the New Testament has been overly shaped by a sixteenth-century lens. These critiques indicate the need not only to revisit what the biblical texts say, but also to understand properly the history of Christian thought in the development of theology. N.T. Wright, one of the most influential voices in the justification discussions, emphasizes this very need when he states that Alister McGrath's 'remarkable two-volume history of the doctrine . . . is required reading for anyone who wants seriously to engage' with discussions about the doctrine of justification.[1] Wright particularly highlights McGrath's contention in *Iustitia Dei* that '[t]he *concept of justification* and the *doctrine of justification* must be carefully distinguished,'[2] and that the idea of *forensic* justification was 'a remarkable innovation in the western theological tradition' at the time of the Reformation.[3]

Since the time it was first published, McGrath's *Iustitia Dei* has received both praise and criticism. For example, in one of the essays dedicated to McGrath for his 50th birthday, Gerald Bray praised the work for successfully bringing justification back to the center of theological discussion, but also called for further engagement with the recent debates about justification, as well as more in-depth study on some of the historical details.[4] While the recent

---

[1] N.T. Wright, *Justification: God's Plan & Paul's Vision* (Downers Grove: IVP Academic, 2009), 79-80, 83.

[2] Wright, *Justification*, 80. He cites Alister E. McGrath, *Iustitia Dei: A History of the Christian Doctrine of Justification* (Cambridge: Cambridge University Press, 1986), 1.2-3, emphasis original.

[3] McGrath, *Iustitia Dei* (1986), 1.3. In the updated third edition, McGrath refers to the Reformation view of justification as 'a decisive shift' rather than a 'remarkable innovation,' and he considers continuities with the Middle Ages as well as the discontinuities. See McGrath, *Iustitia Dei* (3rd edition, 2005), 2.4.

[4] Gerald L. Bray, 'Alister E. McGrath and Justification', in Sung Wook Chung (ed.), *Alister E. McGrath and Evangelical Theology* (Grand Rapids: Baker Academic,

third edition addresses some of these concerns, McGrath himself notes that 'it is still an uncomfortable fact' that some of the work is based on older scholarship.[5]

## Statement of purpose and significance

This present study seeks to correct some of the historical details in McGrath's work that are based on outdated scholarship. McGrath has oversimplified the portrayal of the teachings in the Reformed tradition coming out of Switzerland—specifically, the teachings of the first-generation reformer from Basel, John Oecolampadius (1482-1531). Oecolampadius was a priest, a professor, a preacher, a pastor, and the author of numerous writings.[6] He studied theology and the biblical languages at the universities of Heidelberg, Stuttgart, Tübingen, and Basel. He was ordained in 1510, first published in 1512, assisted Erasmus on the first edition of the *Novum Instrumentum* in 1515, and earned his Doctorate of Divinity at the University of Basel in 1518 while serving as the confessor priest at the cathedral in Basel. Already as early as 1518, Oecolampadius had significant connections with Martin Luther, most notably their common friendship with Melanchthon. By May 1519, he was teaching doctrine that was more evangelical than traditional. After a brief time at a monastery, his controversial writings forced him to flee and he returned to Basel near the end of 1522. He was soon appointed as Lecturer in Holy Scripture at the University of Basel where his lectures drew overflow crowds of more than 400 people. His rare trilingual skills in Greek, Hebrew, and Latin enabled him to explain the meaning of the Scriptures in a way that was distinctive for his time. Many of his lectures were eventually published as fifteen different commentaries covering twenty-one books of the Bible.

Oecolampadius' attempts to persuade the city council of Basel to embrace the Reformation were finally achieved on April 1, 1529. He became highly involved in the debates about the Lord's Supper, most notably disputing alongside Zwingli at the Marburg Colloquy in October 1529. He died only two years later, at the age of 49, just a few weeks after Zwingli, his close friend and colleague. Oecolampadius was praised regularly by his contemporaries for his theological scholarship and frequently considered among the most influential

---

2003), 24-32. See, also, the paper delivered at the 2010 Evangelical Theological Society previously published as John Warwick Montgomery, *Christ Our Advocate: Studies in Polemical Theology, Jurisprudence and Canon Law* (Bonn: Verl. für Kultur und Wiss., 2002), 292-302.

5 McGrath, *Iustitia Dei*, x.

6 The best biography of Oecolampadius is Ernst Staehelin, *Das Theologische Lebenswerk Johannes Oekolampads* (Quellen und Forschungen zur Reformationsgeschichte, 21: New York: Johnson, 1939). The best English biography is E. Gordon Rupp, *Patterns of Reformation* (London: Epworth Press, 1969), 3-47.

reformers of the time.[7] As an important voice during a time when significant transitions were happening in the church and in theology, Oecolampadius ought to be correctly understood in order to recognize the ways the doctrine of justification developed at the time of the Reformation.

## Categorization of the doctrine of justification

McGrath asserts that Oecolampadius was an early humanist who held to *subjective* views of justification and the atonement. He summarizes that Oecolampadius viewed justification not as an *imputation* of righteousness, but as the *actualization* of righteousness.[8] McGrath's conclusions about Oecolampadius in *Iustitia Dei* are a more succinct version of an article published a few years earlier, where he specifically asserts that Oecolampadius had 'an even greater emphasis upon the ethical nature of justification' than Zwingli.[9] In his *Intellectual Origins of the European Reformation*, McGrath similarly asserts that Oecolampadius and Zwingli 'initially demonstrated a *near-total disinterest* in the doctrine and subsequently appear to have *misunderstood* it, regarding it as *detrimental* to the development of piety'.[10] McGrath supports his categorization of Oecolampadius based on the ideas that justification was not a primary doctrine for Oecolampadius, that he emphasized the new life of faith that produces good works, and that his 'strong emphasis upon the importance of regeneration in the Christian life inevitably led to justification being subordinated to regeneration'.[11] He deduces from the theology of Oecolampadius and Zwingli that '[t]he tendency to equate justification with piety, or to make justification dependent upon piety, ultimately arises from the absence of a clear concept of imputed righteousness'.[12] He specifically observes that it is possible that they under-

---

[7] Examples could be given from Wimpfeling, Erasmus, Luther, Melanchthon, Zwingli, Bucer, Calvin, Bullinger, Turretin, Arminius, and many others. For several examples, see J. Brashler, 'Oecolampadius, Johannes (1482-1531)', in Donald K. McKim (ed.), *Dictionary of Major Biblical Interpreters* (Leicester: InterVarsity Press, 2007), 782; L. Miller (ed.), 'Oecolampadius: The Unsung Hero of the Basel Reformation,' *Iliff Review* 39.3 (Fall 1982), 6, 12; Amy Nelson Burnett, *Teaching the Reformation: Ministers and Their Message in Basel, 1529-1629* (Oxford: Oxford University Press, 2006), 26, 47-48.

[8] McGrath, *Iustitia Dei* (1986), 2.34.

[9] Alister E. McGrath, 'Humanist Elements in the Early Reformed Doctrine of Justification,' *Archiv für Reformationsgeschichte* 73 (1 January 1982), 9.

[10] Alister E. McGrath, *The Intellectual Origins of the European Reformation* (Oxford: Blackwell, 1987), 198, emphasis added. In the updated second edition, Oecolampadius' name is completely removed from the discussion about the role of humanism and justification in the Swiss Reformation. See McGrath, *Intellectual Origins* (2nd edition, 2004), 187-88.

[11] McGrath, *Iustitia Dei* (1986), 2.34. Note that at the time of the Reformation, regeneration and sanctification were often used interchangeably. This is why McGrath writes in terms of regeneration, piety, and moral living as all being similar.

[12] McGrath, 'Humanist Elements,' 17.

stood an *ethical doctrine of justification* to be inconsistent with a *forensic doctrine of justification*. McGrath's claim, that neither Oecolampadius nor Zwingli held to a forensic doctrine of justification, supports his assertion that their humanist emphasis on ethical living was a primary reason for their confusion about the nature of justification. It also allows him to conclude that it is probable that the idea of forensic justification had not yet arrived in Switzerland prior to 1530 when it first became particularly evident in the writings of Melanchthon.[13]

McGrath's depiction of Oecolampadius' doctrine of justification is almost entirely based on the conclusions of Henri Strohl's work, published in 1951.[14] McGrath reiterates the same conclusions that Strohl made, and uses the same references to Oecolampadius' writings as Strohl had. For example, McGrath's claim that justification and regeneration cannot be separated is based on Strohl's description of Oecolampadius' comments on Hebrews 10.24.[15] When Strohl's own work on Oecolampadius' view of justification is considered, it becomes apparent that Strohl drew most of his conclusions from selected portions of the biography by Staehelin, published in 1939. Strohl states that his conclusions are based on themes found in Oecolampadius' teaching on 1 John, Mark, Colossians, Hebrews, the catechism he authored, and the new Reformation order.[16] However, a comparison of the summaries of these sources by Strohl and Staehelin reveals a tremendous amount of similarity. Other than the sermons on 1 John, Strohl has no interaction with any portion of Oecolampadius' writings that are not included in Staehelin's biography.[17] So, when Strohl concludes that Oecolampadius was a moralist in his view of justification, McGrath merely imports these arguments and conclusions into his portrayal of the development of justification in the early stages of the Reformation. However, this categorization of Oecolampadius needs to be revised when his writings are more fully explored.

Very few scholars have done much research on Oecolampadius in general, so this portrayal by McGrath has essentially gone unchallenged.[18] Only three

---

[13] See McGrath, 'Humanist Elements,' 9-10; McGrath, *Iustitia Dei* (1986), 2.23-24.

[14] See Henry Strohl, *La pensée de la Réforme* (Neuchâtel Delachaux et Niestlé, 1951), 106-108.

[15] Compare McGrath, 'Humanist Elements,' 10, and Strohl, *La pensée de la Réforme,* 108.

[16] Strohl, *La pensée de la Réforme,* 107-108.

[17] See Staehelin, *Das Theologische Lebenswerk Johannes Oekolampads,* 463-64, on the church-visitation policy; 490-92, on Mark; 494, on Colossians; 577-78, on John; 586-88, on the catechism. In every case, Strohl has adopted Staehelin's quotation or description of 'the new life' and identified this as the totality of Oecolampadius' teaching, despite the fact that Staehelin includes much more in his own summaries of these sources. McGrath also cites this as one of his sources in both editions of *Iustitia Dei,* though it does not appear that he interacted with it.

[18] The need for further research on Oecolampadius has been stated repeatedly by Ed Miller (1982), Thomas Fudge (1997), Bruce Gordon (2002), and Amy Nelson Bur-

other authors have observed aspects of Oecolampadius' writings that present a different picture than McGrath has given us. Akira Demura noted in 1997 that some of Oecolampadius' comments on justification are reminiscent of Luther's doctrine of justification, but not quite as forensic as Calvin's.[19] Most significantly, he states that we 'find a clear-cut statement on the imputation theory of justification' in Oecolampadius' comments on Romans 3.21.[20] While Demura does not directly refer to McGrath's portrayal of Oecolampadius, two recent dissertations do. In her dissertation on Oecolampadius' exegesis of Isaiah, Diane Poythress states that McGrath 'wishes to liberalize Oecolampadius's teaching' on justification and contends that Oecolampadius 'held to a fully Reformed view'.[21] She also comments in a later footnote that Strohl's synopsis of Oecolampadius' emphasis on the practical and ethical life of the church is 'an exaggeration of one aspect of the reformer's writings,' which would have been corrected by a broader reading of his writings.[22] Most recently, David Fink's dissertation on the development of the doctrine of justification identifies that both Staehelin's and McGrath's depictions of Oecolampadius's teaching on justification are inadequate. He also reiterates that Oecolampadius is 'one of the most under-studied of the first-generation Swiss reformers,' with no focused study on his doctrine of justification.[23] These scholars who have interacted with the writings of Oecolampadius maintain that McGrath's portrayal of Oecolampadius needs amending. Therefore, it is necessary to look at what Oecolampadius himself taught to ascertain his teaching on justification.

---

nett (2008). See, for example, Amy Nelson Burnett, 'Contributors to the Reformed Tradition', in David M. Whitford (ed.), *Reformation and Early Modern Europe: A Guide to Research* (Kirksville, MO: Truman State University Press, 2008), 35.

[19] Akira Demura, 'Two Commentaries on the Epistle to the Romans: Calvin and Oecolampadius', in Wilhelm H. Neuser and Brian G. Armstrong (eds), *Calvinus Sincerioris Religionis Vindex* (Kirksville, Mo.: Sixteenth Century Journal Publishers, 1997), 169-70.

[20] Demura, 'Two Commentaries,' 170.

[21] Diane Marie Poythress, 'Johannes Oecolampadius' Exposition of Isaiah, Chapters 36-37' (unpublished doctoral dissertation, Westminster Theological Seminary, 1992), 583, 584-85, 589. See fn. 82 for her critique of McGrath. She unnecessarily concedes that Oecolampadius taught that regeneration precedes justification by citing a reference in Staehelin's summary of Oecolampadius' theological views from before his 'breakthrough' to the Reformation.

[22] Poythress, 'Oecolampadius' Exposition', 588. See fn. 99 where she infers that Strohl primarily drew his conclusions about Oecolampadius from the French translation of his sermons on 1 John published in 1540.

[23] David C. Fink, 'Divided by Faith: The Protestant Doctrine of Justification and the Confessionalization of Biblical Exegesis' (unpublished doctoral dissertation, Duke Divinity School, 2010), 258 fn. 11. He also identifies that Oecolampadius recovered 'earlier patristic insights which had become obscured by the ravages of time and the accumulation of corrosive traditions'. See Fink, 'Divided by Faith,' 308.

## Definitions for justification

Since Oecolampadius did not write a systematic theology or a *loci communes*, the categories of subjective, objective, moralist, or forensic will not be derived from Oecolampadius himself. Therefore, it is essential that we understand what we are looking for in order to discern if he can be categorized as a moralist in his view of justification. McGrath explains the moralist doctrine of justification in *Iustitia Dei* as based on Augustine's teaching that a person is justified by love (*caritate*) alone more than by faith alone.[24] Augustine understood the verb *iustificare* to mean 'to make righteous' based on the idea that the suffix *-ficare* was the unstressed form of *facere*, and therefore justification was considered both an event and a process that involved *inherent* righteousness rather than *imputed* righteousness with almost no distinction between justification and regeneration.[25] McGrath identifies this view as essentially the characteristic medieval understanding of justification which remained until the time of the Reformation.[26] In contrast to moralist justification is 'forensic justification', which McGrath identifies as having three key aspects: 1) a forensic declaration of righteousness as a change in *status* not *nature*; 2) a distinction between *justification* and *regeneration*; and 3) a *synthetic* rather than an *analytic* judgment by God based on the alien righteousness of Christ imputed to the believer.[27] These are the elements to be used to categorize the doctrine of justification found in the teaching of Oecolampadius.

## The teaching of Oecolampadius

To assess Oecolampadius' views, we will primarily consider his exegesis from his commentaries on 1 John and Romans. While this is partly due to space constraints, it is also because the Romans lectures provide his interpretation of the biblical book that deals most specifically with the issues at hand and the 1 John sermons are the main sources that McGrath and Strohl identify as the basis for their argument that Oecolampadius held to a moralist view of justification.[28] These two works also represent his earliest teaching after his Reformation breakthrough. Oecolampadius began preaching on 1 John in the winter of 1523 and teaching on Romans in August 1524.[29] While Oecolampadius certainly emphasized right living, ethics, and the new life in Christ, these writings show that Oecolampadius did not hold to a moralist view of justification.

---

[24] McGrath, *Iustitia Dei* (1986), 1.28–30.
[25] McGrath, *Iustitia Dei* (1986), 1.31, 36, 40-41.
[26] McGrath, *Iustitia Dei* (1986), 1.41-47, 51.
[27] McGrath, *Iustitia Dei* (1986), 1.182.
[28] See Strohl, *La pensée de la Réforme*, 107-108.
[29] The 1 John commentary was first published in June 1524 and later republished and translated into German and French. The Romans commentary was published in August 1525 and republished in 1526. Both commentaries are available electronically at http://libguides.calvin.edu/content.php?pid=47579&sid=442083.

When we explore his sermons on 1 John, we readily find that he explicitly does not agree with Augustine's moralist doctrine of justification, that one is justified by love. In his sermon on 1 John 3.10, Oecolampadius writes:

> Indeed we are justified by faith, and we are made sons of God, but justification is not attributed to love (*charitati non tribuitur iustificatio*). Indeed love and the working of righteousness flow from faith, and are evidences of faith. Moreover, however great love is, nevertheless it does not justify (*charitas magna sit, non tamen iustificat*), because no one loves as much as he ought.[30]

He then repeats that it is clear 'that love and the working of righteousness are evidences of faith'.[31] In his next sermon, he reiterates that John is not saying that we are justified by our love, because 'indeed neither love, nor a good conscience justifies'.[32] Both Demura and Staehelin point out this passage to show that while Oecolampadius did 'emphasize responsive human love toward God and charity among men,' he was careful to articulate that love does not justify, but rather that it is an evidence of faith.[33] Using McGrath's definitions, Oecolampadius self-identified that he was *not* moralist in the sense that one is justified by love.

Further evidence that he is not moralist is found in how he understands the relationship between justification and piety. Oecolampadius teaches that true faith will always produce good works, but there are no good works unless one is previously justified. In his fifth sermon on 1 John, he distinguishes between lifeless faith and true faith, explaining, 'In fact good works will be nothing, unless previously you yourself were good . . . unless you were justified by faith (*nisi te fides iustificet*); neither will you be justified (*neque iustificatus eris*) or faithful if something evil was pleasing to you.'[34] Oecolampadius further taught that these good works which proceed from faith after one is justified are *righteous*. For example, in his tenth sermon, he teaches:

> Consequently, if you have faith and that true knowledge that Christ is our righteousness (*quod Christus nostra est iustitia*) . . . know that you ought to be righteous yourselves, and exert yourself to be. . . . [A]nd you will be those who do righteousness, even though our righteousness is nothing compared to his righteousness, nevertheless it is great, because he works it in us.[35]

---

[30] Johann Oecolampadius, *In Epistolam Ioannis Apostoli Catholicam Primam, Ioannis Oecolampadii Demegoriae, Hoc Est, Homiliae Una & Viginti* (Nurenburg: Apud Iohann Petreium, 1524), 52b. All translations from the Latin are my own.

[31] Oecolampadius, *In Epistolam Ioannis Primam*, 52b.

[32] Oecolampadius, *In Epistolam Ioannis Primam*, 60a.

[33] See Demura, 'Two Commentaries,' 174 and Staehelin, *Das Theologische Lebenswerk*, 228. Staehelin also notes Oecolampadius' comment that when Peter says that love covers over a multitude of sins, he is not teaching justification by love.

[34] Oecolampadius, *In Epistoalm Ioannis Primam*, 25b.

[35] Oecolampadius, *In Epistoalm Ioannis Primam*, 48b.

It is important to notice that he identifies two distinct kinds of righteousness here: Christ as our righteousness and the righteousness that we do by Christ working in us. Oecolampadius is apparently compelled to explain in this sermon the difference between these two kinds of righteousness. He writes:

> And whoever believes, he actually works righteousness by faith, and his works become just and holy (*fiuntque opera illius iusta & sancta*), which otherwise would merit damnation, since the deeds were resulting from faith . . . [but] one is not justified as a result of them, one is justified by faith (*qui non iustificabatur ex se, fide iustificatur*).[36]

Oecolampadius is seeking to make it clear that doing righteousness is distinct from justification, because the righteousness of justification is by faith alone, while doing righteousness is a later result of that faith. In fact, what he teaches here is very similar to what John Calvin would later teach on this topic. Calvin comments on this same verse that the author 'proves by many arguments that faith is necessarily connected with a holy and pure life. The first argument is that we are spiritually begotten after the likeness of Christ; it hence follows, that no one is born of Christ but he who lives righteously.'[37] Like Calvin, Oecolampadius makes specific distinctions between the acts of righteousness which follow justification and the righteousness of justification.

These statements strongly suggest that Oecolampadius understood justification to be a change in *status* more than a change in *nature*. And though they do not reveal a thorough view of forensic justification, there is a glimpse of the concept of imputation. This glimpse is also evident in his sixteenth sermon where he preached, 'Indeed Christ came, who appeased the Father, and who reconciled us to him, whose righteousness is our righteousness (*cuius iusticia, nostra est iusticia*), who as redeemer and priest made satisfaction for sins by one sacrifice.'[38] Oecolampadius does not provide an explanation for *how* Christ's righteousness is ours, so it would be difficult to categorize his view as 'forensic,' but the fact that he teaches that Christ's righteousness is our righteousness in multiple places suggests that a forensic view of justification was developing. It is evident, though, that even with his ethical emphasis, Oecolampadius does not teach a moralist view of justification in his sermons on 1 John.

When we consider Oecolampadius' lectures on Romans, we find further evidence that he does not hold to a moralist view of justification and we get a fuller picture of what his objective views include. The most relevant places in Oecolampadius' teaching to consider when assessing his doctrine of justification undoubtedly include his explanations of *iustitia Dei* and *iustificatio* in his

---

[36] Oecolampadius, *In Epistoalm Ioannis Primam*, 48b.
[37] Jean Calvin, *Commentaries on the Catholic Epistles* (Edinburgh: Calvin Translation Society, 1855), 201-202.
[38] Oecolampadius, *In Epistoalm Ioannis Primam*, 77.

Romans commentary.[39] Oecolampadius offers specific remarks under the heading *Iustitia Dei* in three different places. In his exegesis of Romans 1, he echoes the view of Luther when he writes:

> Take care not to understand here by the righteousness of God, the judgment of God by which he punishes the guilty, or righteousness, by which his own self is his righteousness. . . . Indeed, the gospel declares that God is a friend to the believing ones, but angry with the unbelieving ones: and so here the righteousness of God is placed opposite the wrath of God. And it is the righteousness of God which justifies the impious by grace without respect to works (*Et est iustitia dei, quae gratis iustificat impium, absque operum respectu*).[40]

Then in his comments on Romans 3.21-23, Oecolampadius writes, 'Again in this place, righteousness is where God considers us justified (*iustos reputat*), when certainly we are in his grace (*quando scilicet in eius gratia sumus*).'[41] Finally, he comments on Romans 3.26 that 'because God promised salvation through his Son, and not through our works, this is correctly called righteousness'.[42] From these statements, we see that Oecolampadius understood the righteousness of God as that which fulfills the promises of salvation through his Son and justifies the one who believes by considering the believer righteous when they are not actually righteous. Once again this is contrary to the moralist view of justification described by McGrath.

We also find that Oecolampadius makes a distinction between justification and piety, because he affirms that justification by faith alone is sufficient *and* that living rightly is required for those who have been justified. In order to maintain both these assertions, there must be a distinction between justification and piety. Fink identifies that while Oecolampadius creatively appropriates Ambrose and 'takes much of his language directly from the Wittenberg school,' he acquired his particular view from Origen.[43] Oecolampadius appealed to Origen as one who 'explains this text clearly, saying that the justification of faith

---

[39] McGrath, himself, notes the importance of commentaries, especially those on Romans, for the development of the doctrine of justification. See McGrath, *Iustitia Dei* (1986), 1.39-40. However, neither Strohl nor McGrath interact with Oecolampadius' commentary on Romans.

[40] Johann Oecolampadius, *In Epistolam B. Pauli Apost. Ad Rhomanos Adnotationes à Ioanne Oecolampadio Basileae Praelectae* (Basel: Andream Cratandrum, 1525), 10a. Compare this idea of the *iustitia Dei* to that expressed by Luther in his comments on Romans 1.17 in Martin Luther, *Luthers Vorlesung über den Römerbrief*, 1515/1516 (Leipzig: Dieterich, 1908), 2.14. This does not necessarily mean that Oecolampadius used Luther's commentary, but that he was expressing similar disagreement with previously held understandings of *iustitia Dei*.

[41] Oecolampadius, *In Epistolam ad Rhomanos*, 34b-35a.

[42] Oecolampadius, *In Epistolam ad Rhomanos*, 35b. Staehelin also notes that Oecolampadius expresses God's righteousness as the faithfulness of God to his promises. See Staehelin, *Das Theologische Lebenwerk*, 215-16.

[43] Fink, 'Divided by Faith,' 128-29, 257-58.

alone is sufficient, so that the one who only believes is justified, even if he has not completed a single work'.[44] Fink points out that Oecolampadius responds to the concern that someone might claim they were justified and yet act unrighteously with 'a nearly verbatim restatement of Origen's crucial qualification to this doctrine'.[45] Following Origen, Oecolampadius contends that such a person 'without a doubt has spurned the grace of justification. Obviously, for that reason, pardon is not given so that one is allowed to sin again. Indeed remission is not promised to us for future crimes, but past crimes.'[46] Fink argues that Oecolampadius' adoption of Origen's exegesis demonstrates not only that Oecolampadius was 'operating with a different set of priorities' than Luther, but also that he clung to a traditional medieval view which insisted 'that sin *must not* remain after justification: justification, after all, only wipes the slate clean for prior sins'.[47] For Fink, this establishes that Oecolampadius 'viewed justification primarily in terms of forgiveness for past sins only'.[48]

However, this appeal to Origen on justification by faith is not the complete picture. While Oecolampadius adopted Origen's notion that justification does not promise forgiveness for future sins, he did not understand this to mean that sin must not remain after justification. In fact, he declared that 'the life of the justified is perpetual wrestling: indeed being urged by the Holy Spirit to do good, the flesh hinders and spoils the work'.[49] He assured that 'as long as we live, faith is unfinished and able to be increased: nevertheless it still saves, even if it was as a grain of mustard, as long as it is true faith'.[50] When he developed the 'chief thought that we are justified by faith alone,' in his exposition of Romans 4, Oecolampadius expressed:

> Afterwards grace succeeds, which pardons sins and grants righteousness: but as long as we live, carnal desire remains in us: which although it is still called sin, it is not counted as sin (*imputatur in peccatum*). Finally, we receive peace from all sordid carnal desire, and that [happens] at death and the resurrection.[51]

Similarly, in his explanation of Romans 7, Oecolampadius identified that 'even the justified apostle (*apostolus etiam iustificatus*) still recognizes in himself sin

---

[44] Oecolampadius, *In Epistolam ad Rhomanos*, 37b.
[45] Fink, 'Divided by Faith,' 259.
[46] Oecolampadius, *In Epistolam ad Rhomanos*, 35b. See, also, 34b where Oecolampadius wrote, 'This indeed is righteousness in the present time. For in the future time after this life, the righteousness of God is such that each one is given according to his works. [Paul] alludes to the ceasing from sin and not returning to vomit as in 1 Pet 4[1-3].'
[47] Fink, 'Divided by Faith,' 261, original emphasis.
[48] Fink, 'Divided by Faith,' 261, 264, 308.
[49] Oecolampadius, *In Epistolam ad Rhomanos*, 57a.
[50] Oecolampadius, *In Epistolam ad Rhomanos*, 12a.
[51] Oecolampadius, *In Epistolam ad Rhomanos*, 41a, 53a.

and the desire of sinning'.[52] And in chapter 8, he affirmed that for 'the old man to be crucified and abolished' means that 'we cease from sinning,' but then explained that this does not mean 'that evil affections die all at once, because this is not granted to us in this life'.[53] Rather than teaching that sin must not remain after justification, Oecolampadius' view was that the believer is considered righteous though still affected by sin, and that even though impure and ungrateful acts are mixed in, the one who has been justified will always strive to do good works. Demura affirms that Oecolampadius' comments on *Iustitia Dei* are 'an unmistakable echo of Luther's "*simul iustus ac peccator*" (at the same time, justified and sinner)'.[54] The reason Oecolampadius insisted that justification was for past sins only was so that one would continue to demonstrate true faith by striving to do good works. He is not teaching that justification is the actualization of righteousness, but rather emphasizes that justification is *sola fide* (by faith alone) but can never be *vana fides* (empty faith) or *fictitius fides* (false faith).[55]

It would not be too much to say that Oecolampadius was seeking a solution to the same problem about which Melanchthon would later write. McGrath includes an excerpt from Melanchthon's *Loci Communes* in the *Christian Theology Reader* to show that 'Melanchthon aims to set out the place of good works in the Christian life, avoiding any suggestion that justification takes place on their account—while at the same time stressing that they have a real and significant role within the context of Christian living.'[56] This could just as easily summarize what Oecolampadius is aiming to teach here.[57] Demura maintains that Oecolampadius' perspective is similar to Calvin's 'ethical code,' which taught that one is not justified by works, but the one who is justified is never without works.[58] Similar to Melanchthon and Calvin, Oecolampadius understood justification as a change in *status* more than a change in *nature*, but for the change in status to be genuine, there must be evidence of the faith that justified.

While his sermons on 1 John did not demonstrate all three elements of 'forensic justification,' his lectures on Romans do, even if it is not as strong as in

---

52 Oecolampadius, *In Epistolam ad Rhomanos*, 56b-57a.
53 Oecolampadius, *In Epistolam ad Rhomanos*, 62a-62b.
54 Demura, 'Two Commentaries on Romans,' 171.
55 For example, see Oecolampadius' comments in *In Epistolam ad Rhomanos*, 59a. Staehelin, *Das Theologische Lebenswerk*, 216, broadly summarizes all of Oecolampadius' comments on Romans 6–8 as his exposition on faith that is not empty.
56 Alister E. McGrath, *The Christian Theology Reader* (Malden, MA: Blackwell, 2007), 444-45.
57 For example, Oecolampadius begins his comments on Romans 5, 'He transitions now to works and the fruit of faith, more correctly, the blessings, which come forth from faith [which] first justifies'. See Oecolampadius, *In Epistolam ad Rhomanos*, 47a. See, also, the comments in Fink, 'Divided by Faith,' 129-30.
58 Demura, 'Two Commentaries', 171.

later reformers.[59] Any indication of the imputation of Christ's righteousness was fairly muted in his sermons on 1 John. In his Romans lectures, though, it is more pronounced. While Oecolampadius used the term *imputat* most often in reference to sin that is not counted against those who believe,[60] like Erasmus, he changed the Latin translation of Romans 4 from *reputatum* to *imputatum*. He comments that Paul 'insinuates that if for Abraham, who abounded in all good works, faith alone was imputed as righteousness (*sola fides ad iustitiam imputata est*), then no one else remains to be justified by works'.[61] Oecolampadius states more specifically in his comments on Romans 5.19:

> The righteousness of Christ was obedience all the way to death on the cross, and it works in those who believe, so that they already do not want to be disobedient but obedient to God. Nevertheless, however much our obedience may be, it is not sufficient to save, because it still always has attached some degree of disobedience. Further, the obedience of Christ is imputed as righteousness to those who believe (*obedientia Christi credentibus imputatur ad iustitiam*).[62]

Using the same terminology as he did with reference to Abraham's faith being imputed as righteousness, here he expressly declares that the obedience of Christ is imputed as righteousness to those who believe, even while they are still marred by disobedience.

Though this is the clearest statement of external imputation, in other sections of his commentary on Romans, Oecolampadius states that Christ's merit is given to us, that Christ *is* our righteousness, and that Christ's righteousness is ours. For example, he comments on Romans 8.1, 'Therefore all our merit is in Christ, who is our righteousness (*omne nostrum meritum est in Christo, qui nostra iustitia est*).'[63] And in his comments on Romans 12.1, he teaches that we offer ourselves as sacrifices because 'we learned by faith that Christ is the sacrifice for us and our righteousness'.[64] So, while his terminology of imputation is not as frequent or as precise as Melanchthon or Calvin, the *concept* of Christ's righteousness being imputed to the believer is present in Oecolampadius' teaching on Romans.

---

[59] See, for example, the comments in Fink, 'Divided by Faith,' 136, where he explains how Oecolampadius' description of the relationship between faith and righteousness is 'far less precise than the explanation' of Melanchthon.

[60] See, for example, Oecolampadius, *In Epistolam ad Rhomanos*, 33a, 44a, 49b, 65b. The idea of sin not being imputed to believers was the most common use of the term at the time.

[61] Oecolampadius, *In Epistolam ad Rhomanos*, 43a. See, also, 40a.

[62] Oecolampadius, *In Epistolam ad Rhomanos*, 50b-51a.

[63] Oecolampadius, *In Epistolam ad Rhomanos*, 64b-65a. See, also, 36a, 44a, 49a, 63b. In addition to other references to Christ as righteousness, in his comments on Romans 4.14, 5.12, and 8.17, Oecolampadius refers to God's grace granting righteousness (*tribuit iustitiam*) and Christ as the giver of righteousness (*dator est iustitiae*).

[64] Oecolampadius, *In Epistolam ad Rhomanos*, 92b.

As opposed to any of the passages above from Romans that could have been used, the key passage Strohl selected to prove that Oecolampadius held to a moralist view of justification was Hebrews 10.24.[65] This is a peculiar choice to draw any conclusion about one's view of justification since the verse is about encouraging one another toward love and good deeds. If the same verse were used to identify Calvin's view of justification, for example, we would only find some brief comments about Jews allowing other nations to be included in the church and an exhortation to emulate godly living.[66] This would not help us determine very much about Calvin's doctrine of justification. Similarly, Oecolampadius' comments on this verse provide us with his explanation for why Christians need to admonish one another and continually examine themselves.[67] He is not equating justification and regeneration as McGrath and Strohl suggest,[68] but rather Oecolampadius is merely reiterating a theme which was also common in his early writings that 'faith may not be idle (*fides non sit ociosa*), but must continuously work through delight'.[69] Oecolampadius repeatedly taught that justification and regeneration are distinct, because good works cannot justify or save, even though they must be evident *after* one has already been justified.[70]

## Conclusion

A fuller study of Oecolampadius' commentaries from the early 1520s demonstrates that McGrath's conclusions about Oecolampadius were unfortunately based on a very limited reading by Strohl, which was not even a very close reading. According to Oecolampadius, a person is justified by faith alone with-

---

[65] McGrath and Strohl, also, incorrectly claim that the first catechism of Basel supports their conclusions, but the actual questions and answers of the catechism reveal much more 'objective' teaching. See Johann Oecolampadius, *Institutio Christiana sive Catechismus Puerorum Reipublicae Basiliensis* (Basil: Oporinus, 1561), 4, 9-10.

[66] Calvin, *Commentaries on the Epistle of Paul the Apostle to the Hebrews* (Grand Rapids, Mich.: Eerdmans, 1948), 238-39.

[67] Oecolampadius, *In Epistolam ad Hebraeos Ioannis Oecolampadii* (Strassburg: Apud Mathiam Apiarium, 1534), 112b. He is addressing 'what kind of faith ought to be in each one . . . so that it may be effective through love'.

[68] See McGrath, 'Humanist Elements,' 9; McGrath, *Iustitia Dei* (1986), 2.33; Strohl, *La pensée de la Réforme*, 107.

[69] Oecolampadius, *In Epistolam ad Hebraeos*, 112. This phrase and very similar phrases are found throughout his lectures, sermons, and the catechism from the time of his Reformation breakthrough to his death.

[70] It can also be said that Oecolampadius taught that justification *precedes* regeneration. In his lectures on Job, he provides his 'order of justification' (*ordinem iustificationis*): 'First God sends preachers, they teach, God gives growth and shows mercy, he justifies, regenerates, and reforms (*iustificat, regenerat, reformátque*), so that, the one who was perishing is born again.' See Johann Oecolampadius, *In Librum Iob Exegemata. Opus Admodum Eruditum, ac Omnibus Divinae Scripturae Studiosis Utile* (Geneva: Ex Officina Ioannis Crispini, 1554), 180.

out works, and despite the ongoing presence of sin, the one who believes is considered righteous because of Christ's righteousness. He specifically taught that one is *not* justified by love, that the righteousness of justification is *not* *inherent*, nor is it an *actualization* of righteousness. While living righteously and giving evidence of piety is essential for Oecolampadius, good works and righteousness are only possible *after* one has already been justified. While it is difficult because of the transitional time period in which he was teaching, if forced to categorize his views on the doctrine of justification, Oecolampadius cannot rightly be called a moralist, but rather his teaching conveys all the features of 'forensic justification'. Though the imputation of the alien righteousness of Christ to the believer is less pronounced, the foundational concepts are all present.

A more thorough study of Oecolampadius' writings shows that McGrath's suggestion that it was possible that the ethical emphasis of Oecolampadius was detrimental to, or inconsistent with, a more forensic doctrine of justification needs to be amended. Oecolampadius holds to both. This study also shows that the concept of imputed righteousness and forensic justification was already being taught in Switzerland by 1524, and a version of justification that is explicitly not moralist in 1523. While this specific study does not overthrow McGrath's major arguments about the development of the doctrine of justification, it does offer a necessary correction to the portrayal of Oecolampadius. It provides evidence that the forensic view of justification was compatible with the humanist emphasis on ethical living; and it sheds further light on the timeframe for the decisive shift in the sixteenth century on the teaching of justification.

# CHAPTER 5

## Justification as liberation in Pilgram Marpeck

*Kirk R. MacGregor*

The last six decades have seen a dramatic resurgence of interest in the life and thought of Pilgram Marpeck (c.1495-1556), a South German Anabaptist leader notable for developing unique positions on spirituality, Christian freedom, and love through a combination of diverse influences, ranging from medieval mysticism to Hutterite communitarianism.[1] Arguably, Marpeck's defining doctrine was the 'spiritual, essential justice' (*geistlicher wesentlicher gerechtigkeit*) which consummated in the creation of the 'new being' (*neues wesen*).[2] In conceptualizing this process of thoroughgoing personal transformation, Marpeck wove together many doctrines, including regeneration, justification, and sanctification, into a coherent unity. As a result, it becomes difficult to tell where one doctrine ends and another begins or to discern the precise theological content Marpeck assigned to each doctrine. This is especially true of the doctrine of justification. Hence Stephen Boyd reports that Marpeck 'insists that the Spirit comes in to reorder the human being and therefore tends to conjoin justification and sanctification'.[3]

Although he conjoined these two doctrines, Marpeck did not equate justification with sanctification, as demonstrated by two lines of evidence. First, linguistically, Marpeck avoided describing justification in terms of *Frombma-*

---

[1] This resurgence has generated major monographs on Marpeck's hermeneutics, social thought, Christology, theological method, and practical theology in formulating a feasible urban form of Anabaptism. See William Klassen, *Covenant and Community: The Life, Writings, and Hermeneutics of Pilgram Marpeck* (Grand Rapids: Eerdmans, 1968); Stephen B. Boyd, *Pilgram Marpeck: His Life and Social Theology* (Durham: Duke University Press, 1992); Neal Blough, *Christ in our Midst: Incarnation, Church, and Discipleship in the Theology of Pilgram Marpeck* (Kitchener, ON: Pandora, 2007); Malcolm B. Yarnell III, *The Formation of Christian Doctrine* (Nashville: Broadman and Holman, 2007); Walter Klassen and William Klassen, *Marpeck: A Life of Dissent and Conformity* (Kitchener, ON: Herald Press, 2008), respectively.

[2] *Pilgram Marbecks Antwort auf Kaspar Schwenckfeld's Beurteilung des Buches der Bundesbezeugung von 1542* (ed. Johann P. Loserth; Vienna: Carl Fromme, 1929), 261; my verdict is confirmed by Boyd, *Marpeck*, 147-67.

[3] Boyd, *Marpeck*, 79; cf. 29, 41.

*chung* (making pious) and *Rechtmachung* (making right), words specifically used by those (particularly Catholics and Anabaptists) who insisted on the equation of justification and sanctification.[4] Instead, Marpeck employed Luther's forensic term *Rechtfertigung* to indicate a once-for-all legal and unilateral act of God; however, even a cursory reading of Marpeck's work shows that, whatever his view of justification, he meant something different from Luther.[5] Second, structurally, whenever Marpeck described justification and sanctification in the same context, he consistently listed justification and sanctification as two separate events in the *ordo salutis*.[6]

Notwithstanding its distinctiveness as a theological category in his mind, Marpeck never specifically defined the term 'justification' nor explained its precise function in his doctrinal system. Thus Marpeck's understanding of justification constitutes an underlying presupposition of his writings which never explicitly surfaces. Accordingly, through careful detective work, this piece aims to unearth Marpeck's doctrine of justification. Tools prominent in our search will include the process of elimination and the rules of logical inference. In other words, we shall observe the definitions Marpeck gave to the doctrines surrounding justification (which doctrines are well-defined) in his *ordo salutis* and then subtract this content from his overarching process of personal transformation. Of the ideas which remain, those which exhibit no ties to any other component doctrine of the transformation process must, by elimination, be the parts which together comprise Marpeck's doctrine of justification. We shall then logically piece together these ideas to reconstruct this doctrine in complete and coherent form. In the process, we shall argue that justification for Marpeck is, in a word, liberation—namely, the liberation from the powers of darkness that exclusively occurs through properly undertaking believers' baptism.

## Setting the stage

To understand Marpeck's *ordo salutis*, we must first grasp what humanity needs to be saved from, therefore raising the question of anthropology. Marpeck insisted that human beings were created body, soul, and spirit in the *imago Dei*, specifically construed as the ability to participate in the divine nature by virtue of their spiritual marriage with God, a marriage into which God created them.[7] Thus, for Marpeck the *imago Dei* does not entail that humans were created as gods—such human deification this Anabaptist deemed the su-

---

[4]  Kirk R. MacGregor, *A Central European Synthesis of Radical and Magisterial Reform* (Lanham, MD: University Press of America, 2006), 115-16.

[5]  Thomas N. Finger, *A Contemporary Anabaptist Theology: Biblical, Historical, Constructive* (Downers Grove, IL: InterVarsity Press, 2004), 124-25.

[6]  *The Writings of Pilgram Marpeck* (trans. William Klassen and Walter Klaassen; Kitchener, ON: Herald Press, 1978), 89, 119, 556, 559.

[7]  *Writings*, 530-31, 408.

preme blasphemy[8]—but entails a participatory divinization. Nothing is added to mere human nature; however, on the analogy of common property in marriage, humans legally possessed all God's communicable attributes and, to whatever degree God saw fit, they could access and employ those attributes. This *imago Dei* remained in tact so long as humans lived in the kingdom of God, which Marpeck designated as a transcendent moral state of undivided goodness.[9] In this state distinctions between specific good acts and specific evil acts do not exist because evil is largely unknown; the only known evil would be choosing to leave this state and find out what existed beneath it.[10] Consequently, living in such a transcendent state is the *sine qua non* condition of fidelity to the spiritual marriage. To be in this moral state meant being spiritually married to God, while to be outside this moral state meant being spiritually divorced from God, no longer possessing the *imago Dei*.[11]

On Marpeck's reading of Genesis 2–3, then, eating from the tree of the knowledge of good and evil metaphorically spelled Adam and Eve's decision to spiritually divorce God and degenerate to the lower epistemic realm.[12] In this realm the highest and undifferentiated good does not exist; rather, this highest good is broken down into individual goods, which in turn are paired with their opposites, or corresponding evils.[13] For Marpeck, this lower realm is the kingdom of the world, the abode of darkness ruled by Satan.[14] On account of entering this realm, Adam and Eve became slaves to Satan.[15] However, Marpeck maintained that Adam and Eve did not transmit their enslaved condition to their progeny; as a result, every human is born in exactly the same condition as Adam and Eve before the Fall.[16] Nonetheless, Marpeck alleged that every human

---

[8]  *Writings*, 79.
[9]  *Writings*, 516-18, 532, 536.
[10]  *Writings*, 113, 246.
[11]  *Writings*, 475-77, 531.
[12]  'Because he wanted to be his own lord and god, and because of the cunning deceit of the serpent, he became ashamed and fearful, and, together with all the creatures, fled before God in the knowledge of good and evil'—*Writings*, 113-14. Marpeck also finds this notion substantiated in God's barring Adam and Eve access to the Tree of Life after the Fall—*Writings*, 477.
[13]  *Writings*, 108, 114, 131, 206, 336-37.
[14]  *Writings*, 538.
[15]  *Writings*, 322, 494.
[16]  '[T]he children never bear the penalty of the parents . . . they are like Adam and Eve before the transgression . . . the good and pure creation of God [who] still exist in their created innocent state . . . who stand in all created simplicity, knowing neither good nor evil. . . . Since God ordained that they be born in created innocence, God will refrain from accusing this innocence, since sin has its origin in the knowledge of good and evil'—*Writings*, 127, 208, 252, 257. Hence Marpeck proclaimed that all who die as children are saved: '[T]hey are without justification pronounced blessed by Christ, and regarded as belonging to the sanctified of the kingdom of God: "For to such belongs the kingdom of God." Christ gives no reason from either the Old or New Testament; He simply says, to such belongs the kingdom of God'—*Writings*,

freely chooses to make the same decision as their primal ancestors, abandoning the ethically pristine kingdom of God for the ethically ambivalent kingdom of the world. Hence each individual stands fully responsible for her or his condition of spiritual alienation and so cannot blame Adam and Eve.[17] Such spiritual alienation Marpeck dubbed 'original sin,' original to the human race in general and to each person in particular.[18]

To explain the damage original sin inflicts on each component of tripartite humanity, Marpeck drew, *mutatis mutandis*, on the medieval Cistercian reformer Bernard of Clairvaux.[19] In Bernardian fashion, the body loses its right to partake in the resurrection of the righteous after death.[20] The soul morphs into what Marpeck called 'reason,' by which he does not, in a Kierkegaardian vein, connote the seat of rationality but the insatiable will to scheme, commit, and rationalize evil. This, Marpeck emphasized, is the serpentine part of each person that needs to be killed.[21] The serpentine part infects the body, orienting the body toward evil; that orientation is what Marpeck styled the flesh.[22] The spirit surrenders the *imago Dei*, such that it cannot participate in the divine nature.[23] However, Marpeck hastened to add that the spirit retains as an inalienable attribute the likeness of God, or the potential to be remade in the *imago Dei*.[24] Moreover, unlike Luther and Calvin, the spirit inalienably retains freedom of choice, or the ability to choose anything on the spectrum spanning absolute good, absolute evil, and all points in between.[25]

---

128; *cf.* 116, 131, 140, 143. Children, 'consequently, cannot be damned'—*Writings*, 251.

[17] '[E]very man himself takes and eats of the forbidden fruit, the knowledge of good and evil, and does not eat through the fault of Adam and Eve'—*Writings*, 131; *cf.* 246, 336-37.

[18] 'Original sin is inherited only when there is knowledge of good and evil. Adam and Eve, our father and mother, inherited it when, contrary to the command of God, they ate the fruit of the knowledge of good and evil. . . . But, prior to the knowledge of good and evil, neither inherited sin nor actual sin is reckoned before God. Only when man, in his carnal nature, leaves the good and adopts the bad is God's reckoning forthcoming'—*Writings*, 206-207.

[19] *Writings*, 521. Here Marpeck specifically relied upon Bernard's *De gratia et libero arbitrio* (*On Grace and Free Choice*), which is unsurprising given the fact that, in the words of Jean Châtillon, 'L'influence de S. Bernard,' *Analecta sacri ordinis cisterciensis* IX (1953), 280-81, *De gratia* 'always remained the work most frequently cited and most constantly used' by the sixteenth-century reformers.

[20] *Writings*, 531.

[21] 'Before it submits to the simplicity of faith in Christ, reason is the head of the serpent. . . . Thus, man fell out of the intention and will of God into ignorance and into the intention, cunning, deceit, and will of the serpent, and became its head'—*Writings*, 337, 114.

[22] *Writings*, 73, 121, 165.

[23] *Writings*, 240, 211.

[24] *Writings*, 391.

[25] *Writings*, 257, 494.

This spiritual divorce from God, slavery to Satan, and anthropological damage comprises the condition from which humans need salvation. Hence it follows that salvation must thoroughly transform human nature by holistically reintegrating its fragmented moral experience and heal the divine-human relationship by restoring the divinization individuals once enjoyed.

We are now in a position to spell out Marpeck's *ordo salutis*, noting the content of the well-defined terms, subtracting it from his transformation process, and so deciphering the doctrinal substance he ascribed to justification. His *ordo salutis* may be delineated as follows:

law → 'first grace'[26]/'a spark of grace'[27] → conversion of repentance → believers' baptism → regeneration → justification → love 'in grace and truth'[28] → sanctification → new being

Law, for Marpeck, followed Luther's definition of all Scripture (whether in the Old or New Testament) that convicts sinners of their wrongdoing, burdening them with guilt and terrifying them with the hellish consequences of their actions.[29] By 'first grace' or 'a spark of grace' Marpeck referred to what is classically called prevenient grace. Despite their horror at the prospect of hell, Marpeck claimed that, due to their twisted 'reason,' humans would never, sans divine assistance, find the Gospel of Christ sufficiently attractive to embrace it, albeit their freedom to do so. Rather, humans devise mechanisms of self-salvation, attempting, for example, to earn God's favor or to declare or make themselves divine.[30] According to Marpeck, the history of Israel's wandering in the wilderness is littered with such attempts at self-salvation.[31] Thus the Holy Spirit gives all persons a spark of initial grace that displays the attractiveness of the Gospel; while resistible, it woos persons with Christ's love and motivates them to accept the Gospel.[32]

---

[26] *Writings*, 439. It should be pointed out that, unlike 'a spark of grace,' Marpeck utilized the phrase 'first grace' equivocally, elsewhere taking it to mean the Old Testament—*Writings*, 123.

[27] *Writings*, 425.

[28] *Writings*, 486.

[29] *Writings*, 120–22; Paul Althaus, *The Theology of Martin Luther* (trans. Robert C. Schultz; Philadelphia: Fortress Press, 1966), 254.

[30] 'Because reason presumed to be a god, and to have the power which belongs to God alone . . . [s]he imagines that she can be saved or condemned by her own power, and not by God's, who alone has all power. That is why God has likened our reason to the head of the serpent. This old serpent constantly resists God, and now presumes to be saved through its own ability'—*Writings*, 317; cf. 318.

[31] *Writings*, 106.

[32] Marpeck emphasized that God, who wills for all to be saved and has ordered that will in Scripture (1 Tim. 2.4; 2 Pet. 3.9), gives every individual prevenient grace—*Writings*, 61. Such an emphasis Marpeck made over against Calvin's doctrine of double predestination, which the Anabaptist scathingly denounced: 'It is not as the

This factual assent to the truths of the Gospel, while not, in itself, sufficient for salvation, prompts individuals to undergo the conversion of repentance. Here individuals forever renounce their sin and commit to replace their past way of life with one marked by God-centeredness and other-centeredness, even at the cost of personal suffering. As a result, individuals love their neighbor as themselves.[33] The hardships involved with both giving up one's past lifestyle and embracing future suffering Marpeck denominated 'sharing in the sufferings of Christ'.[34] Only after authentically becoming believers—namely, persons who not merely assent to the Gospel but have forsaken sin, cultivated love of neighbor, and pledged their lives to Christ as a bride pledges herself to her groom—must individuals receive baptism.[35] Marpeck explicitly endorsed baptismal regeneration and baptismal justification, which combine to yield salvation.[36] All of the aforementioned conditions, Marpeck insisted, must be met for the salvific effects of baptism to obtain; if any is lacking, baptism is salvifically null and void.[37] Hence, proper baptism is the wedding between Christ and the believer.[38] When an individual is properly baptized, the Holy Spirit regenerates that person by killing and burying the 'old man' or 'stony heart' of reason in

---

predestinarians and others say, without any discrimination, that God has the right to all salvation and damnation. He has, certainly, but not outside of His order and will, to which His power is subordinated. . . . There is no sharper nor more deceitful article of false teaching than to use and preach the power and omnipotence of God outside of the order of God's Word'—*Writings*, 341.

[33] 'The salvation of the soul depends upon love for the neighbor'—*Writings*, 54.
[34] Marpeck went on to posit the necessity of such suffering: '[W]hoever does not suffer (meaning through a genuine act of repentance) will not rule with Him (Rom. 8). Since not all men repent, not all will share in the sufferings of Christ. Neither can God be gracious to such unrepentant, unrighteous men nor (as He promises in Hebrews 8) will He forget their sins (Ezek. 33)'—*Writings*, 61.
[35] *Writings*, 117, 171-72.
[36] 'Thus, when we are baptized, we are born of His Holy Spirit . . . one goes justified through baptism into the church or into the kingdom of God'—*Writings*, 322, 199.
[37] 'For whoever would enter into baptism, and lay off evil and be cleansed from sin, he must assuredly first be converted, through true repentance, and he must die to sin; otherwise, baptism does not wash away sins. . . . This portal without doubt is very narrow, for you cannot go through it with the old sinful man of the old life; everything must be laid aside and buried before one enters through this gate'—*Writings*, 205, 200.
[38] 'Baptism is similar to a betrothal or a marital union between the believer and Christ. . . . Now listen to what Peter says. He says that baptism saves us. Why? Is it because we are dunked into water or because it is poured over us? Oh no, for he differentiates between true baptism and the mere shedding of the pollution of the flesh. This last act alone cannot do it; only the covenant of a good conscience with God has the power to save. Therefore, baptism saves when, through it, the believer unites himself with God and henceforth denies the desires of the flesh and the lust thereof, and desires with his whole heart to carry out the will of God'—*Writings*, 186-87; *cf.* 295-96.

Christ's death and forming the 'new man' or 'soft heart'.[39] This 'new man' refers to the remade soul, now just as motivated to pursue good as the reason was motivated to pursue evil. Although it is not impossible for the new man to commit evil (just as it was not impossible for the reason to perform good), the new man gains no joy from committing evil and thus will typically avoid it. Hence good constitutes the remade soul's *modus operandi*, with any occasional evil serving as the exception proving the beneficent rule.[40]

Having defined the elements in Marpeck's *ordo salutis* preceding justification, we shall now turn to observing the elements following justification. By love 'in grace and truth' Marpeck meant that, having been translated out of the kingdom of darkness and into the kingdom of light, one spiritually sees God as he is and thus loves God for his own sake, rather than loving God for the compassion and lovingkindness he has first showed the individual. Such is to love God in truth.[41] The 'grace' aspect indicates the individual seeing oneself and others through God's 'eyes,' no longer either loving oneself for one's own sake or loving one's neighbor as one loves oneself but loving oneself *because and just as* God loves one and loving one's neighbor *because and just as* God loves one's neighbor.[42] Hence the individual begins to experience what the medieval spiritual tradition described as the *unio mystica*, participating in the divine nature in such a way that God allows one to employ his attribute of love.[43] But the flesh persists, causing the body to remain geared toward sinful desires.[44] Consequently, sanctification for Marpeck is the lifelong process of growing in God's love—namely, the undifferentiated realm of goodness itself—such that one gradually kills the flesh and becomes increasingly holy just as God is holy.[45] This process culminates in the general resurrection, where the perfected soul is joined with the perfected (i.e., morally pure and immortal) body to yield

---

[39] *Writings*, 94, 112. Hence Marpeck stated that reason 'has died, been crucified, fastened with Christ to the cross, and buried in His death. The birth of the Spirit is the comfort of future life, and itself brings to life'—*Writings*, 138.

[40] *Writings*, 347.

[41] *Writings*, 529-30, 517.

[42] *Writings*, 513, 553.

[43] Paraphrasing from Bernard's *Sermons on the Song of Songs* (2:I.1.1-2, II.2.3; 8:I.1-2), Marpeck explained, 'Nearly the whole of the Canticle presents and illustrates the real, supernatural love by means of the natural parable of love. By this means, all faithful hearts are led into the real, supernatural love, into God Himself; yes, into God Himself, and God into them. First, the Holy Spirit says: "He kisses me with the kiss of his mouth." The eternal Word has gone forth, and continues to go forth, from God Himself. With [this Word], He kisses the hearts of all the faithful. Thus, the divine nature of the children of God is conceived and born from the love of the Word, the imperishable seed'—*Writings*, 393; cf. 391-92.

[44] *Writings*, 364-65, 354.

[45] *Writings*, 581-82, 403. Other Anabaptists would famously describe this as *Gelassenheit*. See Robert Friedmann, *The Theology of Anabaptism* (Scottdale, PA: Herald Press, 1973), 76-77.

the new being. While merely human by nature, the new being participates fully in the divine nature, availing itself of all God's communicable attributes in the new heaven and new earth.[46]

## Piecing together Marpeck's doctrine of justification

Observing the theological content on either side of justification, we detect a number of gaps that, for Marpeck, the doctrine of justification must link. In regeneration, one's 'reason' or old man is buried with Christ, and one's soul is remade via his death. However, one is still a slave of Satan in the kingdom of the world bearing the guilt for one's sin, the spirit still lacks the *imago Dei*, and the body cannot participate in the general resurrection. But it is presupposed by the doctrine of love in grace and truth that one is a free and forgiven citizen of God's kingdom bearing the *imago Dei* with guaranteed participation in the general resurrection. Thus justification must comprise liberation from the kingdom of the world into the kingdom of God and all the forensic elements that logically accompany this transition, including remission of sin, restoration of the *imago Dei*, and the right to partake in bodily resurrection. In sum, we perceive that justification is participation in Christ's resurrection, just as regeneration is participation in Christ's crucifixion and burial. Employing the symbolism of baptism, one is regenerated when one goes down into the water, and one is justified when one comes up from the water. Given the structure of this doctrine, we shall now unpack each facet of Marpeck's justification in turn.

Marpeck insisted that justification comes through faith—namely, believers' baptism is the necessary expression of true faith[47]—and makes the believer a 'free man in Christ Jesus'.[48] This freedom, Marpeck declared, transpires because 'the justification which leads to true devotion and which proceeds from faith, transfers man from the earthly to the eternal, heavenly state'.[49] Marpeck expanded on the liberation the transfer of justification accomplishes for the individual as follows:

---

[46] 'Thus the elect, who have been justified and who live in love in God and God in them, enter into the one eternal real love which remains eternally and is God Himself. But it is impossible to have or come by the power of love, which God has and Himself is eternally (as stated earlier), wholly in this time. . . . But [we can] follow her path with sincere desire . . . and never to lose sight of her until we completely possess her in that day with Christ'—*Writings*, 531-33; cf. 225, 523, 293.

[47] Believers' baptism is the 'recognized, unconcealed confession of faith in Christ' described in Romans 10:9, and 'only in the confession of Christ does salvation by faith consist'—*Writings*, 239, 208. Thus an essential fruit of true faith is baptism, such that the notion of a genuine believer who was unbaptized represented for Marpeck a contradiction in terms. Marpeck frequently drew on the Markan appendix (16.16) to legitimate this reasoning—*Writings*, 89, 93, 95, 111, 146, 155, 189, 190, 247, 335, 438.

[48] *Writings*, 319; cf. 471.

[49] *Writings*, 430.

> If God . . . liberates him from the bonds, cords, and power of the devil, and if Christ lives in him again through His Holy Spirit, he is justified through Christ and no longer a sinner. His sins and the stain of his wickedness have been washed away and cleansed through the blood of Christ, and God does not hold sin against him (Ps. 32[2]). . . . For whomever the Son sets free is truly free; he is released from what possesses him, from sin, death, and hell, which possess all men outside of Christ.[50]

Here we perceive that the effects of justification are predicated on 'the blood of Christ,' which raises the issue of Marpeck's atonement theory and its relationship with justification.

Marpeck held to a version of penal substitutionary atonement where God's wrath is not poured out on Christ himself (i.e. the second Person of the Trinity, who is the spirit of Jesus) but on the human body and soul which Christ bore. Since Christ was God's intended representative of the entire human race (and actual representative of all who properly identify with him in baptism), his body and soul potentially represented the bodies and souls of all individuals. Due to each individual's treasonous choice to reside in the kingdom of the world, God's justice demanded that each person's body and soul (or its equivalent) be destroyed, the body by physical death and the soul by hell. Accordingly, Marpeck insisted that, after the destruction of his body on the cross, Christ descended into hell, where his soul suffered destruction.[51] (Thus both the body and soul of Christ find restoration in his resurrection.) Marpeck thus summarized his theory of the atonement:

> Christ remained in death and hell until He had completely paid, for our sake, the guilt of sin. Thus, the Father did not spare the Son, but gave Him up so that all who believe in Him may have eternal life. The Father sealed the guilt of sin in death and in the prison of hell forever. In His human poverty, the payer of the debt, the true warrantor, went Himself into the depths of hell with our sins, and yet without any sin of His own, through His torment on earth in order to make payment. . . . The Son conquered the sin of many precisely by this descent into the depths.[52]

From this it follows that atonement is linked ontologically to regeneration and forensically to justification. Ontologically, the atonement destroys the 'old man' or 'reason,' thus enabling the soul to be born again.

Forensically, the atonement removes our guilt and the body-soul death sentence for that guilt, as Christ took both upon himself as 'the Lord who in His innocence gave Himself for us the guilty, accepted our guilt, and suffered, the

---

[50] *Writings*, 469, 319; cf. 110.

[51] On this score Marpeck rhetorically queried, 'And what would happen to the saying in Acts 2: "You did not leave his soul in hell" (2.27) if Christ had not descended into hell?'—*Writings*, 557; cf. 85.

[52] *Writings*, 432-34.

66

just one for us the unjust'.[53] By sacrificing his body and soul as a substitute for ours, Christ 'assuaged the wrath of the Father'[54] and procured 'the acquittal' of our sins from the divine tribunal.[55] Elaborating on these points, Marpeck insisted that believers do nothing to earn this acquittal:

> They are made righteous without any contribution on their part [Rom. 3.23f.]; understand clearly that they were made righteous through the redemption which took place through Christ whom God has set as a mercy seat through faith in His blood; Christ demonstrates the righteousness which God demands in that He forgives sin. Before Christ, no sin was forgiven; He Himself, Christ, forgives sins which occurred before, under the patience of God [1 Pet. 3.20]. This sin He carried in order that the righteousness which God requires be demonstrated only in these times and in order that He alone might be just and justify him who has faith in Jesus.[56]

Moreover, Christ's sacrifice ransomed us from the kingdom of the world. Marpeck, however, is no proponent of the ransom-to-Satan theory, since he believed that Satan's ownership of humanity was *de facto* and not *de jure*. In other words, Satan possessed humanity in precisely the same sense as a warden possesses his prisoners; it is only because of God's wrath against humanity that Satan has any power over them.[57] Thus the full penalty for our sins, which Christ paid to God (not simply to the Father, but to himself and the Holy Spirit as well, as this payment is required by God's perfect justice), comprises the ransom necessary to liberate us from the powers of darkness.[58] Accordingly, 'all are justified by God's free grace alone, through his act of liberation in the person of Christ Jesus'.[59] Synthesizing the forensic aspects the atonement lends to justification, Marpeck proclaimed:

---

[53] *Writings*, 526.
[54] *Writings*, 175.
[55] *Writings*, 550.
[56] *Writings*, 136. For Marpeck, Christ's righteousness does not comprise his active and passive obedience to the law imputed to believers, but rather comprises his free decision to forgive our sins by taking them upon himself and paying their legally prescribed penalty. Marpeck's remark that '[b]efore Christ, no sin was forgiven' illustrates his conviction that the Old Testament saints went to hell and there waited for their salvation to materialize; when Christ rose from the dead, he harrowed hell by bringing up with him the Old Testament saints and transferring them to heaven—*Writings*, 108-09, 115-19, 231.
[57] *Writings*, 561.
[58] According to Marpeck, humankind 'remained in bondage and sold under sin, death, and hell until the work of restoration through [Christ's] humanity, in which the Son of God had to be revealed for the redemption through His blood. . . . Christ made atonement for sin by Himself *and to Himself* through His blood'—*Writings*, 115; emphasis added; cf. 467. Note Marpeck's affirmation that Christ, as God, paid the ransom to himself, as well as to the Father and the Holy Spirit—*Writings*, 24-25, 452.
[59] *Writings*, 236.

[T]he Son . . . was born to the Father from the race of man, for the sake of man. He was born to liberate man from the power of the devil, sin, death, and hell. . . . [They have come into it] because of the guilt of sin, and because of the pains of hell and death which were laid on men. Men have been given over to the devil, who has the power of death and torment as well as of sin. And it is sin which causes the wrath of God. . . . Thus, the wrath of God delivers to sin, death, hell, pain, and the devil. . . . Even today, man is utterly under the wrath of God and because of sin, man is outside of Christ, the Lord and Savior. However, because of our sin, the Father did not spare the Son. He has given Him for the sake of man, and delivered Him into the suffering and pain of death, even to condemnation, as a salvation for men.[60]

Marpeck stressed the once-for-all and irreversible character of both the ontological and forensic aspects of atonement. Ontologically, the reason can never spring to life again once it dies. Forensically, after Christ secures and grants our pardon for all past, present, and future sin, no sin can henceforth be charged against us.[61] Since these aspects culminate in justification, Marpeck maintained that justification brings eternal security, such that all who are justified will never, in fact, fall away: '[H]aving died to sins, you henceforth live a new God-fearing life and, willing to walk in it and abide by it, continue therein until the end of your life. . . . No one will tear from His hands those who are given to Christ by the Father (Jn. 10.20).'[62] Marpeck captured this idea in the phrases 'eternal justification'[63] and 'eternal liberty and glory'.[64] But Marpeck simultaneously asserted that it is possible for true believers to fall away, as indicated by the warnings against such in Hebrews 6.4-8 and 2 Peter 2.20-22.[65] Marpeck resolved this tension by arguing that the scriptural warnings constitute the means whereby God ensures that true believers choose never to fall away. For Marpeck, God knew in his omniscience prior to the creation of the world that if scriptural warnings were not given, true believers would freely fall away, but if warnings were given, true believers would freely endure.[66] As a result of this scheme, Marpeck averred that any ostensible believer who later apostatizes could never have truly been justified in the first place:

---

[60] *Writings*, 429-30.
[61] *Writings*, 556.
[62] *Writings*, 207, 85-86; cf. 227, 399, 421, 423, 435, 458, 536, 548.
[63] *Writings*, 453.
[64] *Writings*, 476.
[65] *Writings*, 335, 182-83.
[66] 'Those are all terrible and hard sayings which cause consternation and fright when one seriously considers them. Happy are those who thus allow themselves to be alarmed by the Word of God and who are earnestly shocked because of it. . . . Afterward, however, says Saint Paul, it yields the peaceable fruit of eternal blessedness'— *Writings*, 488, 496; cf. 358.

The true believers will not leave Christ and all His teachings, for Christ does not lose anyone except the children of perdition. . . . Some of these false prophets have gone out from us, but they were not of us, for, if they had been of us, they would indeed have remained with us. . . . They were not, however, of the truth. Had they been of the truth, they would have remained with the truth, as John himself says (1 Jn. 2.19).[67]

Consequently, Marpeck posited that justification is the *ratio praedestinationis*, or the foreseen ground on which God elected individuals, writing their names in the Book of Life, before the foundation of the world. This Book of Life, in turn, becomes a 'book of replication' which God copies onto the spirits of the elect at the moment of justification.[68] This copying accomplishes three important realities, all simultaneously legal and ontological. First, it restores to the spirit the *imago Dei*, or the ability to participate in the divine nature. Marpeck explained: 'The Holy Spirit Himself no longer takes from the image or the mediation of angels, nor does he take it in fire, clouds or darkness, as Moses received it and took it from God. He takes it from the Father and the Son, and gives it to the hearts of all the faithful.'[69] Since this ability is predicated upon being spiritually married to God, Marpeck stipulated that the replication is the legal seal of the spiritual marriage, analogous to a marriage license in our day.[70]

As a result, second, one acquires citizenship in the kingdom of God, or the undifferentiated realm of good emanating from the perfect character of God. Hence the 'Spirit of Christ justifies them to be heirs of Christ's eternal kingdom,' such that each believer is 'enrolled as an heir to the eternal kingdom'.[71] In this kingdom we are free, for Christ 'has given us the privilege to live in His house of peace (yes, in the house of grace and love), not as slaves, strangers, or hirelings, but as friends, children, brothers, and sisters . . . whom the Son makes free is free indeed'.[72] Here we recall that the believer's soul, by virtue of regeneration, already desires to do the good, but it does not yet fully perceive what the good is. Now as one starts living in the realm of undifferentiated good, the believer perceives the good she or he longs to do and performs that good, which fulfills the desire of the soul and generates a robust moral experience.[73] As Christ's spiritual spouse who desires, knows, and accomplishes the good, the believer is henceforth qualified to live forever with God in the new heavens and new earth.[74]

---

[67] *Writings*, 106, 71, 209; cf. 423.
[68] *Writings*, 460; *cf.* 437.
[69] *Writings*, 459.
[70] *Writings*, 525, 63.
[71] *Writings*, 470-71, 199.
[72] *Writings*, 413, 85; cf. 134, 403.
[73] *Writings*, 532, 535, 327.
[74] *Writings*, 112.

Third, therefore, the body receives both the right to participate in the general resurrection and the guarantee that it will so participate because of Christ's resurrection. Hence, just as Christ rose triumphantly from the dead, so the justified believer emerges triumphantly from the realm of spiritual death, presently engaging in new spiritual life with the assurance of new bodily life in the future:

> Thus, we now participate in the first resurrection, which began with Christ. We are the firstborn from the dead. The second death no longer has power over us because of His liberating power, delivered from above. . . . Death is no longer death for us. Rather, through faith in Christ, we have struggled from death to life.[75]

## Concluding reflections

This piece has demonstrated that, on Marpeck's formulation, justification is a multifaceted reality, all of whose facets fall under the broad umbrella of liberation. Justification, like regeneration, occurs through the baptism of sincere believers in Christ. According to Marpeck, this does not mean that justification occurs through works, since believers' baptism is simply the Christ-ordained external expression of faith that any true believer will necessarily show. Hence baptism is not something a person does to earn salvation but is rather simply the means of receiving it. The fundamental role of justification is to liberate the believer from the kingdom of the world, or Satan's dark domain, and to transfer her or him into the kingdom of God, or the divine realm of unalloyed goodness. It accomplishes this liberation through Christ's meeting the demands of divine justice for our sin. Divine justice demands that we, or our substitute, be punished through the destruction of our bodies and souls. By taking a human nature, Christ became the federal head of the human race; by arranging our forgiveness, Christ displayed God's righteousness. This arrangement entailed that Christ bore our sins and received the due penalty thereof via the destruction of his body on the cross and the destruction of his soul in hell. Through this twofold destruction, Christ ransomed believers from the divine wrath, which had previously consigned them to slavery under Satan, and so obtained pardon for their past, present, and future sins. Since no further charge can be brought against believers, justification supplies them with eternal security and serves as the *ratio praedestinationis*. As such, justification restores to the believer's spirit the *imago Dei* which it had surrendered through its own sin and makes the believer a citizen in the kingdom of God. Further, justification raises believers from the dead in new spiritual life and ensures their participation in the general resurrection.

Once pieced together, then, we find that Marpeck conceived a distinctive and original doctrine of justification which, though appropriating insights from various theological streams, does not precisely correspond to any previous category. His doctrine of justification is forensic, but not in the Protestant respect

---

[75] *Writings*, 414; cf. 83.

of imputed righteousness, a respect which Catholic reformers contested.[76] It is also ontological, but not in the Catholic vein of a process whereby the believer is transformed into an actually holy individual, a process denied by Protestant reformers.[77] Marpeck's doctrine of justification is thus a rapprochement between the Protestant and Catholic views which arguably captures the strengths of both while avoiding their potential weaknesses.[78]

---

[76] Jaroslav Pelikan, *Reformation of Church and Dogma (1300-1700)* (The Christian Tradition, 4; Chicago: University of Chicago Press, 1984), 283-89.

[77] Pelikan, *Reformation*, 139, 151.

[78] Interestingly, both the notions of justification as the imputation of Christ's righteousness and of justification as a process of transforming a sinner into a saint have come under sharp challenge in contemporary New Testament studies, particularly in the New Perspective on Paul movement. For representative examples see E.P. Sanders, *Paul and Palestinian Judaism* (London: SCM, 1977), 75, 422; James D.G. Dunn, *Jesus, Paul, and the Law* (Louisville: Westminster John Knox, 1990), 190-98; and N.T. Wright, *Justification* (Downers Grove, IL: InterVarsity Press Academic, 2009), 184-86. Hence, Marpeck's doctrine of justification may well be commended to those who find persuasive the critique of the New Perspective.

# CHAPTER 6

## 'Abba Father': Calvin's biblical understanding of the Fatherhood of God

### Karin Spiecker Stetina

'And because we are his children, God has sent the Spirit of his Son into our hearts, prompting us to call out, "Abba, Father"' (Gal. 4.6, NLT).

'I believe in God, the Father Almighty, the Maker of heaven and earth, and in Jesus Christ, His only Son, our Lord; who was conceived by the Holy Spirit.' This ancient declaration about God has long been an essential affirmation of the Christian faith. This creed affirms Paul's teaching in 2 Corinthians 5.21, 'For he [God the Father] made him [Christ] who knew no sin to be sin for us, that we might become the righteousness of God in him [Christ]' (ESV). Faith in God the Father, Son, and Holy Spirit, unites us to Christ's salvific work. But what if your earthly experience of fatherhood has made it difficult for you to confess a belief in 'God, the Father Almighty'? How does our understanding of fatherhood impact our faith?

Margot Starbuck recounts her struggle with the Fatherhood of God in her spiritual memoir, *The Girl in the Orange Dress: Searching for a Father Who Does Not Fail*, writing:

> Are you like the string of human fathers I've experienced, or are you something else? . . . Are you like the first father who couldn't be bothered to lay eyes on me? Are you like the daddy I loved who left me? Are you like the ill-equipped stepfather who left me? Maybe you're like that first father who, decades later didn't even want the second chance he'd been given.[1]

Margot's disappointing experience of earthly fatherhood is not uncommon. Even for those who have not been adopted, have not been subjected to the devastating effects of divorce, or have not had an alcoholic father, like Margot, it is not difficult to relate. Frequently our earthly experiences serve as the lens by which we perceive our heavenly Father.

---

[1] Margot Starbuck, *The Girl in the Orange Dress: Searching for a Father Who Does Not Fail* (Downers Grove, InterVarsity Press, 2009), 159.

Starbuck, like many Christians, desired to discover in God, a Father that transcends our human paternal experiences. The reformer, John Calvin, found such a Father in God's self-revelation given in the Holy Scriptures. In contrast to some scholars' suggestion that the Reformation caused a shift towards a more oppressive patriarchal understanding of God, Calvin's biblical portrayal of God emphasizes the faithful, tender-loving care of the heavenly Father. In a culture that is struggling with the concept of fatherhood, Calvin's biblically-grounded approach to knowing God stands as an appropriate model for the church today.

## Current perceptions

John Calvin's belief in scriptural authority and the necessity of God's self-revelation for true knowledge of God has undergirded Christianity from the early Church. In recent years, however, this presupposition has been challenged by the idea that knowledge is grounded solely in human experience. Some theologians insist that male God-language is human-derived and its use has absolutized the maleness of God, thereby giving men the right to rule over women. Mary Daly's statement that 'Since God is male, the male is God,'[2] which results in rape, genocide, and war, summarizes well this contention.[3] Scholars such as Eleanor McLaughlin argue that the Protestant Reformation's insistence on *sola Scriptura* resulted in the appropriation of oppressive patriarchal traditions which can only be overcome with female God-language.[4]

It is true, in continuity with the historic Christian tradition, that the reformer, John Calvin, emphasized a biblically-based view of God. Calvin, however, did not see God-language as merely a gender issue, but an epistemological issue. Thus, he did not push gender-specific language into God's nature. Calvin's insistence that God is a spiritual being that is to be known and spoken about in accordance with God's self-revelation is observed in his understanding of scriptural authority and his treatment of the term 'Father'. Distinct from many theologians and even from his earthly experience, Calvin's understanding of the Fatherhood of God is characterized by steadfast love and mercy; a view that

---

[2] Mary Daly, 'After the Death of God the Father', in Carol Christ and Judith Plaskow (eds), *Womanspirit Rising: A Feminist Reader in Religion* (San Francisco: Harper Row, 1979), 54. 'If God in "his" heaven is a father ruling his people, then it is in the nature of things and according to divine plan and the order of the universe that society be male dominated. . . . Within this context, a mystification of roles takes place: the husband dominating his wife represents God himself.'

[3] Mary Daly, *Beyond God the Father* (Boston: Beacon Press, 1973), 97. She argues that when the 'father-god' and all 'his' works are renounced, a new heaven and earth of mutual respect, truth, and vitality will come about.

[4] See, for example, Eleanor L. McLaughlin, 'Male and Female in Christian Tradition: Was there a Reformation in the Sixteenth Century?' in Ruth Tiffany Barnhouse and Urban T. Holmes, III (eds), *Male and Female: Christian Approaches to Sexuality* (New York: Seabury Press, 1976), 50.

stands in opposition to an oppressive, patriarchal view of God. Justification by faith is grounded in understanding this loving Father-child relationship.

## Calvin's earthly experience of fatherhood

Fatherhood was a key issue in Calvin's personal life as well as in his theology. Like Starbuck, the Reformer did not have an idyllic relationship with his earthly father. Gerard Cauvin, Calvin's father, was a well-respected man known for his knowledge and prudence. Though he held an ecclesiastical office for the Lord of Nuyon, he was not known to be particularly pious or warm. From Calvin's writings and historical records, it is known that Gerard provided for his children, but was not demonstrative in his love for his family. This combined with the early loss of his devout, affectionate mother and a stable family life, left a void in Calvin's life.

Calvin knew he had his father to thank for his education and for his vocational opportunities, but he struggled to feel accepted by his father. Gerard's position and ambition for his sons had secured John an excellent education to prepare him for the priesthood; but when his father saw that there were financial advantages in a legal career, he withdrew him from the University at Paris and sent him to Orléans to pursue a course in civil law. Though John wanted to continue his theological studies, out of respect, he acquiesced to his father's wishes and pursued his new studies so diligently that he suffered physically.

Even in the midst of these challenges, however, Calvin recognized God's grace and providence, pointing to this time as important both educationally and spiritually. In a dedication to a commentary, he thanks his mentor Wolmar for teaching him Greek and law.[5] He also describes how he was converted, discovering the heavenly Father, who, unlike his earthly father, revealed himself as merciful and kind.[6] It was not until after his father's death that the Reformer

---

[5]   He warmly dedicates a commentary to Wolmar writing, 'One of the most important things that happened to me was in those early days when I was sent by my father to learn civil law but, . . . you were then professor *summa cum laude*. Nor was it your fault that I did not make greater progress, for you were so kind that you would not have refused a helping hand . . . but the death of my father called me away at an early stage. To you it is, however, that I not a little owe it that I was a least taught the rudiments; and this was afterwards to be a great help to me'—T. H. L. Parker, *John Calvin: A Biography* (Philadelphia: Westminster Press, 1975), 21.

[6]   In his Preface to the Commentary on the Psalms Calvin writes, 'God drew me from obscure and lowly beginnings and conferred on me the most honourable office of herald and minister of the gospel. My father had intended me for theology from my early childhood. But when he reflected that the career of the law proved everywhere very lucrative for its practitioners, the prospect suddenly made him change his mind. And so it happened that I was called away from the study of philosophy and set to learning law: although, out of obedience to my father's wishes, I tried my best work hard, yet God as last turned my course in another direction by the secret rein of his providence. What happened first was that by an unexpected conversion he tamed to teachableness a mind too stubborn for its years-for I was so strongly devoted to the

felt free to abandon his study of law and devote himself fully to the study of Scripture and theology.

This father-son relationship had a strong impact on Calvin's life and theology. He showed a high respect for his earthly father's authority, even when it cost him his freedom and position in the church. Later in his life he experienced a similar relationship with another earthly father figure, fiery French minister, Guillaume Farel. When Calvin attempted to decline Farel's request for him to remain in Geneva to help reorganize and reform the city, Farel threatened to call down the wrath of God upon him. The Reformer was so frightened that he reluctantly stayed to serve God in Geneva. Guillaume Farel, like Gerard Cauvin, used guilt and fear to motivate Calvin to do his will.[7] This authoritarian patriarchal image was further perpetuated by the Church. In the sixteenth century, the Church emphasized the judicial, authoritative nature of God. Calvin was taught a picture of God as Judge, demanding reverence and justice.

Based on his earthly experiences, it would seem logical that Calvin would see God, as McLaughlin suggests, as an oppressive patriarchal figure. It is interesting to see, however, how at odds Calvin's view is with this picture. Though John submitted to these father figures, more out of fear than out of reverence or affection, he saw these relationships as instrumental in knowing and serving God; in part, because God's fatherly nature stood in such sharp contrast to his worldly experiences. He depicts God as kind and warm and even suggests that the guiding hand of God the Father was behind all of the earthly father figures he experienced, revealing his love and providence for him.[8] His spiritual experience of freedom from sin and judgment through Christ's justifying work enabled Calvin to let his understanding of the heavenly Father super-

---

superstitions of the papacy that nothing less could draw me from such depths of mire. And so this mere taste of true godliness that I received set me on fire with such a desire to progress that I pursued the rest of my studies more coolly, although I did not give then up altogether. Before a year had slipped by anybody who longed for a purer doctrine kept on coming to learn from me, still a beginner, a raw recruit'—Parker, *John Calvin*, 163.

[7]  'Until I shall have confessed that I can bear no more, do no doubt that I am performing faithfully what I have promised you. And if in any way I do not match your expectation, you know that I am under your power. Admonish, chastise, do all those things that a father may do to sin him' (written 6 weeks after returning to Geneva; Sept. 2, 1541)—cited in William J. Bousma, *John Calvin: A Sixteenth Century Portrait* (Oxford: Oxford University Press, 1988), 24.

[8]  'The Father does not command us with fearful threatenings but 'calls us with fatherly kindness' to follow him, and we may therefore 'cheerfully and very readily respond to his call and follow where he leads'. God will treat us as 'dear little children', overlooking the imperfection of the service we offer to him, forgiving the sinfulness in it—Parker, *John Calvin*, 70.

sede his earthly experiences.[9] God's self-revelation as Father was transformative to Calvin's understanding of fatherhood and justification.

## Scriptural authority

Historically, proponents of the Christian religion have insisted that God is known most fully by self-revelation. From the burning bush, God is revealed to Moses as 'I am that I am' (Exod. 3.14, NASB)—a name that is beyond human limitations. God alone, not Moses, nor any other human, has the right to name God.

The historical belief that God's self-revelation is necessary in order to be able to speak in truth about God is observed in the writings of Church Fathers such as Origen and Hilary of Poitiers, and then, later, by John Calvin. The developing church of the first centuries held the conviction that God has freely revealed to us what is sufficient for our needs. In this belief, they recognized the extent of God's providential self-disclosure in the Scriptures and the limitations of the human mind and language.

Origen's response to the second century pagan philosopher Celsus, who contended that God 'is not to be reached by word,'[10] exemplifies the patristic understanding of human reliance on God's self-disclosure. When Celsus declared that 'He cannot be expressed by the name,' Origen responded that God can be expressed by the name God names Godself. God's self-disclosure was necessary 'in order to lead the hearer by the hand, as it were, and so enable him to comprehend something of God, so far as attainable by human nature'.[11]

Hilary of Poitiers also discussed the limitations of the human mind and the need for God's self-revelation. On this matter he wrote that 'what man cannot understand, God can be'. He warned that a person,

> Must not measure the Divine nature by the limitation of his own, but gauge God's assertions concerning himself by the scale of His own glorious self-revelation. For he is the best student who does not read his thoughts into the book, but lets it reveal its own, who draws from it its sense, and does not import his own into it.[12]

---

[9] Herman J. Selderhuis, *John Calvin: A Pilgrim's Life* (Downers Grove, IL: InterVarsity Press, 2009), 67; 'I testify and declare that I trust to no other security for my salvation than this, and this only, viz., that as God is the Father of mercy, he will show himself such a Father to me, who acknowledge myself to be a miserable sinner'—Dillenberger, *John Calvin, Selections from His Writings* (Atlanta: Scholars Press, 1975), 35.

[10] Origen, *Against Celsus* in Alexander Roberts and James Donaldson (eds), *The Ante-Nicene Fathers*, vol. 4 (Grand Rapids, MI: Eerdmans, 1956), 6.65.603.

[11] Origen, *Against Celsus*, vol. 4, 6.65.603.

[12] Hilary of Poitiers, *On the Trinity* in (ed.), Henry Wace, *Nicene and Post-Nicene Fathers of the Christian Church*, 2d series, vol. 9 (New York: Christian Literature Publishing, 1899), 3.1.62 and 1.18.45.

The Church Fathers understood God's self-revelation in Scripture as God's accommodation of truth to our human capacity and need. Without this accommodating work we would be without true knowledge of God.

In continuity with the Christian tradition, Calvin insists that God cannot be comprehended unless 'he accommodates himself to our standard' and 'anyone who does not allow God to be silent or to speak as he alone decides is striving to impose order on God'.[13] Calvin believed the apostolic writers to be 'sure and genuine scribes' of the Holy Spirit.[14] When the Spirit enters our hearts, then we realize that the Scriptures are the very word of God.[15] When people fashion Scripture according to their own will, Calvin argues, they 'depart from the true God and forsake him . . . having nothing left except an accursed idol'.[16]

Scripture functions like spectacles, bringing clarity to the otherwise confused knowledge of God.[17] God, as the author of Scripture, has given the testimony of the Holy Spirit in order that we 'seek our conviction in a higher place than human reasons, judgments, or conjectures'.[18] This conviction coupled with Calvin's interpretative skills shaped his use of God-language in general and the term 'Father' in particular. Embedded in Calvin's notion of Scripture is the concept of biblical infallibility and a new emphasis on our reliance on the Word and Spirit for true knowledge of God.[19]

## Calvin's depiction of Father

Calvin's biblical epistemology deeply impacts his view of the Fatherhood of God. Many scholars have insisted that Calvin's strong view of God's sovereignty and immutability leaves little room for a personal, responsive Father.[20] It is indisputable that Calvin emphasizes the sovereignty of God in reaction to the

---

[13] *Comm. Ezek.*, 9.3,4, XL.196d.

[14] *Inst* 1.8.9; 1.8.13.

[15] *Inst* 1.7.5; 1.8.13.

[16] Without the Word people are 'worshipping not God but a figment and a dream of their own heart'—*Inst* 1.4.1-3.

[17] *Inst* 1.4.1-3.

[18] *Inst* 1.7.4. 'Let this point therefore stand: that those whom the Holy Spirit has inwardly taught truly rest upon Scripture, and that Scripture indeed is self-authenticated; hence, it is not right to subject it to proof and reasoning. And the certainty it deserves with us, it attains by the testimony of the Spirit'—*Inst* 1.7.5.

[19] Calvin claimed that we are given direct intuitive knowledge of God through Scriptures, where we experience God speaking to us personally. Calvin believed, however, that historic and philological scholarship is necessary in order to remove the opaqueness of scriptural language ('which is ancient and foreign and full of unfamiliar idioms, habits and toms') so the truth of God's Word may show through clearly (*Inst* 1.6.1). He also discussed how the human condition stands in the way. Only through God's self-revelation and accommodation can humans can have true knowledge of God—*Comm. Ps.* 78.60.

[20] See, for example, W.B. Selbie, *The Fatherhood of God* (London: Duckworth Press, 1936).

medieval view of God, which left God at the mercy of the actions and attitudes of humanity. Unfortunately, the recognition of this emphasis has tended to hinder scholars from recognizing Calvin's conception of the benevolent Father as the supreme, determinative relationship in which God stands to humans.[21] Christ justifies the sinner by faith in order to restore the Father-child relationship.

While the Fatherhood of God is one of the primary themes in Calvin's writings, he never treats it as a separate topic. Calvin employs the concept primarily in two ways: in discussing the intra-Trinitarian relationships and God's relationship with creation. It is the second of these that is more pertinent to a personal apprehension of the Fatherhood of God. Yet, in both instances, Calvin grounds his assertions in Scripture; never promoting male supremacy, nor female oppression.

### The Father in relation to creation: universal and particular Fatherhood

#### The Father in the Trinity

The primary explicit treatment of God as Father comes in Calvin's treatment of the Trinity. He frequently uses the word 'Father' in his first chapter on the Trinity in order to distinguish the first person of the Trinity from the others. While Calvin acknowledges distinctions within the Trinity, he does not see a division in essence.[22] The beginning of divinity is attributed to the Father yet in the Scriptures the Son and Spirit share the name 'God' with the Father.[23] Furthermore, the three share in the activity of creating, providing for, and redeeming humanity.[24] What is particularly noteworthy in Calvin's Trinitarian view is his identification of the Father as a personal, caring member of the Godhead who shares the attributes of graciousness and mercy.[25]

While the primary explicit treatment of God as Father comes in Calvin's discussion of the Trinity, he does not limit the concept of the paternity of God to the Trinitarian relationships. He sees the Fatherhood of God as the completion of the Old Testament and as a normative revelation in the New Testament. It determines the whole teaching of Christ and his apostles as to the relationship of God with humankind. Calvin describes this relationship in a two-fold manner—the universal and particular Fatherhood of God. Both of these roles are characterized by God's unfailing love and mercy.

---

[21] Scott J. Lidgett makes a similar observation in *The Fatherhood of God in Christian Truth and Life* (London: Epworth Press, 1903), 242.

[22] *Inst* 1.13.2, 19.

[23] *Inst* 1.13.24.

[24] '[To] the Father is attributed the beginning of activity, and the fountain and wellspring of all things: to the Son, wisdom, counsel and the ordered disposition of all things; but to the Spirit is assigned the power and efficacy of that activity'—*Inst* 1.13.18.

[25] *Inst* 2.6.1-2, 2.8.21, 3.12.4-8.

## Universal Fatherhood: God the Father as Creator & Provider

John Calvin asserts that the universal Fatherhood of God is evidenced in God's creation and providence of the world. The idea of God as the universal Father of creation, Calvin believes, is proved by the universality of religion, although this idea is corrupted by ignorance and wickedness.[26] Calvin asserts that God shows universal 'fatherly care toward mankind' by the very order of creation.[27] By these, God's government, power, eternity, and goodness are made manifest.[28]

### Providence

Calvin sees the knowledge of God as Creator as intimately tied to God's fatherly providence. The knowledge of this fatherly providence brings comfort to the believer.[29] Calvin sees God's all-pervasive providence in terms of God's paternal favor and care for the offspring.[30] In discussing the Lord's Prayer he writes of God as, 'Our most gracious Father [who] does not disdain to take even our bodies under his safe keeping and guardianship in order to exercise our faith in these small matters, while we expect everything from him, even to a crumb of bread and a drop of water.'[31] In meeting our physical needs, God acts as a caring Father.

Summing up his doctrine of creation, Calvin points to the same theme, that by the order of creation God shows universal fatherly care in that God created all things for humankind's sake. He writes, 'the dispensation of all those things which He has made is in his own hand and power and that we are indeed his children, whom he has received into his faithful protection, to nourish and educate'.[32]

God's paternal concern and care for God's own children lies at the heart of Calvin's conception of Christian devotion. Calvin sees God's universal Fatherhood, as exemplified in God's providential care, as a call to reverence and god-

---

[26] *Inst* 1.4.1-4.

[27] '[He] did not create Adam until he had lavished upon the universe all manner of good things. For if he had put him in an earth as yet sterile and empty, if he had given him life before light, he would have seemed to provide insufficiently for his welfare. Now, when he disposed the movements of sun and stars to human uses filled the earth, waters and air with living things and brought forth an abundance of fruits to suffice as good, in thus assuming the responsibility of a forewing and diligent father of the family he shows his wonderful goodness toward us'—*Inst* 1.14.2.

[28] *Inst* 1.5.

[29] '[Set] free not only from the extreme anxiety and fear there were pressing him before, but from every care. . . . His solace, I say, is to know that his Heavenly Father so holds all things in his power, so rules by his authority and will, so governs by his wisdom, that nothing can befall except he determine it'—*Inst* 1.17.11.

[30] *Inst* 1.2.2; 4.16.32.

[31] *Inst* 3.10.44.

[32] *Inst* 1.14.22.

liness.[33] He writes, 'let the first step towards godliness be to recognize that God is our Father to watch over us, govern and nourish us, until he father us unto the eternal inheritance of his Kingdom.'[34]

In the context of creation, Calvin connects the universal Fatherhood with love and benevolence. This emphasis, however, has often been overlooked because he ends his doctrine of God as Creator with the way God uses the deeds of wicked men to carry out divine judgment.[35] Yet, Calvin did not intend for the more severe image to take precedence over God's fatherly care for creation.

### Particular Fatherhood: special adoption by God the Father as Redeemer

While God displays a universal paternal care for creation, Calvin acknowledges that humans cannot infer that God is Father by merely contemplating the universe.[36] For, 'in this ruin of mankind no one now experiences God either as Father or as Author of salvation, or favorable in any way, until Christ the Mediator comes forward to reconcile him to us'.[37] The true knowledge of God as a loving Father is known, according to Calvin, in the particular Fatherhood of God, in justification. Calvin sets forth this idea in terms of Christ and humanity's special relationship to the Father.

In his answer in the Geneva catechism to the question, 'Why do you call him Father?' Calvin responds:

> We infer, however, that, as God is the Father of Jesus Christ, he is our Father also. That we are the sons of God . . . not from nature but from adoption and grace only. . . . But the Lord Jesus who was begotten of the substance of the Father and is one essence with the Father is by the best title called the Son of God, because He alone is his Son by Nature.[38]

The reformer teaches, as Scripture reveals, that our special relationship with the Father is based upon the intimate relationship of the Son with the Father. When we are united to Christ by faith, we are reunited with our heavenly Father.

### The Father and fallen creation

God reconciles humans in Christ, because the Lord desires not to lose what is his in us. Calvin proclaims that out of paternal benevolence, the Father still finds something to love in fallen humanity and goes before and prepares for our

---

[33] In reference to piety he writes, 'I call "piety" that reverence joined with love of God which the knowledge of his benefits induces. For until men recognize that they owe everything to God, that they are nourished by his fatherly care, that he is the Author of their every good, that they should seek nothing beyond him, they will never yield him willing service'—*Inst* 1.2.1.

[34] *Inst* 2.6.4.

[35] *Inst* 1.17.1, 'either fatherly favor and beneficence or severity and judgment often shine forth'.

[36] *Inst* 2.6.4; 2.9.1.

[37] *Inst* 1.2.1; 2.6.1-2.

[38] *Calvin's Treatises* (Philadelphia: Westminster Press, 1954), 2.40.

redemption in Christ.[39] Originally God was the common Father of humans and angels. However, the 'natural' relationship was forfeited when humans turned from being God's obedient children to God's enemies by sinning.[40] He proclaims that 'the efficient cause of our obtaining eternal life is the mercy of the heavenly Father and his freely given love toward us'.[41] According to Calvin, Scripture reveals that the center of divine Fatherhood is God's grace and mercy towards fallen creation.

## The Father in the Son through the Holy Spirit

The particular divine Fatherhood, that finds its source in Christ's relationship with the Father, according to Calvin, is communicated in the Son and through the Holy Spirit. It is always Christocentric, as is his whole theology. God is our Father only in Christ, for only in and through Christ might believers, be persuaded that he is their Father.[42] In redemption, Christ is the article of our faith and the Father is the source of our trust.[43]

God would have remained hidden, according to Calvin, if Christ's splendor had not shined upon us. Fortunately, God revealed 'himself in Christ so that Christ, by communicating his Father's benefits, might express the true image of his glory'.[44] For Calvin, the very heart of the Gospel is the proclamation of God's Fatherhood in Christ.[45] Calvin insists that our adoption into the Father's family is only realized in the Holy Spirit.[46] Based on his understanding of the Pauline epistles, Calvin explains that the Spirit is the 'spirit of adoption,' and the 'witness' to us of God's paternal benevolence, by which we are embraced as children of God by being united to the Father's beloved only-begotten Son, Christ.[47]

## The Father and adoption

Calvin frequently uses the Pauline concept of 'adoption' to express our new relationship with God the Father.[48] We are assured of our inheritance through

---

[39] *Inst* 2.16.1-3.

[40] *Inst* 2.14.5.

[41] *Inst* 3.14.17.

[42] This is evident especially in *Inst* 2.6-17. A similar point is made in B.A. Gerrish (ed.), *Reformers in Profile* (Philadelphia: Fortress Press, 1967), 6.

[43] Garret A. Wilterdink makes a similar point in 'The Fatherhood of God in Calvin's Thought,' *Reformed Review* 30 (1976), 13.

[44] *Inst* 3.2.1.

[45] *Inst* 2.10.4. '[The] evangelical proclamation is nothing else than to announce that by the fatherly indulgence of God, sinners are justified apart from their own merit: and the whole sum of it is included in Christ'—*Inst* 3.10.4; See, also, *Inst* 2.6.4.

[46] He writes that 'the Holy Spirit is the bond by which Christ effectually unites us to himself'—*Inst* 2.1.1.

[47] *Inst* 3.1.3.

[48] *Inst* 3.2.11, n. 25; 2.6.1, 2.7.15, 2.9.9, 2.12.2, 3.1.3, 3.2.22, 3.11.6, 3.11.6, 3.14.18, 3.17.6, 3.18.2, 3.20.36f., 3.21.7, 3.22.1.4.

the natural Son of God, Jesus Christ, adopting us as his brother.[49] In our adoption, Calvin explains, God the Father is gracious and merciful in willing us to be redeemed and in restoring our freedom.[50] As Romans 8.14-17 proclaims, Christians gain the right to call God 'Abba Father' through their adoption.[51] While God was known as Father by the Israelites, Calvin declares, the advent of Christ is now the key for humans to have an intimate knowledge of God as Father.[52]

In the face of the awesome and threatening hiddenness of God, Calvin encourages the believer to look to the Fatherhood of God. Calvin sees Christ as the mirror of the Father's benevolence and the means by which the incomprehensibility of the Infinite is overcome.[53] Through faith in Christ we are justified and become children of God, knowing God as Christ does, as 'Our Father.' Listen to the picture of the heavenly Father that Calvin discovers in the Word:

> God both calls himself our Father and would have us so address him. By the great sweetness of this name he frees us from all distrust, since no greater feeling of love can be found elsewhere than in the Father. Therefore he could not attest to his own boundless love toward us with any surer proof than the fact that we are called 'children of God' (I Jn. 3.1). But just as he surpasses all men in goodness and mercy, so is his love greater and more excellent than all our parents' love. Hence, though all earthly fathers should divest themselves of all feeling of fatherhood and forsake their children, he will never fail us (cf. Ps. 27.10; Isa. 63.16), since he cannot deny himself (2 Tim. 2.13). [54]

Though God is far beyond us and human fathers often fail us, as he himself had experienced, Calvin points out that we have an opportunity to experience heavenly love here and now through our adoption by the heavenly Father. This is a love that is trustworthy and sets the standard for all other paternal relationships.

*The Lord's Prayer*
One of the primary ways we can know this paternal love is by learning about the Father through Christ's communication with him. Jesus, with the one ex-

---

[49] *Inst* 2.12.2.
[50] *Inst* 2.12.2; 2.6.1; 2.12.2; 2.11.9.
[51] '[Believers] also called God Father under the law, but not with such free confidence, since the veil kept them far from the sanctuary. But, now, when an entrance has been opened to us by the blood of Christ, we may glory with familiarity and in full voice that we are the sons of God'—*Comm. Rom.* 8.14-17, 170.
[52] '[After] the only-begotten Son of God was brought into the world, the heavenly Father has become more clearly known. Accordingly, Paul assigns privilege, as it were, to Christ's kingdom. Yet this ought to be unwaveringly maintained: to neither angels nor men was God ever Father, except with regard to his only-begotten Son; and men, especially, hateful to God because of their iniquity, become God's sons by free adoption because Christ is the Son of God by nature'—*Inst* 2.14.5.
[53] *Inst* 2.6.4.
[54] *Inst* 3.20.36.

ception of the cry from the cross, always invokes God as 'Father' in his record-
ed prayers.[55] Calvin recognizes the Lord's Prayer as particularly important to
our understanding of the Father. In this prayer Jesus shares his own relationship
with the Father and shows God's paternal care for his children.

In his *Commentary on the Gospels*, Calvin discusses at length the importance of Christ's words, 'Our Father, which art in heaven, hallowed be thy
name.' 'Our Father,' Calvin insists, points to the larger sphere of reality.
'Heaven' should conjure up in our minds the most mighty, lofty, and incom-
prehensible things we know and raise our thoughts beyond human experiences.
However, as Calvin points out, we, with imperfect minds, have a tendency to
imagine God after humankind.[56]

Calvin sees the Lord's Prayer as a witness to God's greatness as well as
God's care for God's children. He draws a parallel between Christ's invocation
of God as our Father and the parable of the Prodigal Son. The title 'Father' in
both cases, involves an image of God as compassionate, embracing his children
with open arms, and pardoning them for their sins.[57]

By looking to Christ's references to God as Father, Calvin believes that we
can avoid conceiving of God as earthly or physical and conforming him to our
imagination.[58] Calvin recognizes that in the Lord's Prayer Jesus is accommodating his Father's greatness to our capacity. Yet, in his accommodation, Christ
is portraying God, not as a male human father.[59] God is spiritual in nature, and
'Our Father' is a form of address that is intended to encourage us and set us in
fellowship with one another.[60] Calvin points out that in addressing God as 'our
Father,' Christ invites us to know first-hand God as an unfailing Father upon
whom we can assuredly trust.

---

[55] Mk. 15.34, Mt. 27.46, which is a quotation of Ps. 22.1.

[56] 'He is given the name Father. Now in this epithet alone Christ is supplying us with
ample found for our full assurance, but, as our dependence on God's goodness is only
half of our situation. He commends his power to us in a further phrase. When Scripture says God is 'in heaven', it means that all things are subject to his command. . . .
For as is could be foolish, nay crazy, presumption to invoke God as Father, except as
far as we know ourselves to be engrafted into the body of Christ as sons, we conclude
that were is no other means of prayer than to come to God relying upon his mediation'—*Commentary on the Gospels*, Mt. 6.9-13, Lk. 11.1-4, 206.

[57] *Inst* 3.20.37.

[58] *Inst* 3.20.40.

[59] *Inst* 1.10.2. God is 'shown to us not as he is in himself, but as he is toward us'.

[60] *Inst* 1.13.1. 'Under the name "Father" is set before us that God who appeared to us in
his own image that we should call upon him with assured faith. And not only does
the intimate name "Father" engender trust but it is effective also to keep our minds
from being drawn away to doubtful and false gods, permitting them to rise up from
the only-begotten Son to the sole Father of angels and of the church'—*Inst* 3.20.40.

## Calvin as a model for theology today

Calvin sees the Father of Christ, not earthly fathers, as determinative of our knowledge of the Fatherhood of God. In looking at Scripture's depiction of Christ's relationship with the Father and our adoption, God is revealed as both sovereign and personal; trustworthy and compassionate; just and merciful. Calvin rightly acknowledges that God's Fatherhood is an essential biblical belief that is prevalent throughout the Word. It is time that Calvin's traditional, biblical approach to God-language is recognized and re-appropiated by the Church. In doing so, the Church would reject both an oppressive, male god and an androgynous deity and 'let God be God'. Calvin gives us a beautiful example of this when he writes:

> For He is not only a father but by far the best and kindest of all fathers, provided we still cast ourselves upon his mercy. . . . And to strengthen our assurance that he is this sort of father to us if we are Christians, he willed that we call him not only 'Father' but explicitly 'our Father'. It is as if we addressed him: 'O Father, who dost abound with great devotion toward thy children, and with great readiness to forgive, we thy children call upon thee and make our prayers, assured and clearly persuaded that thou bearest toward us only the affection of a father, although we are unworthy of such a father.[61]

Isn't this the kind of father that we each desire to know and hope to see imitated here on earth: a father that is faithful, kind, and loving, even though we do not deserve such treatment? A father that will never leave us, but one who holds out his arms to welcome us back, even when we have strayed. Though this is a picture of strength, it is certainly not a picture of male-genderized oppression. When one opens the Word of God and allows God to speak, one has the opportunity to discover, as Calvin, Abba Father.

Margot Starbuck, like Calvin, found this very Father in Scripture. Her agonizing search for a trustworthy father came to end, when she, as Calvin, discovered God's revelation, 'I am,' wasn't just for Moses. She writes, 'In that moment those ancient, typeset words lifted off the Bible's inanimate pages to satisfy the deepest thirst of my heart. "I am for you Margot."'[62] Starbuck's journey, serves as a powerful reminder, that we can know an unfailing Father. God the Father seeks us out, desiring to answer our agonizing questions with the response, 'I am' for you. Starbuck stands on the shoulders of biblical theologians who have sought an understanding of God that is not dependent upon our flawed human relationships. If we follow Calvin's example and turn back to the Word to understand fatherhood, we too can find comfort, security, and wholeness; and proclaim, as children of God, 'I believe in God, the Father Almighty!'

---

[61] *Inst* 3.20.37.
[62] Starbuck, *The Girl in the Orange Dress*, 181.

Calvin modeled a reverent trust in the heavenly Father throughout his life. His entire ministry was dedicated to knowing who God really is, Abba Father. In April of 1564, Calvin gave expression to his faith in the Father in his last testament:

> I testify and declare that I trust to no other security for my salvation than this, and this only, viz., that God is the Father of mercy, he will show himself such a Father to me who acknowledge myself to be a miserable sinner. As to what remains, I wish that after my departure out of this life, my body be committed to the earth, (after the form and manner which is used in this city) till the day of a happy resurrection arrive.[63]

This should be the testimony of the church in life and death: that we are saved by the mercy of Abba Father.

---

[63] Quoted in Theodore Beza, *The Life of John Calvin, in Selected Works of John Calvin* (ed. H. Beveridge and J. Bonnet; Grand Rapids, MI: Baker, 1983), 1.xxxvi-xxxvii.

# CHAPTER 7

## Calvin's *praxis* of the Lord's Supper and the *duplex gratia* of salvation

### *Mary Patton Baker*

What was so important about the Lord's Supper that it would be the one issue that would tear apart the unity of the young Reform movement in 1529 at Marburg? The violent disagreement between Zwingli and Luther over the Lord's Supper began as a matter of hermeneutics. Zwingli, viewing Christ's statements rhetorically, insisted on interpreting 'This is my body' to mean, 'This is the figure of my body.' For Luther, the words of Jesus stood alone in their veracity: 'the real body is present by virtue of the word of Christ'. After all, Christ did not say, 'This is the figure of my Body.'[1] But there actually were very strong Christological and soteriological differences underlying their bitter debate.[2] Martin Bucer failed to heal the fissure, but seven years later his younger friend, John Calvin, would attempt to find the middle ground between Luther and Zwingli, drawing the discussion away from how to interpret 'This is my body' to discourse about the divine and human actions that take place in the celebration and to point to the purpose of the Eucharist in the life of the believer.

As early as 1536, in the first edition of his *Institutes of the Christian Religion*, Calvin declared, 'If this *force* of the sacrament had been examined and weighed as it deserved, there would have been quite enough to satisfy us, and these frightful contentions would not have arisen which of old, and even with our memory, have miserably troubled the church, when men in their curiosity endeavored to define how Christ's body is present in the bread.' For 'those who feel thus, do not pay attention, in the first place, to the necessity of asking how Christ's body, as it was given for us, became ours; how his blood, as it was

---

[1]   Hermann Sasse, *This is My Body* (Adelaide: Open Book Publishers, 1977 [Augsburg, 1959]), 188, 196. Sasse reconstructs the debate at Marburg from the Weimar edition of *Luther's Works*, supplemented by other primary sources from the period.

[2]   See W. Peter Stephens, 'The Soteriological Motive in the Eucharistic Controversy', in Willem van't Spijker (ed.), *Calvin: Erbe und Auftrag: Festchrift für Wilhelm Neuser Geburtsag* (Kampen: Kok, 1991), 203-13; Joseph McLelland, 'Lutheran-Reformed Debate on the Eucharist and Christology', in *Marburg Revisited*, 42; Mark Garcia, *Life in Christ: Union with Christ and Twofold Grace in Calvin's Theology* (Milton Keynes: Paternoster, 2008), 150.

shed for us, became ours. But that means to possess the whole Christ crucified, and to become a participant in all his benefits.'[3] For Calvin, *possessing Christ* was the force of the sacrament and thus frequent celebration of the Eucharist was necessary for believers to grow in their union with Christ, for union with Christ is 'the special fruit of the Lord's Supper'.[4] Major disputes over the Supper, then, distracted believers from enjoying the purposes for which Christ instituted it.[5]

My purpose in this essay is to explore the connections Calvin makes between the celebration of the Lord's Supper and our union with Christ in regard to the ongoing sanctification of the believer.[6] In the Eucharist Calvin understood the Holy Spirit to be dynamically witnessing to the *duplex gratia* of salvation by assuring believers of their justification and, secondly, by drawing believers into closer communion and enjoyment of our union with Christ.[7] The source of our growth in holiness for Calvin always centered upon our present tense union with Christ, participation in his life through the fellowship of the Holy Spirit. Due to his close identification of participation in the Eucharist to growing in this holiness, Calvin was clearly interested in the practice of the Eucharist as well as its theology: that the celebrations and liturgies of the Lord's Supper bring believers into this experience of their union with Christ. This essay will highlight three areas: Calvin's doctrine of union with Christ, its correlation to his Eucharistic theology, and its significance in the *praxis* of the Lord's Supper.

## Calvin's Doctrine of Union with Christ

Briefly stated, Calvin understood the content of our salvation and the foundation for our Christian life as our union with Christ. Through the gift of faith, we lay hold of Christ and the Holy Spirit makes us one with Christ. It is in this union that we receive two blessings, the *duplex gratia* of justification and sanctification. Calvin's gaze was always directed towards the perfect salvation achieved for us by Jesus Christ, decreed by the Father from eternity, accom-

---

3   1536 *Inst.*, 104.
4   This is the focus of section 4.17.2 of the 1559 *Institutes*. The editors of the 1960 Battles' edition sub-titled the section: 'Union with Christ as the Special Fruit of the Lord's Supper.'
5   Calvin expresses this sentiment in the opening paragraph of his *Short Treatise on the Holy Supper of Our Lord Jesus Christ*, T&T 2:164.
6   Two recent monographs have made very important contributions in the understanding of Calvin's doctrine of union with Christ and the sacraments: J. Todd Billings, *Calvin, Participation, and the Gift: the Activity of Believers in Union with Christ*, Changing Paradigms in Historical and Systematic Theology (New York: Oxford University Press, 2007) and Mark Garcia, *Life in Christ*. My particular contribution here is to draw attention to the significance the connection held for Calvin for the piety of the believer.
7   See 1559 *Inst* 4.17.11.

SINCE WE ARE JUSTIFIED BY FAITH

plished in time by the God-man Jesus Christ, and applied to us through our union with Christ, wherein the Holy Spirit gives to us all that he has received from the Son. Jesus Christ himself *is* our salvation: 'we see that our whole salvation and all its parts are comprehended in Christ'.[8] No benefit of salvation, neither justification nor sanctification, can be received outside of communion with him: 'we must understand that as long as Christ remains outside of us, and we are separated from him, all that he has suffered and done for the salvation of the human race remains useless and of no value for us. Therefore, to share with us what he has received from the Father, he had to become ours and to dwell within us.'[9] This 'joining together of Head and members, that indwelling of Christ in our hearts—in short, that mystical union,' must be understood as the highest value of salvation. 'We do not therefore contemplate him outside ourselves from afar in order that his righteousness may be imputed to us,' but rather 'we put on Christ'.[10]

It is because we receive Christ himself in salvation that justification and sanctification cannot be separated. Quoting 1 Corinthians 1.30, 'Christ is given unto us for righteousness, wisdom, sanctification, and redemption,' Calvin adds, 'Therefore Christ justifies no one whom he does not at the same time sanctify. These benefits are joined together by an everlasting and indissoluble bond.'[11]

Thus Calvin rather remarkably asserts that justification and the first gift of sanctification, regeneration, are given at the same time in the one act of salvation. He explains in his 1541 *Geneva Catechism* that 'when by faith we receive Christ as he is offered to us, he not only promises us deliverance from death and reconciliation with God, but also the gift of the Holy Spirit, by which we are regenerated to newness of life; these things must necessarily be conjoined so as not to divide Christ from himself'.[12] Calvin then differs from emerging sixteenth-century Lutheran doctrine in that he does not see 'justification as the de facto sum-total of salvation'.[13] Further, to pit the primacy of union with Christ against the primacy of forensic justification in Calvin is unfounded.[14] Calvin affirms that the legal pronouncement in justification that we are found righteous *ex nobis* is not made any less true by also affirming that in the first

---

[8] 1559 *Inst* 2.16.19.
[9] 1559 *Inst* 3.1.1.
[10] 1559 *Inst* 3.11.10.
[11] 1559 *Inst* 3.16.1.
[12] 1541 *Geneva Catechism*, *T&T* 2.55.
[13] Garcia, *Life in Christ*, 260. For the nuances between Calvin and Luther on justification and sanctification in salvation, see Garcia, 258-62, and Jonathan H. Rainbow, 'Double Grace: John Calvin's View of the Relationship of Justification and Sanctification,' *Ex Auditu* 5 (1989), 99-105.
[14] An example of this can be found in Thomas L. Wenger, 'The New Perspective on Calvin: Responding to Recent Calvin Interpretations,' *Journal of the Evangelical Theological Society* 50.2 (2007), 311-28.

gift of sanctification, regeneration, Christ becomes *in nobis.*

But why does Calvin equally assert that the two gifts of justification and sanctification are also distinct? Calvin and Luther both rejected the Catholic theology of infused grace as a prior condition to justification. To establish sanctification/regeneration as the cause of justification would breach the central affirmation of the Reformation that justification is forensic.

However, inversely, Calvin just as strongly asserted that sanctification was not an effect of justification because that would mean that when someone is justified they are not yet regenerated. This, then, would imply that our justification is a legal fiction, which Calvin firmly rejected. Calvin uses the pneumatologically dynamic words he finds in Paul to describe the Father's actions in justification: the believer is *engrafted into, adopted* and *joined to* Christ.[15] These words refer to the divine action of the Father that truly brings a change not only in our status before God, but also involves a true transformation of the human soul in regeneration, as it is vivified by the Spirit. Calvin is clear this union is not 'substantialist,' that is, to be understood in the sense of a mixing of essences. Rather Calvin refers to actions of God in salvation as the 'mystical union,' for 'as soon as we receive Christ by faith, . . . we are truly made his members'.[16] In our union with Christ we are now adopted into the life of God. This is not an external relationship, but a true familial communion through the fellowship of the Holy Spirit.

While Calvin understood being brought into union with Christ as the definitive action of God in salvation, he also identifies another aspect of this union 'which is the fruit and effect of the former. For after Christ, by the interior influence of his Spirit has bound us to himself and united us to his Body, he exerts a second influence of his Spirit, enriching us by his gifts.'[17] This Calvin sometimes refers to as our 'spiritual union' and he often uses the Latin words *participatio* and *communio* to denote this present tense 'spiritual union' which every believer enjoys. It is in this 'second communion, by which Christ dwelling in us not ineffectually, brings forth the influence of his Spirit in his manifest gifts,' that the believer is enabled to be 'strong in hope and patience,' to 'temperately keep ourselves from worldly snares, ... strenuously bestir ourselves to the subjugation of carnal affections,' and to continue 'earnestly in prayer, that mediation on the life to come which draws us upward'.[18] Consequently, Calvin

---

[15] For example, for references to 'adopted,' see *Inst* 3.3.9 and 3.8.1; for 'joined,' see 3.2.30 and 3.6.2; and for 'engrafted,' see 3.2.30 and 3.2.24.

[16] Calvin to Vermigli, 8 August 1555, *CO* 15.723. English translation from George Cornelius Gorham, *Gleanings of a Few Scattered Ears, During the Period of the Reformation in England* (London: Bell and Daldy, 1857), 349-50, cited in Garcia, *Life in Christ,* 284-85.

[17] Calvin to Vermigli, 8 August 1555, *CO* 15.723, cited in Garcia, *Life in Christ,* 285.

[18] Calvin to Vermigli, 8 August 1555, *CO* 15.723. English translation from Gorham, *Gleanings,* 351, cited by Richard Gamble, 'Sacramental Continuity Among Re-

believed that the initial act of regeneration in salvation was just the *beginning* of a pilgrimage to becoming more like Christ. The source of this transformation is found in the *deepening of our union with Christ through our 'spiritual communion' with him.*

There is a Trinitarian focus in Calvin's understanding of our union with Christ. Our union with Christ is through the Spirit just as Christ's relationship with the Father is through the Spirit: 'we infer that we are *one* with the Son of God; not because he conveys his substance to us, but because, by the power of his Spirit, *he imparts to us his life* and all the blessings which he has received from the Father'.[19]

Thus it is the *person* of the Spirit who binds us to Christ and brings us in communion with him. Contra any idea of deification that would unite us to Christ's divinity (a very un-Calvinistic idea), our union with Christ's humanity allows us to replicate the human life Jesus lived; *a life lived in communion with the Holy Spirit.* Our *participatio in Christus* is not one of consubstantiality with the divine Godhead, but one of communion.[20]

Repeatedly Calvin specifies that our union with Christ is a union with his human nature. What we receive from Christ corresponds with what he has received *from* the Father according to his human nature, not what he has possessed *with* the Father from all eternity. There is first a soteriological reason for this. We could not become children of God unless the 'Son of God became the Son of Man, and had not so taken what was ours as to impart what was his to us, and to make what was his *by nature* ours *by grace.*'[21] Christ in his assumed humanity possessed no 'stain' of sin because he was 'sanctified by the Spirit'.[22] And in our union with Christ as humans, we are also given that same Spirit: 'we are furnished, as far as God knows to be expedient for us, with the gifts of the Spirit. . . . Then, relying upon the power of the same Spirit, let us not doubt that we shall always be victorious over the devil, the world, and every kind of harmful thing.'[23]

Thus our sanctification is not founded on simply imitating Christ in our ac-

---

formed Refugees', in Frank A. James (ed.), *Peter Martyr Vermigli and the European Reformations* (Leiden: Brill, 2004), 108.

[19] *Comm. John* 17.21, CTS, emphasis added.

[20] Calvin only advocated a deification that paralleled the theology of union expounded herein. For two excellent treatments of the 'certain kind of deification,' Calvin advocated (Calvin, *Comm. 2 Peter* 1.4, CNTC 12:330). See J. Todd Billings, 'John Calvin: United to God through Christ', in Michael Christensen and Jeffery A. Wittung (eds), *Partakers of the Divine Nature: the History and Development of Deification in the Christian Tradition* (Grand Rapids: Baker Academic, 2008), 200-218; Jonathan Slater, 'Salvation as Participation in the Humanity of the Mediator in Calvin's *Institutes of the Christian Religion*: a Reply to Carl Mosser,' *Scottish Journal of Theology* 58.1 (2005), 39-58.

[21] 1559 *Inst* 2.12.2, emphasis added.

[22] 1559 *Inst* 2.13.4.

[23] 1559 *Inst* 2.15.4.

tions, but upon our participation in Christ's humanity, humanity lived in fellowship with the Spirit.[24] The *imitatio* is the work of the Spirit as we share in the same Spirit who shaped Jesus' human life.

There is a genius in this insistence by Calvin of the *distinctio sed non separatio*, distinct but not separate *duplex gratia* of salvation. Calvin challenged all who heard him to grasp onto the understanding that while their salvation is assured by the Father's free adoption given in justification through Christ's obedience, he also calls them into a relationship of transformation with the Holy Spirit. Through this *koinōnia*-faith-relationship with the living Christ and his Spirit, good works *will* be manifest.

In this brief introduction to Calvin's soteriological emphasis on our union with Christ as the sum of salvation, I have laid a needed basis for next probing Calvin's theology of the Lord's Supper. In Calvin's pneumatological emphasis on our union with Christ, he highlights the participatory fellowship of the Holy Spirit between Christ and the Father, and Christ and the believer. The ongoing reality of our participation in Christ is founded in communion rather than essence. This 'spiritual union' is the only source of our growth in sanctification. We are to live our life as Christ did, governed by the Holy Spirit. At the center of our life in Christ is our encounter with the Triune God.

### Calvin's Eucharistic theology and the *duplex gratia*

The Eucharist was certainly important to John Calvin. In fact, Calvin's main stumbling block to joining the young reform movement in Paris in the early 1530s was Zwingli's doctrine of the Eucharist. When Calvin read that 'Zwingli and Oecolompadius left nothing of the sacrament but bare and empty figures,' this so profoundly disturbed the young man's sacramental piety that he turned away for a time from reading the reformers.[25] Every year, from 1536 until his death in 1564, Calvin wrote something about the Eucharist.[26]

But in all of Calvin's vast number of works on the Lord's Supper, he never strayed far from this central point: in the celebration of the Supper, the believer is nourished with real spiritual food, the enjoyment of one's union with Christ.

---

[24] R. Michael Allen, *The Christ's Faith: a Dogmatic Account* (London: T. & T. Clark, 2009), 121-32; Julie Canlis, *Calvin's Ladder: A Spiritual Theology of Ascent and Ascension* (Grand Rapids: Eerdmans, 2010), 96-100; Garcia, *Life in Christ*, 139-45.
[25] *Second Defense of the Sacraments*, T&T 2.252, cited in Bernard Cottret, *Calvin: A Biography* (Grand Rapids: Eerdmans / Edinburgh: T. & T. Clark, 2000), 66.
[26] Thomas J. Davis, *The Clearest Promises of God: The Development of Calvin's Eucharistic Teaching* (New York: AMS Press, 1995), 6. Davis's excellent account of the development of Calvin's theology demonstrates where Calvin's thought varied over the course of his writings. But Davis's conclusions correspond with the thesis here, that Calvin's theological movement in his eucharistic thinking can be attributed to 'Calvin's desire that the Christian, first of all, know what it is that makes a Christian—union with Christ' (212). To demonstrate this theme is present over the entire course of his career, I include quotations from 1536 onwards.

Consistently Calvin emphasized the sacramental act did not take place merely in the arena of human movement towards God, but rather, in the Lord's Supper a true communion between believer and Christ took place that spiritually strengthened and nourished the believer. In this, Calvin followed Paul—that the cup of blessing and the bread that we break is a true participation in the body and blood of Christ. Commenting on Paul's exhortation to the Corinthians, Calvin asserts that 'the source of that *koinõnia* which exists among us, is that we are united to Christ . . . not a mere human fellowship, but the spiritual union between Christ and believers'.[27] Calvin understood that the translation of the word *koinõnia* in this passage was something much stronger than human fellowship; it denoted rather our possessing Christ through the indissoluble bond of the Holy Spirit.

Thus the very words Calvin uses in describing union with Christ are replicated in his theological account of the divine/human encounter enjoyed in the celebration of the Lord's Supper. Accordingly, there are specific theological convergences between Calvin's theology of union with Christ and his Eucharistic theology.[28] Below I will summarize a few of these convergences as a window into the heart of Calvin's teaching on the Eucharist, that the special gift of the Eucharist is both a personalized and corporate, dynamic experience of our union with Christ. Along the way, I will show how Calvin integrated his positions vis-à-vis the soteriological and Christological debate between Luther and Zwingli into his own conception of the divine action and Christ's presence in the Eucharist. For as much as Calvin sought to find common ground, he did not shy away from disagreement when he saw other doctrinal issues at stake.

### The first gift: justification

Calvin believed that in the Lord's Supper the Spirit assures believers of their justification while offering them the opportunity to express humiliation and gratitude for this gift. In the opening words of Calvin's first theological offering on the Eucharist (the 1536 *Institutes*), significantly, Calvin chose these words to introduce the subject:

> We call it the Lord's Supper or the Eucharist because in it we are both *spiritually fed by the Lord's goodness*, and give thanks to him for his kindness. The promise added thereto very clearly asserts for *what purpose it has been instituted*, and the goal to which it looks, namely, to confirm us to the Lord's body was once for all

---

[27] *Comm. 1 Cor.*, 10.16, CNTC, 9.216.

[28] See, also, Garcia, *Life in Christ*, 160-170 and Billings, *Calvin, Participation*, 116-43, for a more extensive treatment of the convergences than space allows here. Garcia draws more structural comparisons; while Billings, on the other hand, explores the analogical similarities in both Baptism and the Lord's Supper. But my purpose is to demonstrate how through these convergences Calvin understood that the 'special gift' of the Lord's Supper is a present tense experience of our union with Christ.

so handed over to us, *as now to be ours*, and also forever to be so; that his blood was once for all so poured out for us, as always to be ours.

As Calvin continues in this passage he provides hints at what will be developed in full later, that the Eucharist enables us to enjoy our union with Christ: 'Great indeed is the fruit of sweetness and comfort our souls can gather from this sacrament; because we recognize Christ to have been so engrafted in us as we, in turn, have been engrafted in him.'[29]

Unmistakably, for Calvin the chief function of the Spirit's actions in the sacrament is not 'simply to exhibit (*exhibere*) to us the body of Christ'. Rather it is 'to seal and confirm (*obsignare et confirmare*), that promise by which he testifies that his flesh is food indeed and his blood is drink'.[30] Calvin therefore understands that in our Eucharistic celebrations we experience the dynamic aspects of our justification and the assurance of our faith is strengthened and nurtured. In the celebration participants are invited into a place of rest from all their efforts at self-justification.[31]

### The second gift: sanctification

The idea of spiritual nourishment and strengthening in the Lord's Supper fits the connection Calvin makes between union with Christ, sanctification, and the Lord's Supper. For, as I related above, Calvin understood that it is through our participation with Christ that our sanctification grows and our faith is strengthened. For Calvin, the spiritual food of the sacrament is Christ himself. Calvin insisted that 'to receive any fruits from the sacrament *is to have received him*. After anyone deeply grasps this thought and meditates upon it, he will readily understand how the body of Christ is offered to us in the sacrament, namely truly and effectively.'[32]

Calvin criticized Zwingli for reducing participation in the Eucharist to simply an act of remembering and believing: 'the true participation in himself which he gives us, which he has signified by the words "eating" and "drinking" does not consist in mere knowledge. For eating the bread, not looking at it, ministers nourishment to the body.'[33] Calvin maintained that we are truly partaking of Christ in the sacrament just as our union with Christ is a true participation in Christ, and not a fictional courtroom finding. While he agreed with Zwingli

---

[29] 1536 *Inst.*, 102.

[30] 1536 *Inst.*, 103 (CO 120). Note however, that *exhibere* is an active verb meaning 'offers, presents, and delivers'. As such, Calvin is emphasizing the effects of the sacrament's offering, to seal and confirm. *Exhibere* does not mean simply to 'symbolize', or 'represent', as it is often translated. See Leo F. Stelton, *Dictionary of Ecclesiastical Latin* (Peabody: Hendrickson, 1995), 93. As such, the sacrament 'delivers' God's promises from his Word.

[31] Billings, *Calvin, Participation,* 142.

[32] 1536 *Inst.*, 104, emphasis added.

[33] 1541 *Inst.*, 12.553.

(and Luther) that the sacraments held no intrinsic power unto salvation, contrary to Zwingli's formulation, Calvin believed the Supper was not a figure of our salvation, but rather that in it we receive Christ himself.

Calvin develops a line of theological argument to counter Zwingli's concern that *any* elevation of the sacraments above human activity challenged the doctrine of salvation through Christ alone. His resource for this was to draw upon the Augustinian understanding of the Eucharist as a sign *joined* to the reality of that which it signifies: the body and blood of Christ. Zwingli clearly misunderstood the difference between an Augustinian sign and a figure of speech. Signs for Zwingli are not operative or instrumental; rather, they refer only to a past event, not the present communication of the Spirit. But Calvin clearly understood Augustine's distinction between sign and reality, and their conjunction: 'the figure and the truth are contained in the sacrament'.[34] Through proclamation of the Word and the performance of the liturgical act 'God therefore truly executes whatever he promises and represents in signs; nor do the signs lack their own effect in proving their Author truthful and faithful.'[35] Calvin asserted, '[W]hen we have received the symbol of the body, let us no less surely trust that the body itself is also given to us.'[36] This partaking was then a true participation in the life of Christ.

### The fellowship of the Spirit

But Calvin needed to solve the problem of understanding the conjunction of sign and signified in a way that did not invoke local presence and yet helped his readers understand that the sign indeed was joined to the reality it signified. Just as the Holy Spirit is the one who unites us to Christ and the Father, the Spirit is also the agent who joins the *signa*, the communion elements, and the *res*, Christ's flesh and blood.

Calvin's specific reference to Christ's flesh and blood is a reference to our union with Christ's humanity, a union we truly enjoy with him through the Spirit. Christ's 'flesh' functions in Calvin's formulation of the *res* of the Eucharist as a synecdoche for Christ's true humanity.[37] As we have seen above, Christ's assumption of our flesh is of prime importance soteriologically and in our understanding of the nature of our participation in Christ. Thus also in the Sacrament, 'the same flesh breathes life into us,' the substance of that flesh that he is *as* the Son of God in our humanity.[38]

Calvin agreed with Zwingli that Luther's doctrine of ubiquity challenged the doctrine of the bodily ascension of Christ's body in his claim that Christ's body can be everywhere. Calvin believed that after the ascension Jesus did not cease

---

[34] 1559 *Inst* 4.14.15.
[35] 1559 *Inst* 4.14.17.
[36] 1559 *Inst* 4.17.10.
[37] Canlis, *Calvin's Ladder*, 101.
[38] *Exposition of the Mutual Consent, T&T* 2.238.

his assumption of a human body, and therefore in his humanity he is still 'circumscribed by the measure of a human body,' somewhere beyond the created order accessible to us.[39] Even as the glorified Christ he cannot be on the altar or in many places all simultaneously.

In the *Geneva Catechism* Calvin poses this question for the young child: 'Wherefore I doubt not that as he testifies by words and signs, so he also makes us partakers of his substance, that thus we may have one life with him.' How can this be the catechist asks, 'when the body of Christ is in heaven and we are still pilgrims on the earth'? The child answers: 'This he accomplishes by the secret and miraculous agency of his Spirit, to whom it is not difficult to unite things otherwise disjoined by a distant space.'[40]

In a sense Calvin is saying that spatial distance is simply the wrong category with which to understand Christ's presence.[41] To advocate any kind of local presence is to deny the Spirit's bond of efficacy in bringing true communion between Christ and the believer. We are united to Christ's humanity through the same fellowship of the Spirit that the risen Christ also enjoys. We are not to bring Christ 'back down to earth' by claiming local presence, but rather to understand the Spirit's activity as the mode of 'descent by which he [Christ] lifts us up to himself'.[42] Ronald Wallace identifies this mode as 'celestial presence,' because Calvin claimed that the eating of Christ's flesh is a 'heavenly act'.[43] Calvin maintained the distinction between the humanity and divinity of the risen Christ as to space and time, but not as to power or presence.[44] Even as we feed on our oneness with Christ's flesh we are also to be drawn up to the contemplation of his divinity; that as the *Logos*, self-identified as the man-God Jesus Christ, he has redeemed us from all eternity. To this end, Calvin insisted that every Communion service include the ancient hymn of the church, the *Sur-*

---

[39] 1559 *Inst* 4.17.30.
[40] *Geneva Catechism, T&T* 2.91.
[41] Billings, *Calvin, Participation*, 138.
[42] 1559 *Inst* 4.17.16.
[43] Ronald S. Wallace, *Calvin's Doctrine of the Word and Sacrament* (Grand Rapids: Eerdmans, 1957), 208. The reference in Calvin to the Supper as a 'heavenly act' can be found in *Comm. 2 Cor.* 11.24, CNTC 9.247.
[44] See 1559 *Inst* 4.17.30 and *Comm. Eph.* 4.10, CNTC 11.177. Unlike Luther, Calvin emphasized the communication of attributes takes place at the level of the person, not the two natures. Consequently he still maintained the unity of Christ's human and divine nature in the second person of the Trinity, the One who chose to be our Mediator in the eternity of time. Calvin is careful to protect the distinctness of the two natures so that our identity with Christ according to his human nature does not 'in any way compromise his being *homoousias* with the Father' (Slater, 'Salvation as Participation,' 46). What is referred to as the '*extra-Calvinisticum*' is simply Calvin's way of identifying the unity of Jesus' natures: the assumed humanity in space and time with the Eternal Son, who as mediator fills the whole world. See, also, Joseph N. Tylenda, 'Calvin's Understanding of the Communication of Properties,' *Westminster Theological Journal* 38.1 (Fall 1975), 54-65.

*sum corda*, albeit modified for Reformed worship.[45]

In sum, I have drawn out the connections Calvin drew between his doctrine of union with Christ and the importance he places on the celebration of the Lord's Supper. In his Eucharistic theology Calvin offers a grammar for understanding how believers substantially partake of Christ's flesh and blood in the Lord's Supper that follows the logic of his theology of the *duplex gratia*. Even more, he emphasizes how participation in the Eucharistic celebration reinforces our understanding and our experience of our union with Christ; for in the Eucharist we receive Christ himself so that he may continue his work of transforming us ever more into his image. Calvin explains that though what we receive is that which we have every day, the Eucharist *'admonishes and incites us more strongly* to *recognize* the blessings, which we have received, and receive daily from the Lord Jesus'.[46] It is communion enjoyed in a unique way.

The gift of communion is intensified in the Eucharistic act because of its accommodation to our human senses. 'Now there cannot be a spur which can pierce us more to the quick than when he makes us, so to speak, see with the eye, touch with the hand, and distinctly perceive this inestimable blessing of feeding on his own substance.'[47] Calvin describes our communion with Christ in the Lord's Supper as one in which the Triune God *'nourishes'* our faith, *'confirms'* to us our redemption, *'renews'* his covenant, and *'assures'* us that through 'feeding on Christ' we will be 'refreshed by partaking of him, so we may repeatedly gather strength until we shall have reached heavenly immortality [and that] we will endure to the end'.[48] And, just as we enjoy food and are 'gladdened' by wine, we are to be made happy by our response of gratitude as we celebrate the Lord's Supper and become prepared to go out into the world and spread God's justice.

### The *praxis* of the Lord's Supper in worship

Calvin was a true liturgical theologian in that he was concerned that the words of our mouths and the actions of our bodies correspond to a heart of piety and obedience towards God. In the celebration of the Lord's Supper Calvin sought to draw emphasis away from what he perceived as magical superstitions in the Roman church that lead to the worship of the earthly elements to a new focus on the participant's living communion with Christ and each other. To this end, he vastly simplified the liturgy of the Lord's Supper and rid the churches of all images, altar cloths, vestments, church ornaments, candles, and the like. And

---

[45] For the history of the use of the *Sursum corda* in the Reformed churches, see Christopher Elwood, *The Body Broken: The Calvinist Doctrine of the Eucharist and the Symbolization of Power in Sixteenth-Century France* (New York: Oxford, 1999), 43-44.
[46] *Short Treatise, T&T* 2.173
[47] *Short Treatise, T&T* 2.173.
[48] 1559 *Inst* 4.17.4.

yet he insisted that though he had 'abolished' the mass, he had not 'destroyed the Sacrament'.[49] By requiring this simplicity, Calvin hoped to keep the focus turned away from the trappings of the mass that served to elevate the physical elements of the bread and wine, apart from their spiritual significance. Rather, Calvin wished to turn the believer towards Christ's 'celestial presence' and the communion each believer experienced with Christ in the consumption of the elements. On the Sundays Communion was celebrated the communion table was set in front of the pulpit. Gathered together before the table of the Lord, fellowship in Christ also took on corporate meaning. The sacraments were the 'visible Word,' which enabled participants to realize their oneness with Christ and each other, constituted by the fellowship of the Holy Spirit.

The Communion services (as well as every other morning service of the Lord's Day) began with a corporate confession. As the service brings each participant through a remembrance of the gifts of justification and sanctification, the journey of worship begins, as does the moment of coming to faith, with an acknowledgement of the sinful state and the need for forgiveness. The Minister's words of absolution remind the worshipper that through Jesus our sins are wiped away, and appeal for 'daily increase of the gifts of the Holy Spirit,' so he 'may produce in us the fruits of righteousness and holiness'.[50]

After the Confession the service proceeded forward with corporate singing of the Psalms followed by the reading and preaching of the Scriptures, corporate prayer, reciting or singing the Lord's Prayer and the Apostle's Creed.[51] Accordingly, Calvin's worship services were marked by their corporate and participatory nature. Unlike the Roman Mass, the participant did not simply watch most of the service or listen to professional choirs sing the liturgy. At every point in Calvin's service, the congregation is worshipping and responding, enjoying in all aspects of their worship their true communion with God. Calvin did not disparage the value of religious emotion in worship. He wrote that 'a happy emotion toward God is not a dead or brutish thing, but it is a living movement, proceeding from the Holy Spirit, when the heart is deftly touched and the understanding illuminated'.[52]

---

[49] *Manner of Celebrating the Lord's Supper, T&T* 2.122.

[50] *Forms of Prayer, T&T* 2.100.

[51] James H. Nichols, 'The Intent of the Calvinistic Liturgy', in John H. Bratt (ed), *The Heritage of John Calvin: Heritage Hall lectures, 1960-70* (Grand Rapids: Eerdmans, 1973), 101-103. There were variations upon the order of these segments as further editions of the *Forms of Prayer* were implemented over the years in Geneva. For these variations see Christian Grosse, *Les Rituels de La Cene: le Culte Eucharistique Reforme a Geneve (XVIe - XVIIe siecles)* (Geneva: Droz, 2008).

[52] *La Forme Des Prieres et Chantz Ecclesiastiques, Epistre Au Lecteur, CO* 6.166; English translation from Auguste LeCerf, 'The Liturgy of the Holy Supper at Geneva in 1542,' reprinted in Richard Gamble (ed.), *Calvin's Ecclesiology: Sacraments and Deacons* (Articles on Calvin and Calvinism, 10: trans. F.D. Shafer: New York: Gar-

When Communion was celebrated the service continued with a specific exhortation to 'receive this great blessing with true sincerity of heart and ardent desire,' and to 'enjoy together his body and blood, or rather himself entire'. As the exhortation continued Calvin's liturgy once again reminds the congregation that to receive Christ entirely, is to receive the *duplex gratia*.

> It is truly the holy bread of heaven that gives us life, that we may no longer live in ourselves . . . but that he may live in us and conduct us to a holy, happy, and ever-during life, thus making us truly partakers of the new and eternal covenant . . . and in feeling fully persuaded that thou art pleased to be forever a propitious Father to us, by not imputing to us our offences, and to furnish us, as dear children and heirs.[53]

And at this point each participant is appropriately asked again to examine their consciences, to see whether he or she desires to live a life of holiness, and whether they seek 'salvation entirely in Jesus Christ'. Repentance is what constitutes a 'worthy partaker,' not that one is 'perfect or righteous' in their own self. Rather the sacrament is 'medicine for the poor spiritual sick,' and all that is required is a desire to 'have all our pleasure, joy, and contentment in him alone,' and to receive the sacrament knowing that 'although we see only bread and wine,' we 'possess him entirely'. Therefore, 'let us present ourselves to him with ardent zeal, in order that he may make us capable of receiving him'. At this point the *Sursum corda* is recited: 'Let us raise our hearts and minds on high, where Jesus Christ is, in the glory of his Father, and from whence we look for him at our redemption.'[54] Each participant then comes forward to receive the bread from the pastor and the wine from an elder, while psalms are sung.

In his liturgy as well as his theology, the highest value for Calvin was participation in Christ in whom we find both justification and sanctification in our union with him. The Eucharist was given to the church for this very reason. It is in the Eucharist, as embodied persons, we enter into a communicative event with the living God who uses embodied instruments to convey his grace.

As early as the 1536 *Institutes* Calvin urged his readers to participate weekly in the Eucharistic celebrations. He advocated this because of the important benefits received: the strengthening of faith, the urging of 'themselves to sing thanksgiving and to proclaim his goodness; finally, by it to nourish mutual love, and among themselves give witness to this love'.[55] Subsequently, when Calvin first arrived in Geneva he proposed that Communion be celebrated once

---

land, 1992), 213. Original French essay by Lecerf, 'La Liturgie de Cène de 1542', in A. Schlemmer (ed.), *Etudes Calvinistes* (Aix-en-Provence: Kerygma, 1999), 52.
[53] *Forms of Prayer*, T&T 2.105.
[54] *The Manner of Celebrating the Lord's Supper*, T&T 2.120-21.
[55] 1536 *Inst* 112.

a week.[56] Even though at Strasbourg the Eucharist was celebrated weekly, when he returned to Geneva in 1541 Calvin proposed a compromise of monthly celebrations.[57] But in Geneva, where Calvin did not always get his way with the city's magistrates, he had to settle for quarterly celebrations. As late as his 1559 *Institutes* he was still complaining about the infrequent practice.[58]

Unfortunately, the differences at Marburg between Zwingli and Luther are still with us. To this day our own continued theological debates over Christ's real, true, or symbolic presence in the Eucharist eclipse its importance in spiritual formation. The frequency of practice in Reformed churches reflects the design of Zwingli and the town magistrates in Geneva. Now more than ever we need to turn to John Calvin to discover why he believed the Eucharist was important. Far from a simple memorial ceremony, Calvin places participation in the Lord's Supper at the heart of our knowledge of ourselves as redeemed children of God and our sanctification as followers of Christ.

---

[56] Jean Calvin, 'Articles Concerning the Organization of the Church and of Worship at Geneva', in *Calvin: Theological Treatises* (trans. J. K. S. Reid; Library of Christian Classics, 22: London: SCM Press, 1954), 48.

[57] '1541 Draft Ecclesiastical Ordinances', *Theological Treatises,* 66.

[58] 1559 *Inst* 4.17.44.

# CHAPTER 8

# Explicit and implicit appendixes to Calvin's view of justification by faith

## David W. Hall

A search for the term 'justification' in the data base of Calvin's major writing[1] shows that the term 'justification' is used over 200 times in the *Institutes*— certainly indicating that this concept was of dominant interest to Calvin. This and other considerations have given rise to the claim that the doctrine of justification is the most important doctrine for the Protestant Reformation, in general, and for Calvin, in particular. If that claim is sustained, then it would also stand to reason that other correlates, properly tied to justification, would consistently reflect both the meaning and the thrust of Calvin's denotation of justification.

The preponderance of this term's occurrences appears primarily in the middle of the *Institutes* in Book 3, chapters 11-12. Accordingly, once this doctrine is constructed in principle in those sections, other correlates are subsequently built on that supporting foundation. Thus, if the faith rises or falls with justification by faith, certain other implied Christian teachings might be expected to give way (or be strengthened) depending on how this teaching is maintained. Similarly, if these correlates reflect Calvin's homology a stronger understanding of his view of justification ensues. Moreover, the importance of many of these auxiliary doctrines is seen by the depth that Calvin devotes to these areas in the second half of the *Institutes*, following his explanation of justification. Indeed, most of the normal topics of Christian living are impacted by the meaning of justification, and practical theology is infused by the semantic content of this notion.

To better understand Calvin on this topic, in this essay I discuss, first, Calvin's view of justification, including interactions with current theorists and the *Institutes*. As a vital and critical area, it also begets overflows and correlates; second, what Calvin explicitly calls the 'Proper appendix of justification,' namely, Christian liberty; and, third, other implicit areas in which Calvin draws on justification to make assertions for other *loci*: prayer, election, ecclesiology, civil government, and eschatology.

---

[1] Using http://www.ccel.org/ccel/calvin/institutes.txt

## Summary of Calvin on justification from the *Institutes*

This much debated area, however, may not be as obscure or as difficult as some seem to make it. Whether one begins with Calvin's commentary on Romans or with the *Institutes*, as long as one reads Calvin comprehensively, his view on justification is fairly clear and consistent. While creative theologians may always discover a stray thread or phrase in any theological wardrobe (particularly in the larger *corpae*, say by Augustine, Calvin, Edwards), Calvin's view can safely be categorized as consistent with the forensic view, expressed in later Protestant and Puritan creeds and confessions. It certainly was not a precursor, N.T. Wright notwithstanding, to putative theories about Second Temple of Judaism; nor was this a sclerotic post-reformation Scholastic development.

According to the *Institutes*, Calvin discussed justification following his treatise on the 'Life of the Christian Man.' Along with cross-bearing and self-denial, this Christian life has an eschatological horizon that is never outpaced or forgotten. The Christian, just prior to Calvin's discussion of justification, is to understand and use the good gifts of God without becoming addicted to them.[2] Godly contentment should inspire a Christian to accept poverty or blessing, becoming enchanted with neither but always looking to our heavenly calling. With that backdrop, Calvin then launches into his discussion of justification in Book 3, chapter 11.

Justification is tied to regeneration, as part of a 'double grace (*duplicem gratiam)*'.[3] The first of those graces is that one is reconciled to God 'through Christ's blamelessness,' resulting in a gracious Father instead of a condemning Judge. That seems to be Calvin's beginning definition of justification: the act of God by which he transforms us from criminals to children. The second grace is that 'sanctified by Christ's spirit we may cultivate blamelessness and purity of life,' or regeneration. In this context, Calvin calls this justification 'the main hinge on which religion turns,' asserting: 'For unless you first of all grasp what your relationship to God is, and the nature of this judgment concerning you, you have neither a foundation on which to establish your salvation nor one on which to build piety toward God.' Thus, Calvin begins by contending that justification must be known and was essential both for salvation and for continuing piety.[4]

---

[2]  *Inst* 3.11.2.

[3]  *Inst* 3.11.1.

[4]  Among the recent discussions of Calvin on justification are the following: Mark A. Garcia, *Life in Christ: Union with Christ and Twofold Grace in Calvin's Theology* (Milton Keynes: Paternoster, 2008); A.N.S. Lane, *Justification by Faith in Catholic–Protestant Dialogue* (London/New York: T. & T. Clark, 2002); J. Todd Billings, *Calvin, Participation, and the Gift: The Activity of Believers in Union with Christ* (Changing Paradigms in Historical and Systematic Theology: New York: Oxford University Press, 2008); Michael Horton, *Covenant and Salvation: Union with Christ* (Louisville, KY: Westminster John Knox, 2007); and Dennis E. Tamburello, *Union*

SINCE WE ARE JUSTIFIED BY FAITH

Calvin defines justification initially as both being 'reckoned righteous in God's judgment' and as being 'accepted on account of his righteousness'.[5] Thus God provides both the legal verdict and the moral atonement. As a result, the justified person is 'reckoned in the condition not of a sinner but of a righteous man'. God judicially alters the 'condition' of a sinner, and by the death of Christ 'reckons' that sinner to be righteous. The justified sinner 'grasps the righteousness of Christ through faith . . . is clothed in it, [and] appears in God's sight not as a sinner but as a righteous man'. For Calvin, then, justification is 'the acceptance with which God receives us into his favor as righteous men. And we say that it consists in the remission of sins and the imputation of Christ's righteousness.'[6]

While modern theologians may debate other aspects of the Reformed tradition, Calvin's initial definition is clear, unencumbered, and predictably orthodox. Calvin proceeds to support his view of justification by citing only a few passages, since 'it would take too long to collect all the passages'[7] that exhibit the meaning of justification. Furthermore, he viewed Paul's teaching on justification to be summarized by the term 'acceptance,' further emphasizing the judicial/forensic nature of justification. Said Calvin clearly, 'Therefore, since God justifies us by the intercession of Christ, he absolves us not by the confirmation of our own innocence but by the imputation of righteousness, so that we who are not righteous in ourselves may be reckoned as such in Christ.'[8] Thus, Calvin equates justification with 'acceptance,' 'imputation,' 'pardoning,' 'reckoning,' and the divine commutation of justice.

So careful was Calvin to focus on God's commutation of justice that he provided an extensive critique of Osiander's view. Osiander (1498-1552) taught 'some strange monster' of essential righteousness, in which he advocated that Christ's essence was ontologically mingled with ours in justification. Calvin objected both to 'infusion' of Christ's essence and 'substantial' righteousness.[9] Calvin's point was none other than this: God the Judge justifies, and his act reckons our condition differently than it is. Osiander's problem was his 'dividing' of Christ's natures; in contrast, Calvin emphasized that Christ's atoning work fully comprehended both natures and was performed *qua* Mediator. Christ's obedience and the acts of his human nature were equally central to justification. Instead of an ontological union (Osiander), Calvin taught—and this guards us against the substantialism of Eastern Orthodoxy[10]—that the union

---

with Christ: John Calvin and the Mysticism of St. Bernard (Louisville, KY: Westminster John Knox, 1996).
[5] *Inst* 3.11.2.
[6] *Inst* 3.11.2.
[7] *Inst* 3.11.3.
[8] *Inst* 3.11.3.
[9] *Inst* 3.11.5.
[10] See the paragraphs on McCormack below.

102

was a 'mystical'[11] or spiritual one—much like the logic he employed later in his sacramentology.

Calvin spied 'more poison'[12] in Osiander's view that 'we are righteous together with God'. It could hardly be clearer that Calvin held to a forensic view of justification, especially when one observes this polemic against Osiander in his most important theological treatise. At one point Calvin affirmed that the essential meaning of justification was so clear as 'reckoning' (an 'expression taken from legal usage') that he wrote, 'Anyone moderately versed in the Hebrew language, provided he has a sober brain, is not ignorant of the fact that the phrase arose from this [legal] source, and drew from it its tendency and implication.'[13]

Bruce McCormack has seized on Calvin's critique of Osiander and shows how this refracts Calvin's denotation of justification. Following Calvin's own definition of justification,[14] McCormack recognizes Calvin's emphasis on justification as acquittal—certainly a legal concept, commenting that '"to justify" means nothing else than to acquit of guilt him who was accused as if his innocence were confirmed'. The setting is that of a courtroom. The question is one of guilt or innocence. And the divine verdict is one of innocence. How can this be? It is because the guilt for our sin was imputed to Christ, who then suffered the legal penalty that our guilt required. 'This is our acquittal: the guilt that held us liable for punishment has been transferred to the head of the Son of God [Isa. 53.12].'[15]

McCormack then observes further that the concept of acquittal presumes that 'the righteousness on which it is based be complete'. Accordingly, the acquitted person must truly be innocent of the preferred charges, but

> complete innocence is found in Christ alone. He alone was sinless. His obedience alone is perfect. But that, then, means that the ground of our justification must lie, at every moment of the Christian life, outside of ourselves. . . . Outside of us, Christ's righteousness is complete; in us, it is not. Therefore, if justification does

---

[11] *Inst* 3.11.10.
[12] *Inst* 3.11.11.
[13] *Inst* 3.11.11.
[14] *Inst* 3.11.2.
[15] Bruce McCormack, 'Union with Christ in Calvin's Theology: Grounds for a Divinization Theory?' in David W. Hall (ed.), *Tributes to John Calvin: A Celebration of his Quincentenary* (Phillipsburg, NJ: Presbyterian & Reformed, 2010), 517. See, also, Bruce McCormack, *Justification in Perspective: Historical Developments and Contemporary Challenges* (Grand Rapids, MI: Baker, 2006) and 'What's at Stake in Current Debates over Justification: The Crisis of Protestantism in the West', in Mark Husbands and Daniel J. Treier (eds), *Justification: What's at Stake in the Current Debates* (Downers Grove: InterVarsity Press, 2004).

indeed consist in acquittal, then the ground of our justification must be found to lie in the alien righteousness of Christ and in it alone.[16]

Moreover, McCormack confirms that,

> The mechanism by means of which Christ's perfect righteousness is made to be ours is that of imputation. Imputation is a concept drawn from the realm of accounting (of book-keeping). Guilt is not credited to the account of the sinner; Christ's righteousness is. The same mechanism is employed by Calvin to explain how our guilt is made to be Christ's—in other words, how he who knew no sin was made sin on our behalf. . . . That is, he who was about to cleanse the filth of those iniquities was covered with them by transferred imputation. . . . Our guilt was made his by imputation. . . . In any event, atonement and justification are twin doctrines for Calvin. Both are construed in strictly forensic terms.[17]

Finally, citing Calvin's critique of Osiander's view that the 'essential righteousness' of Christ is taken to our nature, McCormack analyzes:

> Against this conception, Calvin says that Osiander ought to have been 'content with that righteousness which has been acquired for us by Christ's obedience and sacrificial death'. The *acquired* righteousness of Christ: by this phrase Calvin clearly means to refer to the righteousness that accrues to Christ's sinless obedience in life and in death—in other words, to his *human* righteousness, that which is added to his divine righteousness.[18]

Cornelis Venema has recently summarized that, for Calvin, any discussion of faith would be barren, deformed, and useless should it fail to include an elaboration of this two-fold benefit as Calvin did.[19] Richard Gaffin similarly clarifies, notwithstanding, that Calvin did not teach that justification fails to lead to sanctification. Returning to the term 'regeneration,' he believes that God always produces moral reform in the life of the truly justified: 'He does not justify in part but liberally. . . . From this it follows that the doctrine of justification is perverted and utterly overthrown when doubt is thrust into men's minds, when the assurance of salvation is shaken and the free and fearless calling upon God sufferance hindrance—nay, when peace and tranquility with spiritual joy are not established.'[20] To be sure, for Calvin

> justification and sanctification are inseparable. As such, however, they are not confused but distinguished. Accenting inseparability, Calvin speaks not of two

---

[16] McCormack, 'Union with Christ,' 517.

[17] McCormack, 'Union with Christ,' 518.

[18] McCormack, 'Union with Christ,' 518-19.

[19] Cornelis P. Venema, 'Union with Christ, the "Twofold Grace of God," and the "Order of Salvation" in Calvin's Theology', in Joel Beeke (ed.), *Calvin for Today* (Grand Rapids: Reformation Heritage Press, 2010), 93.

[20] *Inst* 3.11.11.

graces but of 'two-fold grace' in the singular, although later in this section he does refer to regeneration as 'the second of these gifts' or better, this 'second grace,' signaling some distinction. The nature of both this difference and inseparability, as well as the nature of the underlying union involved, Calvin will clarify as his discussion unfolds.[21]

Venema agrees that justification, the first benefit, is always accompanied by the second benefit, sanctification—although justification has a logical priority that the French reformer could not ignore.[22] Such justification—juridical in nature—'consists in the remission of sins and the imputation of Christ's righteousness'.[23] Standing against the received medieval confusion of justification with a condition of possessing righteousness, Calvin saw justification as including divine acquittal as well as acceptance and reconciliation. Venema warns of the practical ills that flow from confusing justification with either sanctification or apotheosis: 'Unless the difference between justification and sanctification is carefully maintained, the goodness and mercy of God will be seriously impugned and the assurance of faith will be threatened.'[24]

Venema argues convincingly that Calvin expected that his readers would easily conclude, by his sequence of topics, that justification was not by works but by faith alone—but as 'simple pardon'.[25] Furthermore, Calvin believed this precise ordering of topics would underscore the inseparability of justification and sanctification. In short, much of the discussion about Calvin on justification—especially if it leads to minimization of justification or an optimization of external factors—appears, upon calmer understandings to be a Shakespearian 'Much Ado About Nothing.' Or put it this way: looking for Calvin to articulate or support a 'new perspective' on justification is about like expecting Calvin to enunciate a new perspective on creation, the Trinity, inspiration, etc. Richard Gaffin puts things in focus when he summarizes:

---

21 Richard Gaffin, 'Justification and Union with Christ', in David W. Hall and Peter A. Lillback (eds), *A Theological Guide to Calvin's Institutes* (Phillipsburg, NJ, Presbyterian & Reformed, 2008), 253-54.

22 Venema, 'Union with Christ' 144-45.

23 *Inst* 3.11.2.

24 Cornelis P. Venema, 'Union with Christ,' 98. Venema's chapter also provides a helpful summarization of the dialogue between Thomas Wenger and Marcus Johnson. Among other things, Venema makes it clear that the earlier discussion of sanctification before justification in Calvin should not discount how Calvin routinely treats sanctification as an effect of, fruit of, or following from justification (154). Moreover, in *Institutes* 3.3, Calvin explains the order of his loci, and in 3.11.1 when he speaks of justification as 'the main hinge on which religion turns,' while calling for it to have a priority of comprehension given to it, Calvin states: 'For unless you first of all grasp what your relationship to God is, and the nature of his judgment concerning you, you have neither a foundation on which to establish your salvation nor one on which to build piety toward God.'

25 Venema, 'Union with Christ,' 106.

[F]or Calvin sanctification as an ongoing, life-long process follows justification and in that sense justification is 'prior' to sanctification and the believer's good works can be seen as the fruits and signs of having been justified. Only those already justified are being sanctified. But this is not the same thing as saying, what Calvin does *not* say, that justification is the source of sanctification or that justification causes sanctification. That source, that cause is Christ, in whom, Calvin is clear in this passage, at the moment they are united to him by faith, sinners simultaneously receive a two-fold grace and so begin an ongoing process of being sanctified just as they are now also definitively justified.[26]

Gaffin further explains that Calvin called the idea that 'imputation is nonforensic or somehow a nonjudicial transfer or communication' a 'frivolous notion'.[27]

Toward the conclusion of Calvin's discussion of justification, we begin to sense the practical test of doctrine in his writing.[28] Not only is it founded, in Calvin's work, on proper exegesis and systematic consistency, but the practical affect of a doctrine confirms its right understanding. Thus for Calvin the erroneous constructs—whether Osiander's, the Romanist's, or the Enthusiast's—of doctrine falsely conceived is further revealed in its practical bondage and hindrance.

It is this practical test that leads us to the next sections of this paper. Calvin's conclusion to section 3.11.12 illustrates how practical he is: 'In short, whoever wraps up two kinds of righteousness [i.e., Osiander's key flaw] in order that miserable souls may not repose wholly in God's mere mercy, crowns Christ in mockery with a wreath of thorns.'

With a clearer view of Calvin on justification now in view, let us move forward to see how he then builds further on what is already constructed. Moreover, each appendage will corroborate the meaning of justification as explained above.

---

[26] Gaffin, 'Justification and Union,' 256. Gaffin also reports the substantial enlargement and placement of this topic in the second (and other) editions of Calvin's *Institutes*, showing the 'roughly four-fold, expansion of the *Institutes* in the second, 1539 edition. Now and in subsequent editions (1543-45 and 1550-54) there is a separate chapter on justification (6 or 10, depending on the edition), positioned between chapters on repentance and the similarity and difference between the Old and New Testaments. This chapter, with its own title, "Concerning Justification by Faith and the Merits of Works," is approximately 7 times the length of the treatment in 1536 and consists of 87 numbered sections, without subtitling or other internal subdivisions.' Further, Gaffin theorizes that Calvin's crystallization of this topic in his final edition was, in part, a response to the 1547 Council of Trent.

[27] Gaffin, 'Justification and Union,' 263.

[28] *Inst* 3.11.11.

## The explicit appendix: Christian liberty

In his dispute over the meaning of justification with Osiander, Calvin labeled his view a 'strange monster,' thinking that it was tantamount to a revival of Manicheanism. The separation of essential parts, practice from doctrine, was often at the core of accusing one's opponents of Manicheanism. Just as Calvin had a consistent view of justification, he also believed that it consistently had payoff in Christian living.

In two different spheres—the civil sphere and the authoritarianism of Roman ecclesiology—he was challenged to work out an enduring view of liberty. In Book 3 of *The Institutes*, he took up this subject of Christian liberty, and his insights are still helpful today. To begin with, a key distinction must be introduced from the conclusion of chapter 19 of that work.

Calvin spoke of two species of liberty: civil and spiritual.[29] He taught that human government is two-fold: 1) spiritual government is internal, and it trains the conscience in matters of piety and worship; and 2) civil government refers to external matters. The former has its seat in the soul, and the outer government refers to external activity. The church is to teach and handle the spiritual order; and the political rulers care for civil order. Calvin suggested that if we pay attention to this distinction, 'we will not erroneously transfer the doctrine of the gospel concerning spiritual liberty to civil order'. That division of labor would become an essential building block of stable societies; it would also supply ample protection for proper freedom.

With that in mind, it should be clearer that church and state each had a valuable role to play in human life. However, they should not interfere with the proper jurisdiction of the other; God intended it to be that way.

As Calvin began his groundbreaking chapter on Christian liberty, he first sought to explain why this topic was so important. He argued that it was necessary for contemporaries to understand this, even if only on an elementary level, lest they have their consciences burdened by the threat of endless rules and stifling captivity. Indeed, he asserted, this topic was a *proper* 'appendage (Lat. *appendix*) to justification,' meaning that if one knew how he had been truly justified (by God alone), then he might also know that true liberty would result only as one followed God. Thus, from the outset, Calvin believed that liberty was a gift, and one that should be used as God has designed it. It was a natural correlate of the right understanding of justification.

Pastor Calvin was sensitive to the tender consciences of many Protestants. He argued that if one omitted an explanation of this subject, much wavering and trepidation would result.[30] The battle over justification, in other words, could be lost not only over what justification meant in theory but also over how it was practiced. Accordingly, Christians who were justified, if they did not un-

---

[29]  *Inst* 3.9.15.
[30]  *Inst* 3.19.1.

derstand this 'thing of prime necessity,' would 'hesitate and recoil' in many things, hardly being able to undertake anything without crippling doubts. Calvin also taught that once justification is appropriated, then for those who 'seriously fear' God, this topic yielded 'incomparable benefit'. Moreover, he believed that this topic had its rightful place as a corollary or appendix, properly speaking, to justification.

So vital was this doctrine for Calvin that he concluded, 'Unless this freedom be comprehended, neither Christ nor gospel truth, nor inner peace of soul, can be rightly known.'[31] Thus, he advised that this 'so necessary a part of doctrine' not be suppressed. For Calvin, the doctrine of justification—in its correct understanding of the role of law—leads to a Christocentric and ethical liberation.

Being regenerated by God, believers were to 'voluntarily obey the will of God,'[32] not obeying out of a servile fear. Instead of being in terror, the believer should know the love of God; and liberty flowed from that. This also meant the end of various perfectionistic schemes. Calvin's followers were to be perfect in Christ, not in themselves. That also implied the end of legalism. As such, believers were permitted to use things as helpful or omit them, as long as they did not seek to overturn the moral law. Accordingly, there were many things in life that Calvin classified as 'indifferent'. To fail to make that distinction would, he thought, mean 'no end of superstition'.[33] As long as believers used created things properly, liberty was a good rule of thumb. The goal of this liberty was to 'give peace to trembling consciences'.[34]

Calvin also offered a hierarchy of norms to help people make decisions. Matters of Christian liberty had to be subjected to the law of charity;[35] by that, he meant that sometimes we must voluntarily restrict ourselves so that we do not cause others to stumble. Thus, liberty is not absolute in Calvin's scheme. It is good and a gift from God, but even it must be kept in perspective. Moreover, just as the law of liberty must be subject to the law of charity, nevertheless this norm of love is not the final test either; for the law of love 'must in its turn be subordinate to the purity of faith'. Thus, for Calvin a finely nuanced view of liberty and ethics valued the purity of the revealed faith to the utmost. Following that, the rule of charity trumped, and after that came Christian liberty.

Calvin had seen an oppression of liberties—both in Paris and in the eyes of the many refugees who arrived so regularly at Geneva's walls—and he formed his view of liberties based on God's Word and also in a fashion that avoided misuses of it. Christian liberty was the proper appendage of justification. However, Calvin knew that sanctification was always intertwined with justification. Thus, if not careful, other Christian matters of practice could virtually nullify

---

[31] *Inst* 3.19.1.
[32] *Inst* 3.19.4.
[33] *Inst* 3.19.7.
[34] *Inst* 3.19.9.
[35] *Inst* 3.19.13.

justification if not rightly formulated. The final chapters of Books 3 and 4 treat those matters.

## Implicit appendixes

The logic in the final section of this essay is as follows: If we understand justification (J) as Calvin did, it leads necessarily to the doctrine of Christian Liberty (L). If both of those are obtained (J + L), then certain other Implications (I) follow. In each case below, the simple 'J + L → I' logic shows the internal consistency of Calvin's thought. It also serves to liberate each of these individual *loci* from the bondage of medieval practices—a consequence that is not inconsiderable.

*Prayer. The way one is justified affects the way one prays*

Jae Sung Kim has noted the difference that theoretical formulations make for the practice of prayer in his study of Calvin's soteriology and prayer. He notes that 'One of the distinctive contributions of John Calvin to reformed theology is the firm establishment of the doctrine of application of redemption.' In an important essay, Kim seeks to 'expose a distinct aspect of Calvin's soteriology, which emphasizes that justification by faith should be complemented by prayer in the Holy Spirit'.[36] Kim writes that the focus of Calvin's idea on the application of redemption 'starts with recognizing faith as the primary gift and secret work of the Holy Spirit to unite us with Christ. . . . The chief role of the Holy Spirit in the application of redemption is to unite us with Christ.'[37] Moreover, Kim sees both prayer and faith as God's gifts, noting that

> these two subjects are closely related in Calvin's biblical soteriology, especially in his numerous polemical arguments against the Roman Catholics and some radical Lutheran extremes. One of Calvin's controversial arguments on Reformed soteriology shows us a new understanding of justification by faith. The imputation of Christ's righteousness is not only alien but has been compared with the doctrine of infusion and self-attained righteousness of Council of the Trent. In this sense, Calvin's doctrine of prayer is also very different from the Roman Catholics.[38]

Kim's important observation is borne out from a perusal of some of Calvin's 'rules for prayer'. In his third rule for prayer, Calvin taught that any person who 'stands before God to pray, in his humility giving glory completely to God, abandon[s] all thought of his own glory, cast[s] off all notion of his self-worth, in fine, put away all self-assurance'.[39] One observes both the difference between the prevailing Roman view of prayers, as well as how similar the termi-

---

[36] Jae Sung Kim, 'Prayer in Calvin's Soteriology', in Hall (ed.), *Tributes to John Calvin*, 343-55.
[37] Kim, 'Prayer,' 343-55.
[38] Kim, 'Prayer,' 343-55.
[39] *Inst* 3.20.8.

nology (humility, cast off own glory, put away self-assurance) is to that of Calvin's forensic justification. Moreover, he adds that confidence is derived in prayer 'solely from God's mercy'.[40] Is Calvin not calling for *sola misericordae ora* in the same way that he calls for *sola gratia* and *sola fides* concerning justification? It is difficult to imagine a logical disjunction. It is not in our 'own righteousness' that we have the enjoyment of a 'pure conscience before the Lord' in prayer.[41] To the contrary, faith necessarily joins the 'acknowledgement of our misery, destitution, and uncleanness'—the same starting point for forensic justification. Calvin also denied that observing fixed hours for prayer could ever pay 'our debt to God,'[42] drawing clearly and consistently on forensic terminology.

Later, Calvin will argue that appealing to the intercession of Saints (*qua* Romanism) assaulted the dignity of Christ's work. To hold such would imply that 'Christ were insufficient or too severe'.[43] It is a dishonoring of Christ that 'strips him of the title of sole Mediator' to pray to others; moreover this 'obscures the glory of his birth and makes void the cross'.[44] Thus Kim observes that the doctrine of prayer links two important subjects, Christian liberty and predestination in the final edition of the *Institutes.*[45]

Prayer is almost, but not quite (except as a part of sanctification), elevated to the *ordo salutis* in Calvin's work. Jae Sung Kim summarizes:

> In order to escape from Roman Catholic's error, Calvin attacks the practice of penance, especially the three steps of the Scholastics: contrition of heart, confession of mouth, and satisfaction of works. For Calvin, God simply requires repentance and faith. Our sanctification is the object of regeneration and our efforts strive to overcome bad habits. The first step in the Christian life is self-denial, which is the departure from self to thorough obedience to God. Then, bearing the cross leads us to mature trust in God's will.[46]

Thus, justification as a critical part of soteriology has bearing on prayer. It is no coincidence that Romanists and Calvinists view prayer differently. The same would be true for proponents of any of the other differing views of justification. Calvin put it this way: 'God finds nothing in man to arouse him to do good to him but that he comes first to man in his free generosity. For what can a dead man do to attain life?'[47] Calvin applies this scriptural logic further, drawing on Hosea 2.19: 'If a covenant of this sort, which is clearly the first union of us with God, depends upon God's mercy, no basis is left for our righteousness. . . .

---

[40]  *Inst* 3.20.9.
[41]  *Inst* 3.20.10.
[42]  *Inst* 3.20.50.
[43]  *Inst* 3.20.21.
[44]  *Inst* 3.20.21.
[45]  Kim, 'Prayer,' 344.
[46]  Kim, 'Prayer,' 354.
[47]  *Inst* 3.14.5.

If justification is the beginning of love, what righteousness of works will precede it?'[48] The logic of justification, applied to prayer, was subsequently applied to election.

*Election. The way one is justified affects the way one views God's sovereignty*

Calvin's defense of divine election upon review may surprise some by its unanticipated gentleness and pastoral tone. He opines that the only possible way to understand this is for 'reverent minds' to accept what God has written. He also argues practically that one of the benefits of election is the resulting comfort: 'We shall never be clearly persuaded, as we ought to be, that our salvation flows from the wellspring of God's free mercy until we come to know his eternal election, which illumines God's grace by this contrast: that he does not indiscriminately adopt all into the hope of salvation but gives to some what he denies to others.'[49] Moreover, he again reiterates that 'our salvation comes about solely from God's mere generosity' the contrary of which fails to tear pride up by its very roots. Nothing, says Calvin, has more potential to make us humble than to realize that our standing with Christ is undeserved. Furthermore, this teaching, along with forensic justification 'is our only ground for firmness and confidence' and 'alone will free us from all fear'.[50]

Calvin explicitly links election and justification in a key section that draws upon numerous scriptural texts. At one location, he states again that 'freely given mercy' not 'regard to human worth' (the dynamic of justification) is the engine for this loving election that dares to adopt any into God's family.[51] Also, in this context, Calvin speaks of 'justification' as 'another sign of [the] manifestation' of election.[52] In the next chapter, Calvin preaches that 'we were adopted in Christ into the eternal inheritance because in ourselves we were not capable of such great excellence'.[53] The internal consistency between Calvin's view of justification and election demands that we allow his correlates to corroborate his main theorem.

*Church government. The way one is justified affects the way one's life is ordered in the church and how church power is conceived*

The bulk of Book 4, following on the heels of Calvin's elaboration of justification, discusses various matters of church government. One might think that in these areas, the shadow of justification does not extend. *Au contrare.* If for no other reason, the very conception of church power and the ethos of ecclesiology

---

[48] *Inst* 3.14.6.
[49] *Inst* 3.21.1.
[50] *Inst* 3.21.1.
[51] *Inst* 3.21.7.
[52] *Inst* 3.21.7.
[53] *Inst* 3.22.1.

is affected by the subjects and manner of God's justification. A different view of justification would well lead to a different ecclesiology.

Calvin's sixth chapter in his original edition addressed three topics: Christian liberty, ecclesiastical power, and political administration.[54] His teaching on Christian liberty was one of the earliest features of his thought, and it is either an essential part of Gospel teaching[55] or, as it would later become known, an 'appendix to the doctrine of justification'. Calvin's discussion of this topic, which was so important in his day, follows the same outline as his 1559 edition, albeit in slightly compressed form. The longest section in his sixth chapter is on ecclesiology proper. Calvin viewed this in his day as an extension of Christian freedom,[56] for if church masters invaded the conscience, that tyranny threatened Christian liberty. It is worthy of note that Calvin viewed church government as important for spiritual liberty—thus the need to devote so much writing to that subject during the Reformation era. Justification, thus, even overflowed into church order, with proper ecclesiology being infused with theology. It is not too much to assert that Calvin viewed himself as setting forth an ecclesiology of liberty as opposed to the prevailing tyranny of 'innumerable,' 'limitless,' and 'entangling' church governance that 'traps to catch and ensnare souls'.[57] If this language sounds similar to Calvin's comments on justification, there is a good explanation for this found in homology.

His divine-right ecclesiology would later be extended by his disciples, but on the level of principle his advocacy of *sola Scriptura* in this topic is as clear as in other theological *loci*. With Scripture acknowledged as his authority even for ecclesiology, Calvin asserted that 'if faith depends on God's word alone, if it looks to it and reposes in it alone, what place is now left for the word of men?'.[58] That reliance on an alien source (or 'alien righteousness') is similar to his view on justification. Legislative power, thought Calvin, or the authority to 'frame new laws,'[59] was denied to the apostles; only ministerial power—the right to echo and assert what God had already declared—was given to the church. God, the sole ruler over souls, was the sole ruler over the church of all souls.

---

54 See Ford Lewis Battles' edition of Calvin's *Institutes of the Christian Religion* (1536) (Grand Rapids: Eerdmans, 1986). The initial edition is drawn upon to illustrate the continuity of Calvin's thought over time.
55 *Inst* (1536), 176.
56 *Inst* (1536), 184.
57 *Inst* (1536), 185.
58 *Inst* (1536), 189.
59 *Inst* (1536), 189.

*Civil government. The way one is justified affects the way one constructs the role of the civil magistrate*

While it may seem 'alien to the spiritual doctrine of faith,'[60] a certain necessity compelled Calvin to tie political matters to faith. Indeed, for Calvin, the whole plan of God's salvation implied numerous ethical correlates and a correct formulation in governmental matters yields 'greater zeal for piety' that may flourish in us 'to attest our gratefulness'.[61] For Calvin, political matters flow from a proper appropriation of previous doctrines and also produced something as practical as thankfulness.

Moreover, Calvin's naming of magistrates 'the vicars of God'[62] employs terminology that reminds a careful reader of the substitutionist vocabulary that is similar to Calvin's soteriological formulations. Also, for Calvin the very concept that the civil government works for both the saved and the unsaved implies two other very important factors: 1) justification, under that formulation, is an internal-forensic work, not a moralistic one; and 2) Calvin's view permits the non-justified to have equal protection, as Calvinist states have tended to provide.

*Eschatology. The way one is justified affects the expectations of the future hope*

It is well known that Calvin proffered an underdeveloped eschatology, at least in his *Institutes*. Some, of course, claim that he's a modern-day postmillennialist based on remarks in his Commentary on Daniel and other Old Testament prophetic books. Seldom, however, is Calvin viewed as having a premillennial bent, probably because he so frequently lambasted the 'chiliasts'. I am happy to leave to other better scholars the exact determination of his view,[63] if I may make but one note before moving to make some concluding remarks. My only insight into Calvin's eschatology and its affinity to his view on justification is to point out one trenchant and pastoral comment he makes near the outset of this discussion. Calvin castigates being tied to earthly things, and suggests that we would do better spending more time on our 'heavenly life'.[64] Then he shows the pastoral payoff for raw doctrine: 'Accordingly, he alone has fully profited

---

[60] *Inst* 4.20.1.
[61] *Inst* 4.20.1.
[62] *Inst* 4.20.6.
[63] See Heinrich Quistorp, *Calvin's Doctrine of Last Things* (Eugene, OR: Wipf and Stock, 2009). Also, Hank Bowen, 'Calvin's Eschatological World and Life View,' (http://reformedherald.org/index.php/component/k2/item/65-calvin's-eschatological-world-and-life-view); James L. Codling, *Calvin: Ethics, Eschatology, and Education* (Cambridge Scholars Publishing; New edition, January 2010).
[64] *Inst* 3.25.1.

in this gospel who has accustomed himself to continual meditation upon the blessed resurrection.'[65]

In his commentary on Romans 8.30, Calvin has no mental anguish tying justification to glorification. At one point, Calvin defines justification as spanning 'the unremitted continuance of God's favor, from the time of our calling to the hour of our death,' and asserts that since 'Paul uses this word [justification] throughout the Epistle for *gratuitous imputation of righteousness*, there is no necessity for us to deviate from this meaning.'[66] Calvin, of course, did not create this logic of justification. He merely followed the Apostle Paul in Romans 5.1, who enumerated several blessings (peace, access, standing, perseverance) to 'since we have been justified through faith, *therefore* . . .'

### Observations and conclusion

For Calvin, justification caused the recipients to 'turn aside from the contemplation of our own works and look solely upon God's mercy and Christ's perfection'.[67] Accordingly, a certain 'order of justification' is observed, consistent with Calvin's earlier definitions. This orderly design begins with God's 'freely given goodness' to the sinner, finding no good in the human subject. Then God 'touches' the sinner with this goodness, causing him to turn away from any sense of moral virtue. The sinner seeks salvation wholly in God's mercy by faith; and the sinner acknowledges that he has been reconciled to God. He is justified because of Christ's mediatorial activity, and once regenerated 'he ponders the everlasting righteousness laid up for him not in good works to which he inclines but in the sole righteousness of Christ'.[68] Such apprehension leads, then, properly to Christian liberty as an appendage and to many other aspects of true piety.

Without such justification and its appendix, Calvin only sees a 'strange monster' or salvation by works. Assurance of salvation is also assailed: 'for when we rise up toward God [with works], that assurance of ours vanishes in a flash and dies'.[69] In summary, for Calvin 'this whole discussion will be foolish and weak unless every man admit his guilt before the Heavenly Judge, and concerned about his own acquittal, willingly cast himself down and confess his nothingness'.[70] Such is the safeguard afforded by a correct understanding of justification.

Calvin's view of justification is even tied to humility or the thought that we have nothing left to ourselves. In fact, the 'gateway to salvation,' according to

---

[65] *Inst* 3.25.1.
[66] John Calvin, *Commentary on the Epistle of the Apostle Paul to the Romans* (Grand Rapids: Baker, 1979), 19.319, emphasis added.
[67] *Inst* 3.11.16.
[68] *Inst* 3.11.16.
[69] *Inst* 3.12.2.
[70] *Inst* 3.12.1.

Calvin, does not lie open for us 'unless we have laid aside all pride and taken upon ourselves perfect humility; secondly, that . . . this humility is an unfeigned submission of our heart'.[71]

Two correlates of free justification are that 1) God's glory is undiminished; and 2) our consciences have rest and serenity. Drawing on *The Institutes*,[72] Cornelis Venema has recently called attention to how assurance itself is tied, in Calvin's thinking, to a right view of justification.[73] Calvin expected that any inability to discern the difference between justification and sanctification would dramatically reduce a believer's assurance of faith. Moreover, Venema is helpful to note how sanctification, rightly following justification, liberates the believer from being tempted to present God (mercenary-like) with an overdue bill. For when sanctification is within the matrix of free justification, 'it represents the free, Spirit-authored life of a forgiven sinner in the presence of his gracious heavenly Father'.[74] The logic is that if sanctification is not buttressed upon God's prior pardon/acquittal, it invariably 'becomes tainted with the infections of "anxiety" before God ("Have I been sufficiently obedient?"), "pride" ("Surely my good works contribute something to my acceptance with God"), and a "mercenary" spirit ("No doubt, my obedience will prove valuable since God will 'repay' me in kind")'.[75]

For Calvin, the divine righteousness that brings justification is not sufficiently presented unless God 'alone be esteemed righteous, and communicate the free gift of righteousness to the undeserving'.[76] Moreover, 'God's glory is somewhat diminished if man glories in himself.' Thus, Calvin's view of justification is strongly forensic—not ontological—and it results in the fruit of godliness. Justification and its appendixes, rightly understood, can permit no human glorying, and 'man cannot without sacrilege claim for himself even a crumb of righteousness'.[77] Calvin advised seeking peace of soul 'solely in the anguish of Christ our Redeemer'.[78] Most clearly, 'Faith is something merely passive, bringing nothing of ours to the recovering of God's favor but receiving from Christ that which we lack.'[79]

Calvin's theory of justification is clear from his writings. Thankfully, he confirms his forensic view[80] repeatedly as he discusses explicit and implicit ap-

---

[71] *Inst* 3.12.6.
[72] *Inst* 3.13.3.
[73] Venema, 'Union with Christ,' 111.
[74] Venema, 'Union with Christ,' 113.
[75] Venema, 'Union with Christ,' 113.
[76] *Inst* 3.13.1.
[77] *Inst* 3.13.2.
[78] *Inst* 3.13.4.
[79] *Inst* 3.13.5.
[80] In his commentary on James 2.21, Calvin sees a distinction between how Paul uses the term justification ('the gratuitous imputation of righteousness before the tribunal of God') and what James means by it ('The manifestation of righteousness by the

pendixes to justification—all of which form spokes connected to the hub (if I may use an analogy different from the 'hinge') on which our religion rises or falls. Moreover, his doctrine of justification overflows with numerous practical effects.

conduct, and that before men').

# CHAPTER 9

## The suffering church in Calvin's *De Scandalis*: an exercise in Luther's *Theologia Crucis*?

### Bonnie Pattison

In 1982, Brian Gerrish noted that 'Luther's doctrine of the *Deus absconditus* has been subjected to intense study . . . [but] surprisingly, however, there is no such body of literature on what Calvin thought about God's hiddenness.'[1] Furthermore he claims that, 'it could be shown that Calvin's thoughts on hiddenness parallel Luther's in their full range'.[2] Gerrish notes that T.H.L. Parker recognized (almost two decades earlier) that 'the concept of *Deus absconditus* is as native to Calvin's theology as it is to Luther's'.[3] Gerrish concludes that scholars probably have been 'skeptical about the genuine unity of the various motifs' in Calvin's thought, clustered under the 'common rubric of "God's hiddenness"'. Nevertheless, he believes that 'the problem has simply been neglected, at least in its full scope'.[4]

Students of the Reformation know that the concept *Deus absconditus* is fundamental to Luther's *theologia crucis*. It forms the linchpin of Luther's theology of the cross, a constellation of ideas about the nature of God's revelation that gave birth to Luther's clarion call for *sola fide, sola gratia,* and *sola scriptura.* However, regarding Calvin's thought as a second generation reformer, this begs the following question: If Calvin studies has neglected investigating Calvin's understanding of the hidden God as Parker and Gerrish claim, could it also have neglected investigating whether Calvin has a theology of the cross as well? In his book, *Calvin's Theology of the Psalms,* Herman Selderhuis has ventured into this issue by dedicating a chapter to the theme 'God the Hidden.' From studying Calvin's theology of the Psalms, Selderhuis makes the following conclusion: 'Based upon what he says about the hiddenness of God, as well as

---

[1] B.A. Gerrish, '"To the Unknown God" Luther and Calvin on the Hiddenness of God', in *The Old Protestantism and the New: Essays on the Reformation Heritage* (Chicago: University of Chicago, 1982), 141.

[2] Gerrish, 'To the Unknown God', 141.

[3] Gerrish, 'To the Unknown God', 341, fn. 58. See T.H.L. Parker, *Calvin's Doctrine of the Knowledge of God* (Edinburgh: Oliver & Boyd, 1969), 27.

[4] Gerrish, 'To the Unknown God', 141.

his description of the Christian life, it is clear that Calvin holds to a *theologia crucis*.[5] The goal of this study is to provide further evidence to the claim that Calvin, indeed, has a theology of the cross. This study will examine one segment of Calvin's thought—his theology of the suffering church—and demonstrate the echo of Luther's theology of the cross within it. This theme emerges when Calvin is faced with the pastoral challenge of explaining the significance of suffering for the Gospel to the Evangelical Church in France undergoing persecution. This study will suggest that the constellation of theological propositions, which comprise Luther's *theologia crucis*, appear in Calvin's ecclesiology of the persecuted church. This study will not answer the ultimate question Gerrish poses, namely, 'whether Calvin could follow Luther into the sharpest paradoxes of the *theologia crucis*, which culminate in the thought of *dues crucifixus*'.[6] Rather, this study will take the broadest outline of Luther's theology of the cross and will demonstrate its general influence on Calvin's theological understanding of the suffering church.

Since Luther and Calvin were both prolific this study must be limited in scope. First, I will provide a brief discussion of Luther's theology of the cross,[7]

---

[5] Herman J. Selderhuis, *Calvin's Theology of the Psalms* (Grand Rapids: Baker Academic, 2007), 188. This is the first sentence in a chapter subsection entitled '*Theologia Crucis*' in which Selderhuis dedicates about three pages to the topic. Randall C. Zachman also briefly mentions Calvin's theology of the cross in passing but does not develop the theme. See his *John Calvin as Teacher, Pastor, and Theologian: The Shape of His Writings and Thought* (Grand Rapids: Baker Academic, 2006), 194-95; and *The Assurance of Faith: Conscience in the Theology of Martin Luther and John Calvin* (Louisville, KY: Westminster/John Knox, 1993), 11.

[6] Gerrish, 'To the Unknown God,' 341, fn. 60.

[7] Though Luther only uses the term *theologia crucis* four times in his writings—all in 1518, the year after *The Ninety-Five Theses* was published (*Lectures on Hebrews*, early 1518; *Asterisci Lutheri Adverses Obeliseos Eccii*, March, 1518; *Heidelberg Disputation*, April, 1518, Luther's most explicit reference; *Explanations to the Ninety-Five Theses*, August, 1518). See Anna M. Madsen, *The Theology of the Cross in Historical Perspective* (Eugene, OR: Pickwick, 2007), 65-66; Robert Kolb, 'Luther's Theology of the Cross: Fifteen Years after Heidelberg: Lectures on the Psalms of Ascent,' *Journal of Ecclesiastical History* 61 (January 2010), 70, writes, '[A]n examination of his lectures in the Psalms of ascent delivered in 1532 and 1533, which include a use of the phrase "theology of the cross," reveals that the core of his ideas brought together in 1518 under this label remained vital to the structure of his thinking.' Veli-Matti Kärkkäinen provides a good summary of the long and complicated history of interpretation of Luther's Theology of the Cross. Kärkkäinen points out that while there have been four major swings in the interpretation; 'It is a consensus among recent Lutheran scholars that the *theologia crucis*, far more being just a topic among others, is *the* programmatic theme underlying all of Luther's theology.' This study will not be concerned with these swings in interpretation but will only underscore the basic outline of his thought in Kärkkäinen's 'Theology of the Cross: A Stumbling Block to Pentecostal/Charismatic Spirituality', in Wonsuk Ma and Robert

summarized in five propositions.[8] Next, using Calvin's treatise *De Scandalis* (*Concerning Scandals*), this study will show that the contours of Luther's assumptions about the nature of God's revelation in his theology of the cross are echoed in Calvin's thought on the suffering church, which form Calvin's own particular theology of the cross. It will suggest that these echoes influenced Calvin's reading of Scripture and frame his understanding of history regarding God's purposes in the church's suffering. Finally, this study will propose that Calvin possesses his own particular theology of the cross with regard to the suffering church and that it may be distinguished from Luther's only in terms of emphasis.

## Luther's *Theologia Crucis* summarized in five propositions[9]

*1. A theology of the cross is a theology of revelation as opposed to a theology of speculation*

Early in his career, Luther came to realize that the cross not only revealed God's gracious atonement for human sin, but that it had an epistemological dimension as well[10]—namely, it disclosed a mystery, an understanding of the way God manifests God's knowledge or reveals God's self to the world. At the Heidelberg Disputation of 1518, Luther declared the only place a believer may look for a knowledge of God is in the cross of Jesus Christ. Thus, anyone who uses creation alone to speculate about God, according to Luther, has forfeited his or her right to be called a theologian.

*2. God's revelation is hidden, revealed indirectly or under its opposite*

Luther's theology of the cross taught that God is a hidden God; when the knowledge of God is manifested it is revealed paradoxically, made known under the sign of its opposite—namely, the suffering, weakness, folly and ignominy of the cross. This notion comes out of Luther's reflection on God's declaration to Moses in Exodus 33.23: Moses would only be allowed to see God's 'backside' as he passed by, and not his face. Luther concluded that God's 'front side' (God's majestic attributes) is God's invisible nature (cf. Rom. 1.20) and

---

P. Menzies (eds), *Essays in Honour of Russell P. Spittler* (New York: T. & T. Clark, 2004),152-53, especially fn. 10.

8   These propositions are a distillation by leading Lutheran scholars, drawn from theses 19-22 of his *Heidelberg Disputation* and other writings. See fn. 12 for sources.

9   These five propositions are my own summaries dependent upon Walther Von Loewenich, *Luther's Theology of the Cross* (trans. Herbert J. A. Bouman; Minneapolis: Augsburg, 1976), 11-22; Alister E. McGrath, *Luther's Theology of the Cross: Martin Luther's Theological Breakthrough* (Oxford: Blackwell: 1985), 149-52; Robert Kolb, 'Luther's Theology of the Cross: Fifteen Years after Heidelberg,' 75, 85; and his 'Luther on the Theology of the Cross,' *Lutheran Quarterly* 16 (2002), 443-66.

10  Heino O. Kadia, 'Luther's Theology of the Cross,' *Concordia Theological Quarterly* 63 (July 1999), 177.

cannot be seen in itself, even though all creation bears witness to it. However, God's 'backside' (the *posteriora Dei*) is made visible in the cross.[11] Using Paul's insight in 1 Corinthians 1.17-2:8, Luther claimed that the knowledge of God revealed in the cross (God's 'backside') is foolishness and a stumbling block to the world.

*3. The hiddenness of God's revelation means that it cannot be discovered by natural reason but can only be known by faith*

Luther taught that God's revelation is found only in suffering and in the cross, not in works or human moral acts. Luther maintained that the knowledge of God concealed in Christ 'shatters human illusions concerning the capacity of human reason to discern God' anywhere except 'in Christ crucified'.[12] Luther understood the inner relationship between moralism and religious intellectualism: both expect to discover God through reflection upon human moral sense or patterns found in the created order.[13] In both cases, reason is led down the wrong path and unable to discern a true knowledge of God. Luther maintained that the work of concealing God's knowledge is done by both the devil (who wants to see the Gospel suppressed) and by God (who wishes people to come to him by faith).[14] Because reason on its own cannot discern a knowledge of God, it must be led by faith.

*4. A theology of the cross is opposed to a theology of glory*

According to Luther, a 'theology of glory' (*theologia gloriae*) does not recognize God's revelation hidden in Christ's suffering. Rather, it trusts natural reason and seeks a knowledge of God in creation and pursues divine merit through good works. Hence it fosters speculation about God's nature and is attracted to power, splendor and the pride of human achievement. For those who subscribe to a theology of glory, a true knowledge of God's power and glory remains concealed under the foolishness and appalling spectacle of the cross.[15] Furthermore, a theologian of glory sees one's own suffering as a 'nonsensical in-

---

[11] Concerning Luther's thought on the hidden God, Gerrish, 'To the Unknown God,' 140, 340 n. 56, notes, '[I]n his word, the one God has lifted the corner of the veil, taken a step out of his hiddenness. . . . Like Moses we are permitted to catch a glimpse of God's "back parts".' See, also, *WA TR*. 5.294.24, 34; 295.5; 294.4 (#5658a).

[12] McGrath, *Luther's Theology of the Cross*, 150.

[13] Althaus, Paul, *The Theology of Martin Luther* (Philadelphia: Fortress Press.1968), 28; see, also, McGrath, *Luther's Theology of the Cross*, 150.

[14] Robert A. Kelly, 'The Suffering Church: A Study of Luther's *Theologia Crucis*,' *Concordia Theological Quarterly* 50 (January 1986), 4.

[15] Luther wrote, 'Because he [humanity] misused the knowledge of God through works, God wished again to be recognized in suffering, and to condemn wisdom concerning invisible things by means of wisdom concerning visible things, so that those who did not honor God as manifested in his works should honor him [Christ] as he is hidden in his suffering'—*LW* 31.53. See Althaus, *The Theology of Martin Luther*, 25.

trusion' into his or her world rather than as an opportunity to discover a knowledge of God through a patient bearing of a cross. A theologian of the cross, on the other hand, values suffering as his or her most precious treasure. This person sees with the eyes of faith that it is through the experience of suffering that the living God works out his salvation in the lives of those whom he loves.[16]

### 5. *God and self become known in the experience of suffering*

Luther insists that God makes God's-self known in suffering, and therefore our suffering fulfills a special purpose. Suffering, affliction and temptation are seen as a means by which the believer is brought near to God.[17] It is through suffering and affliction (or human *Anfechtung*) that we are made knowledgeable of our sin (*opus alienum*) and subsequently our need for God's grace (*opus proprium*).[18] As McGrath summarizes, 'God assaults man in order to break him down and thus to justify him.'[19] Luther claims that in this way we participate in Christ's cross and thus it is through our sufferings God has chosen to disclose God's self to us.[20]

### B. An examination of the contours of Luther's *Theologia Crucis* echoed in Calvin's theology of the suffering church in *De Scandalis*.

Calvin's treatise *Concerning Scandals* provides one of the most focused and extensive treatments of his perspective on the persecuted church in all of his writings. Though Calvin covers a whole range of scandalous issues in this work this study will concentrate only on his comments regarding Christ, the Gospel and the persecuted church, which comprise nearly half of the book. The subsequent outline will roughly follow Luther's five propositions given above in order to demonstrate the manner in which Calvin echoes Luther's theology of the cross when ministering to the suffering church.[21]

---

[16] McGrath, *Luther's Theology of the Cross*, 151.

[17] McGrath, *Luther's Theology of the Cross*, 150-51.

[18] Though McGrath only speaks of Luther's theology of the cross disclosing a knowledge of God in suffering, Kolb, 'Luther on the Theology of the Cross,' 459, maintains 'Luther's *Deus absconditus* and *Deus revelatus* also reveals a great deal about his understanding of what it means to be human. It might be said that his anthropology taught both a *homo absconditus* and a *homo revelatus.*'

[19] McGrath, *Luther's Theology of the Cross*, 151.

[20] Luther writes, '[L]iving, or rather dying and being damned make a theologian, not understanding, reading or speculating'—*WA* 5.163.28–29. See, also, Loewenich, *Luther's Theology of the Cross*, 22-23.

[21] This section will roughly follow the outline given above for Luther's theology of the cross with some exceptions. Luther's first proposition, 'A theology of the cross is a theology of revelation,' will be discussed last in Calvin's theology of the cross; Luther's propositions three and four on reason and faith will be combined into Calvin's

*1. A true knowledge of Christ and the church is hidden under its opposite*

Calvin describes *Concerning Scandals* as a treatise written to those who 'at one time embraced the gospel of Christ, and . . . yet wish to have it without scandals'.[22] He defines a scandal as anything that presents itself as a stone of stumbling, or an offense that becomes an obstacle in our faith because it 'diverts us from the right direction'.[23] Calvin's argument turns to Christ as the prime example of what people deem to be offensive: though Christ's function is to 'lead us by the hand directly to the Father'.[24] Christ is also 'a rock of offence'.[25] Calvin is adamant: 'Do they want Christ free from every scandal? Let them invent a new Christ for themselves! For he can be no other Son of God than the one made known in the Scriptures.'[26]

What becomes interesting for this study is when Calvin explains why Christ is an offense. Calvin's logic follows the second proposition of Luther's theology of the cross outlined above, namely, *God's revelation is paradoxical, hidden under the sign of its opposite.*[27] Calvin exclaims:

> I know that these things are said to many people in vain. I am quite well aware of the way their derisive laughter pursues us, because we seek life in the death of Christ, grace in his curse, and justification in his condemnation. . . . They therefore conclude that nothing is too silly for us who hope that we shall be given life by a dead man, ask for pardon from a curse, and flee for refuge to a gallows as the one and only hope of eternal salvation. . . . I have already said that there is no other way by which we can attain to the wisdom of God than by becoming fools in this world.[28]

Notice that Calvin's last sentence above is a paraphrase of Paul's words in 1 Corinthians 1.18–2:8, one of the most important biblical seedbeds of Luther's theology of the cross.[29] Calvin recognizes that the faith he has just described *is*

---

second proposition; I have added an extra point as proposition three, a section on Calvin's rejection of a 'theology of glory'.

[22] *Concerning Scandals*, 9 (*OS* 2.166. 32-34).

[23] *Concerning Scandals*, 8 (*OS* 2.165-66.1-2).

[24] *Concerning Scandals*, 8 (*OS* 2.166).

[25] *Concerning Scandals*, 9 (*OS* 2.166).

[26] *Concerning Scandals*, 8 (*OS* 2.166).

[27] Selderhuis, *Calvin's Theology of the Psalms*, 180, observes, 'Calvin's commentary on the Psalms makes it clear in any case that on this point [the hiddenness of God] he is Luther's student, regardless of the differences in emphases which lie between them or the relative brevity of the Genevan Reformer on this matter.' And, again, Selderhuis writes, 'Based on what he says about the hiddenness of God as well as his description of the Christian life, it is clear that Calvin holds to a *theologia Crucis*. It is characteristic of the theology of the cross that reality is manifested in its opposite just as the victory of Christ over death is shrouded itself in the crucifixion' (188).

[28] *Concerning Scandals*, 19-20 (*OS* 2.173).

[29] Robert Kolb, 'God's Gift of Martyrdom: The Early Reformation Understanding of Dying for the Faith,' *Church History*, 64 (September 1995), 409-10, identifies 1 Co-

foolish to the world, because the truth of the Gospel is indeed *paradoxical and hidden under the sign of its opposite.*[30]

This language of paradox, present in Calvin's description of the Gospel, also carries over to his portrayal of the suffering church:

> Let us remember that the outward aspect of the Church is so contemptible that its beauty may shine within; that it is so tossed about on earth that it may have a permanent dwelling place in heaven; that it lies so wounded and broken in the eyes if the world that it may stand vigorous and whole, in the presence of God and his angels; that it is so wretched in the flesh that its happiness may nevertheless be restored in the spirit. In the same way, when Christ lay despised in a stable multitudes of angels were singing his excellence; . . . when the sun failed, it was proclaiming him—hanging on the cross—King of the world; and the tombs opened were acknowledging him Lord of death and life.[31]

Calvin's point is simple: the church is afflicted because Christ was afflicted. Like a true knowledge of Christ, a true knowledge of the church's condition is paradoxical, its real beauty and spiritual vitality is hidden under its weakness, brokenness and worldly contempt.

Luther speaks with a similar voice in his *Commentary on the Psalms*: 'Just as Christ's victory over sin, death, and the devil is hidden under the external appearances of defeat, so the glory of the church is hidden under the sign of its opposite.'[32] Regarding Luther's teaching, Robert Kelly notes,

---

rinthians 1 as one of the most important biblical seedbeds of Luther's theology of the cross.

[30] Calvin's quote echoes Luther's language. As early as 1516, when Luther was lecturing on Romans 9.3, when he spoke of the paradox of the Christian faith, 'He who hates his life in this world will keep it for eternal life' (John 12.25). Luther continued, 'What is good for us is hidden and that so deeply that it is hidden under its opposite. Thus, our life is hidden under death, love for ourselves under hate for ourselves, glory under ignominy, salvation under damnation, our kingship under exile, heaven under hell, wisdom under foolishness, righteousness under sin, power under weakness.' See Luther's *Lectures on Romans, WA* 1[4].392, line 28-32 (*LW* 25.382-83). See, also, Kolb, 'Luther's Theology of the Cross: Fifteen Years after Heidelberg,' 71.

[31] *Concerning Scandals,* 29-30 (*OS* 2.180).

[32] *LW* 11.227-28 (*WA* 4.77-78). Luther commented that 'You see nothing splendid about the church,' and how 'Its value cannot be determined by appearance, by the judgment of the five senses or reason, not by laws, nor by arts or philosophy; but according to God's Word'—*LW* 12.255 (*WA* 40[2].550). See, also, *LW* 27.133-34 (*WA* 40[2].170-71). In 1538 Luther commented that the church must appear to the world just as Christ appeared to the world, 'Hacked to pieces, marked with scratches, despised, crucified, and mocked'—*LW* 54.262 (*WA TR* 3.553, #3709). In speaking about the situation of the German church under the pope, Luther said, 'Truly the image of the church is deplorable! The church lies hidden under very great weakness and offense'—*LW* 54.291 (*WA TR* 3.694, #3900). See, also, Kelly, 'The Suffering Church,' 10.

[The] basic reason for the suffering of the church is that it is the church of Jesus Christ, the same Jesus who died on the cross. Just as the cross determined the work of Christ, so it determines the mission of the church. . . . In the Romans lectures Luther says in a gloss to Romans 8.17 that, for a Christian, *compati* means 'suffering together' with Christ, that is, suffering the same things that Christ suffered.[33]

Calvin's turn to Christology in his argument for why the church suffers squares with his theological conviction that the church truly participates in Christ. Todd Billings notes in his book, *Calvin, Participation and the Gift*, that our union with Christ does not merely mean that Christ's life is an example to be followed but that the church participates 'substantially,' via baptism, in sharing 'Christ's death and resurrection through the Spirit'.[34] This 'substantial participation' in Calvin's thought not only relates to the biblical exhortation to die to the flesh and live by the Spirit, not only is it the means by which God enacts his promises, as Billings well notes;[35] but as demonstrated by Calvin's argument in *Concerning Scandals* it *also* refers to the believer's experience of 'a cross' of suffering. Calvin refuses to lighten the message that the believer will suffer for their faith because this union between Christ and his church extends all the way to the cross:

> Now, if we see Christ in his own body tormented by the insults of the wicked in their arrogance, crushed by cruel tyranny, exposed to derisive behavior, violently dragged this way and that, do not let us be frightened by any of those things, as if they were unusual. On the contrary, let us be convinced that the Church has been ordained for this purpose that as long as it is a sojourner in the world it is to wage war under the perpetual cross.[36]

To the persecuted church in France, Calvin confirms that their suffering is in fact *usual*. This notion that the true glory of the church is hidden under an opposite, namely death and defeat, is not just a passing remark for Calvin. Echoing the insights in Luther's theology of the cross,[37] Calvin makes it clear that

33 Kelly, 'The Suffering Church,' 9. See, also, *LW* 25.72 (*WA* 56.79); *LW* 25.86-87 (*WA* 56.97).
34 Todd Billings, *Calvin, Participation, and the Gift* (Oxford: Oxford University Press, 2007), 122.
35 Billings, *Calvin, Participation, and the Gift*, 122.
36 *Concerning Scandals*, 30 (*OS* 2.180).
37 In his Commentary on Psalm 110.7 Luther writes, 'Having heard that Christ, in His own person, had to enter into His glory through suffering and death (Luke 24.26), we are to know that so it must also be for His entire kingdom on earth, that is, for His Christendom. His person serves as a model, and all those who are Christians must conform to His image. For this reason His kingdom has had to endure the cross and suffering since the beginning of time and we must follow the path to glory and life through misery, persecution, shame, and death. If He, our Lord and Head, had to do this, why should we expect something better?'—*LW* 13.347 (*WA* 41.236-37). See, al-

the despised condition of the church is *normative*. In Calvin's view, like Christ's sojourn in this world, the church has been *ordained* to experience such struggles, while on earth, in perpetuity.

## 2. The hidden knowledge of God cannot be discerned by natural reason, but only by faith

Kelly notes that one of the basic principles in Luther's theology of the cross is that Christians must take the gospel by faith, not by sight—that is, not according to empirical experience.[38] Calvin concurs with Luther. Natural reason and the senses, left unaided by faith, are to be suspect when evaluating the life and death of Christ as well as the spiritual state of the church.[39] In *Concerning Scandals* Calvin writes, 'The situation of the Church Universal contains in itself far greater grounds for offence' than any 'private afflictions of the individual'.[40]

> [The church] never shines with that splendor, which would enable the minds of men to recognize the kingdom of God. Secondly, if ever it succeeds in rising to some modest position, soon afterwards it is either crushed by the violence of tyrants or collapses of its own accord, so that, that situation lasts only for a short time.[41]

According to Calvin, the church has dismal aesthetics and lacks social stature. A few sentences later he notes that even Cicero, one of his favorite philosophers, despised the church, scoffing at the law of God because in his day, Jews were experiencing unfavorable circumstances. Calvin concludes, 'From this man alone one can form an estimate of them all.'[42]

Calvin believes that reason alone, unaided by faith, simply cannot surmount the foolish appearance and claims of the church. A scandal is something our reason deems foolish and therefore we choose not to embrace. Given the apparent foolishness of God's wisdom displayed in the church, Calvin also knows that when the church undergoes severe persecution, even confessing Christians can struggle with their faith. 'What is the reason,' Calvin asks,

> . . . why many people are shrinking today from making a genuine profession of the gospel, except that they see that we are few in number and also have very little authority—indeed no power—while they are admirers of all contrary things on the

---

so, Michael Parsons, *Martin Luther's Interpretation of the Royal Psalms: The Spiritual Kingdom in a Pastoral Context* (Lewiston: Edwin Mellen, 2009), 210-13; especially fn. 213 for an informative discussion on Luther's understanding of a believer's 'bearing the cross'.

[38] Kelly, *The Suffering Church*, 9; *LW* 21.44 (*WA* 32.334).
[39] *Concerning Scandals*, 22-23 (*OS* 2.174-75).
[40] *Concerning Scandals*, 28 (*OS* 2.179).
[41] *Concerning Scandals*, 28 (*OS* 2.179).
[42] *Concerning Scandals*, 28-29 (*OS* 2.179).

opposite side? And certainly, as things are today, there is no need to be surprised if such a deformed state of the Church is frightening them away.[43]

The Reformed Church in Calvin's day was not only unattractive, but its deformed state was downright frightening. Again, Calvin remedies this with a lesson on Christology, and in particular, Christ's kingship:

> In truth, the only people who stumble on this stone and the only people kept back by this stumbling block are those who *do not discern the spiritual kingdom of Christ*. For those who allow neither the stable in which Christ was born nor the cross on which he hung to prevent them from giving honor to the King himself, will not in the least despise the poor condition of his Church.[44]

In Calvin's mind, there is a correlation between 'the spiritual kingdom of Christ' and 'the deformed state of the Church' because he understands that Christ's kingdom is revealed under an opposite and therefore must be an object of faith.[45]

To fully appreciate what Calvin means by the phrase 'the spiritual kingdom of Christ' and the significance it gives to his ecclesiology of the suffering church, this study will pause to briefly examine some of Calvin's comments on this phrase from his commentaries. When speaking of Christ's kingship displayed in the triumphal entry, Calvin specifically highlights the importance of Christ riding on an ass:

> His kingdom will have nothing in common with the pomp, splendor, wealth, and power of the world; and it was proper that this should be made known by an outward manifestation, that all might be fully assured that it is spiritual.[46]

---

[43] *Concerning Scandals*, 29 (*OS* 2.179).
[44] *Concerning Scandals*, 29 (*OS* 2.179), emphasis added. Luther also sees the incongruity of Christ's crucifixion with his kingly office: 'It is most difficult of all to recognize as king, one who died such a desperate and shameful death. The senses are strongly repelled by such a notion, reason abhors it, experience denies it, and a precedent is lacking. Plainly this will be folly to the Gentiles and a stumbling block to the Jews (1 Cor. 1.23) unless you raise your thoughts above this' (*LW* 14.342). See, also, Kärkkäinen, 'Theology of the Cross,' 58, fn. 48.
[45] Concerning the external aspect of the kingdom Calvin echoes what Luther relates in his *Commentary on Psalm* 45.2: 'If you look at the external aspect of this kingdom, everything is opposite: where in this spiritual kingdom life is proclaimed, there, judging by appearances, is death; where glory is preached, there is the ignominy of the cross; where wisdom is preached, there is foolishness; where strength and victory is preached, there is infirmity and the cross; and the same is true of the rest. So everything you will now hear of Christ's kingdom you must understand according to the article "I believe in the holy church." Whoever says, "I believe," does not see what the situation is like, but sees the opposite'—*LW* 12.204 (*WA* 40².482). For a discussion of Luther's thoughts on this passage see Parsons, *Martin Luther's Interpretation*, 132-33.
[46] *Commentary on John* 12.15, *CO* 47.285.

Again, when observing the circumstances surrounding Christ's birth, Calvin declares that God 'stripped him of all earthly splendor, for the purpose of informing us that His kingdom is spiritual'.[47] In other words, Christ's poverty, affliction and lack of splendor, wealth and power were providentially engineered to reveal that Christ was not an earthly king and that the kingdom he rules is not an earthly realm. For Calvin, Christ's poverty, suffering and lack of splendor is a visible mark that his kingdom is indeed *spiritual*.[48] Thus Calvin's *theologia crucis* with regards to the suffering church, is grounded in the incarnation of Christ and the manifestation of Christ's office of kingship revealed to the world under its opposite.

In Calvin's comments on Isaiah 53.2—'he hath no form or comeliness'—he provides a significant clue as to why an understanding of the cross *must* accompany any biblical or historical reading of the suffering church's situation:

> [This] must be understood to relate *not merely to the person of Christ*, who was despised by the world, and was at length condemned to a disgraceful death; *but to His entire kingdom*, which in the eyes of men had no beauty, no comeliness, no magnificence, which, in short, had nothing that could direct or captivate the eyes of men to it by its outward appearance.[49]

Calvin's thoughts on the suffering and outward appearance of the church could not be more clear. The life of the church is bound up with her King and Savior. The church's unfavorable circumstances are necessary for its visible witness to

---

[47] *Commentary on Matthew* 2:1, *CO* 45.81.

[48] See Bonnie Pattison, *Poverty in the Theology of John Calvin* (Eugene OR: Pickwick, 2006), 164-68.

[49] *Comm Isa* 53.2, *CO* 37.256, emphasis added. Calvin has similar logic in *Concerning Scandals* 29 (*OS* 2.179-180), 'And when Paul speaks about the similarity between head and members in bearing the cross (Rom. 8.17), they are all in agreement. When he says that we ought to die with him in order that we may be sharers of his life (2 Tim. 2.11) nobody cries out in protest. When the whole of Scripture compares this present life to a stern warfare and teaches that it is filled with many different struggles, they nod their assent that it is all true and correct. Therefore, the name "Church Militant" is so commonplace and trite that it echoes even on the lips of children. But when it comes to the place of decision, they seem to have forgotten all those things and run away from the image of Christ as though it were some strange monster.' Also, when Luther refers Isaiah 53.2–3 in his *Commentary on Psalm* 45.2 he writes, 'For that reason I have stated that this King is hidden under the opposite appearance: in spirit He is more beautiful than the sons of men; but in the flesh all the sons of men are more beautiful than he, and only this King is ugly, as He described in Isaiah 53.2,3. . . . Therefore we see that delightful and pleasant things are stated of this king in the Psalm, but they are enveloped and overshadowed by the eternal form of the cross. . . . These things are spoken to us, however, to let us know that we have such a king. . . . We must be conformed to the image of this king.' See *LW* 12.208-209 (*WA* 40².487). See Parsons, *Martin Luther's Interpretation*, 134-35, for a discussion of this passage.

the spiritual kingdom of Christ. Since the church's union with Christ is a spiritual union, it must also exhibit the same lack of earthly splendor and majesty that her humbled king exhibited in order to bear witness to the spiritual nature of God's kingdom on earth.[50] In *Concerning Scandals,* Calvin's pastoral challenge is to communicate this vision drawn from the contours of Luther's theology of the cross, to a persecuted church in difficult circumstances, so that they will persevere in faith and will allow their reason and senses to be formed by the Gospel.

### 3. Calvin's rejection of a theology of glory

In *Concerning Scandals,* Calvin reminds his readers that there is something they could experience that is more perilous than persecution:

> To get what . . . [most people] long for, a church well-favored in every way, flourishing with wealth and influence, enjoying unbroken peace—in short, lacking nothing to make its circumstances prosperous and most desirable—will it not have the appearance of an earthly power? Accordingly, *the spiritual kingdom of Christ* will have to be sought elsewhere; and furthermore, the Church will be cut off from its head.[51]

What is worse than persecution for Calvin? Being separated from Christ. Again, Calvin uses the theologically salient phrase, '*the spiritual kingdom of Christ*'. This kingdom has nothing to do with the church that exhibits what Luther would call a 'theology of glory'—namely, being well favored, lacking nothing, enjoying peace and worldly influence, in sum, having no crosses to bear.[52] The cross of suffering, poverty and affliction marks 'the spiritual kingdom of Christ' and, therefore, Christ can be found nowhere else.

In 1539 Luther wrote a treatise, *On the Councils of the Church,* published in German, while Calvin was in Strasburg. Though Calvin could not read German, there were ample colleagues in the city who could have provided Calvin with a basic outline of its contents.[53] In the third section of the treatise Luther lists

---

[50] See Pattison, *Poverty in the Theology of John Calvin,* 185-86.

[51] *Concerning Scandals,* 29 (*OS* 2.180), emphasis added.

[52] Luther claims that when persecution and the cross are not apparent for the church, 'this is a sure sign that the pure teaching of the Word has been taken away'—*LW* 27.43 (*WA* 40².172-73). See Kelly, *The Suffering Church,* 7.

[53] Luther's important treatise *On the Councils of the Church* could have been made know to Calvin by Melanchthon or Bucer who knew German. In the *Institutes* 4.9.8, at the end of a paragraph, Calvin may hint of this when he speaks of the validity of conciliar decisions and adds this sentence in 1543: 'They have surely put forward many impious opinions. And it is not necessary here to collect instances, either because it would take too long or because others have done this so diligently that not much can be added.' Battles, notes that Calvin could have in mind either Peter Crabbe's *Concilia omnia* or Luther's *On the Councils of the Church* (which, also, used Crabbe's work). See *Inst* 4.9.8, fn. 9.

seven marks of the true church;[54] Luther's seventh mark is relevant for this study:

> The holy Christian people are externally recognized by the holy possession of the sacred cross. They must endure every misfortune and persecution, all kinds of trials and evil from the devil, world, and the flesh (as the Lord's Prayer indicates) . . . *in order to become like their head, Christ.*[55]

Luther's seventh mark of the true church is suffering, trials and persecution '*in order [that believers] become like their head, Christ*'. This may explain Calvin's claim that a church characterized by peace, prosperity and social influence 'will be cut off from its head'. If, perchance, Calvin did not have knowledge of the themes in Luther's *On the Councils of the Church*, there are numerous other writings in Latin where Luther discusses the church's suffering for the gospel. In fact, Kelly writes, 'The connection of persecution with the pure Gospel is so strong for Luther that he can say that the absence of persecution [for the church] is a sign of the absence of the Gospel.'[56]

For Luther, as for Calvin, a theology of the cross is always at odds with a theology of glory. The two cannot coexist. They are not only competing value-systems but are expressions of competing kingdoms that mark the church by the way they manifest the church's life to the world. Concerning the contrast between Luther's theology of glory and the cross, Robert Kolb writes,

> First, medieval systems of theology all sought to present a God whose glory consisted in fulfilling what in fact are fallen human standards for divine success: A God who could make his might known, could knock heads and straighten people out. . . . These scholastic theologians sought to fashion—with biblical citations, to be sure—a God worthy of the name, according to the standards of the emperors and kings, whose glory and power defined how glory and power were supposed to look. . . . Second . . . Luther suggested that these medieval systems of biblical ex-

---

[54] Luther's seven marks of the true church are as follows: (1) 'First, the holy Christian people are recognized by their possession of the holy word of God'; (2) 'by the holy sacrament of baptism, wherever it is taught, believed, and administered correctly according to Christ's ordinances'; (3) 'the holy sacrament of the altar [Lord's Supper] wherever it is rightly administered, believed, and received, according to Christ's institution'; (4) 'by the office of the keys [church discipline]'; (5) 'by the fact that it concentrates or calls ministers, or has offices that it is to administer'; (6) 'by prayer, public praise, and thanksgiving to God [public worship]'; (7) 'by the holy possession of the sacred cross'—*LW* 41.148–64 (*WA* 50.628–41).

[55] *LW*, 41.148 (*WA* 50.628), emphasis added. In *Concerning Scandals*, 29 (*OS* 179–80), Calvin refers to Paul's words 'about the similarity between head [Christ] and members [the church] in bearing the cross', and how 'the whole of Scripture compares this present life to a stern warfare and teaches us that it is filled with many different struggles'.

[56] Kelly, *The Suffering Church*, 8. See *LW* 27.180 (*WA* 2.464); *LW* 21.50 (*WA* 32.339); *LW* 27.44 (*WA* 40².54-55).

position taught a human glory, the glory of human success . . . [and] the success of human reason that can capture who and what God is, for human purposes.[57]

This study does not permit me to further delineate this connection between the two kingdoms in Calvin's thought, and the way he echoes the contours of Luther's *theologia crucis* versus *theologia gloriae*. However, this much is clear: a theology of glory belongs to the kingdom of this world and expresses all that this world holds dear, whereas a theology of the cross belongs to the spiritual kingdom of Christ and therefore appears foolish and paradoxical in this world.

Calvin never uses Luther's terminology of *theologia gloriae* in his writings, yet in *Concerning Scandals*, he does use a phrase that appears conceptually congruent with it. In a passage where Calvin discusses the German Protestant debacle of the Schmalkaldic War (1546–1547)[58] he makes the following comment:

> While people's spirits were raised to high hopes for our side, I said publicly on some occasions that more danger threatens us from our own victory than from that of our enemies, and that no disasters are to be feared so much as what I may call *a highly triumphal gospel*, which would transport us to a state of elation.[59]

What does Calvin mean by, 'a highly triumphal gospel'?[60] In the Latin, Calvin hesitates even to put the adjective '*triumphale*' next to the noun '*Evangelium*' without the intervening qualifying phrase '*ut ita loquar*' to clarify its novel character. Regrettably, Calvin does not provide a specific explanation of the phrase, nor does he use it again in his corpus. However, there is good reason to believe, from its context here, that this phrase lies in a similar semantic field as Luther's 'theology of glory'.

This passage appears in a discussion about the spiritual failure of the German nobility in the Schmalkaldic War. Calvin uses these German political leaders as an example for 'the way our unruly spirit [needs to be] tamed and subjugated by the discipline of the cross'.[61] He rebukes them for how they 'haughtily . . . were casting the gospel under a shadow,' and how 'they openly displayed . . . treacherous cowardice'.[62] He concludes,

---

[57] Kolb, 'Luther on the Theology of the Cross,' 446.
[58] A footnote in *Opera Selecta* by Barth-Niesel suggests that this passage refers to the Schmalkaldic War (1546–1547); see *OS* 2.192 fn. 2. See, also, *Concerning Scandals*, 48, n. 39.
[59] *Concerning Scandals*, 48 (*OS* 2.192-93), emphasis added. 'Publicly' in the French version is 'in sermons,' though Fraser notes, that 'no reference is to be found there'. See, also, *Concerning Scandals*, 48, fn. 40 (*OS* 2.192).
[60] To my knowledge, this is the only place where Calvin uses this phrase. The sentence in Latin reads: *Neque enim tam metuendas esse ullas clades, quam nimis triumphale, ut ita loquar, Evangelium, quod nos ad insolescentiam efferret*—*OS* 2.192.40-193.1.
[61] *Concerning Scandals*, 48 (*OS* 2.192).
[62] *Concerning Scandals*, 49 (*OS* 2.193).

If the Lord had not been quick to resist their ungodly presumption, the disease would have become almost incurable in the course of time. Teaching and godly admonitions would have carried no weight.[63]

What is this 'ungodly presumption,' this 'disease' that 'would have become almost incurable' that results in turning a deaf ear to 'godly admonitions'? Was it a false understanding of the Gospel that assumed that Christ's kingdom was compatible with triumph, power and victory in this world? Calvin saw the false assumptions of 'a triumphal gospel' that in essence confused the *spiritual* kingdom of Christ with the kingdom of this world. The worst thing that could happen to those who held to this error was to have history reward such beliefs with power, victory, and triumph.

A theology of the cross understands that the Gospel will never bring earthly power, success or freedom from tyrannical kings. Furthermore, the theologian of the cross understands that suffering for the Gospel is the church's most precious treasure. Calvin recognizes that the German nobility never grasped this meaning of the cross.

In many places, the leading positions were filled by wicked hypocrites. In fact, after suffering defeat, certain leaders of great reputation, the nobles of a state paralyzed by an indefinable fear were immediately demoralized and freely surrendered. . . . In one nation we see more impious and sacrilegious defections from Christ in the space of two years than the histories of all times and peoples narrate.[64]

The German nobility were demoralized because their fallacious triumphal Gospel failed them. They held a theology of glory, a Gospel which reasoned that the true church is a triumphal church. Since suffering is not part of the paradigm of *theologia gloriae*, in their defeat they surrendered their Protestant faith and returned to Catholicism.[65] Calvin stood appalled.

### 4. God and self become known in the experience of suffering

For Luther, the experience of suffering and affliction reveals one's sin (*opus alienum*) and need for God's grace (*opus proprium*).[66] Similarly, in Calvin's *theologia crucis*, suffering produces a knowledge of self.[67] Commenting on 2

---

[63] *Concerning Scandals*, 48-49 (*OS* 2.193).
[64] *Concerning Scandals*, 49 (*OS* 2.193).
[65] In *The Magnificat* (1521) Luther remarks on how prosperity will often not stand up for the Gospel. See *LW* 21.37 (*WA* 7.593).
[66] McGrath, *Luther's Theology of the Cross*, 150-51. See Kolb, 'Luther on the Theology of the Cross,' 459.
[67] Calvin writes, 'Indeed, our very poverty better discloses the infinitude of benefits reposing in God. The miserable ruin, into which the rebellion of the first man cast us, especially compels us to look upward. . . . Each of us must, *then*, be so stung by the conscience of his own unhappiness as to attain at least some knowledge of God. . . . Accordingly, the knowledge of ourselves not only arouses us to seek God, but also,

Corinthians 12.10, Calvin recognizes that 'failure of strength . . . and other afflictions . . . are means for making our own feebleness clear to us'. 'For if God had not exercised Paul with such trials,' Calvin writes, 'he would never have perceived his weaknesses so clearly.' Paul's 'knowledge of self' was made manifest by his trials because they created 'an awareness of [his] own feebleness, self-distrust and humility'.[68] Calvin applies this 'knowledge of self' similarly to the church. When reflecting on the German defeat in the Schmalkaldic War, he states, '*By this testing the Lord revealed* what sort of character each [leader and noble of state] had.' The war revealed 'in many places the leading positions were filled by wicked hypocrites'.[69]

Trials and suffering have a way of separating the wheat from the chaff. Calvin saw the conquest of the German princes at the hand of Charles V as an event where suffering revealed the sin and spiritual failure of the German aristocracy. Instead of clinging to Christ and his grace when their trials manifested their feebleness and lack of power and influence, the German nobility fell into temptation and returned to Catholicism rather than suffer for the Gospel.

Calvin pauses in his astonishment over this scandal in Germany, this cradle of Protestantism, to praise a lone figure: John Fredrick, Duke of Saxony.

> Indeed, . . . *it has been made plain* how faith remains firm and unbroken when hearts are sustained by the power of the Spirit. The heroic magnanimity of soul, *which the Lord made plain for all generations to see* in one man, who was defeated and a captive, would never have been believed except from such an experience of the cross.[70]

Two times Calvin claims the duke's faith *has been made plain* for all to see. At the time *Concerning Scandals* was published, Fredrick had languished in prison for about three years, refusing to recant his evangelical faith or agree to the Augsburg Interim. Such a commitment amidst suffering manifested the Duke's faith for all of Europe to witness. A 'heroic magnanimity of soul,' as Calvin describes it.

Calvin's statement, however, attests that another kind of knowledge is being revealed. The Duke persevered in faith *because*, Calvin claims, he was 'sustained by the power of the Spirit'. Thus, the Duke's faithfulness disclosed God's power. Calvin's last phrase says it all: this 'would never have been believed *except from such an experience of the cross*'. The cross John Fredrick was called to bear had a purpose: to disclose the nature and depth of his faith (a

---

as it were, leads us by the hand to find him. Again it is certain that man never achieves a clear knowledge of himself unless he has first looked upon God's face, and then descends from contemplating him to scrutinizing himself'—*Inst* 1.1.1-2 (*OS* 3.31.16-8, 24-6; 32.7-12).

68 *Comm 2 Cor.* 12.10, *CO* 50, 142.
69 *Concerning Scandals*, 49 (*OS* 2.193).
70 *Concerning Scandals*, 49 (*OS* 2.193), emphasis added.

knowledge of self) *and* thereby, to make manifest the power of the Spirit (a knowledge of God).[71]

Luther expresses similar thoughts on the *Magnificat*. God 'lets the godly become powerless and to be brought low,' and yet 'He is present to them with all His power, yet so hidden and in secret that even those who suffer the oppression do not feel it but only believe.' Luther continues,

> There is the fullness of God's power and His outstretched arm. For where man's strength ends, God's strength begins. . . . And when the oppression comes to an end, *it becomes manifest what great strength was hidden underneath the weakness.* Even so Christ was powerless on the cross; and yet there He performed His mightiest work and conquered sin, death, world, hell, devil, and all evil.[72]

It is an interesting twist of history that John Fredrick's life took on the very pattern of the cross, the very *theologia crucis* Luther addresses. When Luther composed this commentary in 1521, he dedicated it 'to the Serene Highness, Prince John Fredrick, Duke of Saxony, . . . my Gracious Lord and Patron'.[73] Luther died months before the outbreak of the Schmalkaldic War and never saw the day when this once eighteen year-old boy-prince would prove his commitment to the Gospel by demonstrating, by the fortitude of his faith, the very words Luther penned in honor of him nearly thirty years earlier.

According to Luther, suffering is the way God manifests a knowledge that the true power which sustains the church is not human in origin, but rather has its source in Christ, the church's object of faith.[74] According to Kelly, Luther

---

[71]  For both Luther and Calvin, when the cross of affliction and suffering is laid upon the individual there arises a knowledge of self, a revelation of one's sin and spiritual poverty. For both theologians this knowledge should drive the person to Christ and his grace as one's only hope of salvation. As you can see, the experience of suffering and affliction for the Christian embody a parallel function to that of the first use of the law for Calvin, the second use for Luther, namely; the law is meant to reveal a knowledge of our sin so that we are driven to Christ where we find grace. See Pattison, *Poverty in the Theology of John Calvin*, 218-22.

[72]  *LW* 21.340 (*WA* 7.586), emphasis added.

[73]  *The Magnificat* was printed eight times in German and twice in Latin. Luther wrote this treatise to the then young prince John Fredrick (1503-1554) in gratitude for his repeated and outspoken support of Luther and his theology. Fredrick was mentored by George Spalatin, which may explain his tenacious Lutheran faith. Nevertheless it is clear from the way he suffered in prison under Charles V that his commitment to the evangelical faith was not a political commitment but a true conversion of the Spirit and commitment to the gospel. See *LW* 21.XIX.

[74]  Kelly writes, 'It must be made obvious that the power behind the church and the Gospel is God's alone. Christians must be taught not to trust in their own achievements but to put their faith only in Christ. In the same way, *the world must see the church brought low so that no one can imagine that the final victory of the Gospel is the result of human power.* God's work is best done in the midst of poverty and lowliness, not in pomp and power.' See Kelly, *'The Suffering Church,'* 9, emphasis added.

articulates a variety of ways God's power is manifest in suffering.[75] At times Luther claims that this power is a sanctifying power that forms the people of God into the image of Christ.[76] At other times it is the power of the Gospel that provokes Satan's opposition to the church.[77] Sometimes Luther simply reiterates that the power and glory of God is hidden under the suffering church and that it appears offensive to the world.[78] Concerning the event of martyrdom, Kolb notes, that Luther refers to it as a gift of God, literally a 'witness to the faith, the Word of God in action.' Kolb continues, 'According to the theology of the cross, this seemingly foolish and impotent Word is God's power.'[79]

Calvin's message on the suffering church in *Concerning Scandals* also addresses the manifestation of the power of God.

> . . . with an unconquerable firmness of faith, surmounted such a great waves of persecution, and the fact that the church survived all tyrants and heretics in order to pass on the true doctrine of faith to succeeding generations, *provides a shining testimony of the divine power, because it far surpasses all the glories of the world.*[80]

This is not a minor point for Calvin. Rather this 'shining testimony of divine power' which 'far surpasses all the glories of this world' is, in Calvin's eyes, the dénouement of the suffering church. In *Concerning Scandals* Calvin spends approximately fifteen pages,[81] reviewing the history of God's providential pro-

---

75  See Kelly, '*The Suffering Church*,' 13.
76  Kelly, '*The Suffering Church*,' 13. See *LW* 41.165 (*WA* 50.652). *LW* 51.198-99 (*WA* 32.29).
77  Kelly, '*The Suffering Church*,' 13. See *LW* 21.52 (*WA* 32.341); *LW* 21.224-25 (*WA* 32.485).
78  Kelly, '*The Suffering Church*,' 13. See *LW* 54.291 (*WA TR* 3.694, #3900). In Luther's *Sermon on Cross and Suffering*, preached at Coburg in 1530, Luther gives three reasons for suffering: First, God wants believers to be 'conformed to the image of Christ' so they may share in Christ's glory; second, because the Gospel reveals the devil for what he is and so he engages the church in battle revealing that the Word is stronger than the devil; and third, because God disciplines the church to keep it from becoming 'sleepy and secure' in its faith—*LW* 51.206-207 (*WA* 32.36-38). It is unlikely that Calvin read this sermon since it was published in German; nonetheless, it is representative of Luther's thought on the theology of the cross applied to the suffering church.
79  Kolb, 'God's Gift of Martyrdom,' 403-404.
80  *Concerning Scandals*, 47 (*OS*, 191-92), emphasis added.
81  As counted in *Opera Selecta*. See *OS* 2.179.15-194. 9. *Concerning Scandals*, 28–50. Also, Calvin writes as his introduction and thesis statement to a portion of this section: 'For the Church's condition is often calamitous and always unstable; indeed it is being continually tossed about by many different tempests just as in a stormy sea, In the first place, the Lord is showing us in that a clear example of his marvelous providence; and secondly, it provides a useful and indeed necessary exercise for putting our faith and our patience to the test. If the Church had been so established and equipped with aids of every kind that it glittered with its riches, it would be no differ-

tection of the suffering church from the Old and New Testament to his present day. For a man who was relentlessly committed to *brevitas*,[82] it is significant that Calvin relates situation after situation where the church was 'miserably harassed' and God's power and providence sustained it.[83] In the middle of this section, Calvin pauses and restates his thesis: 'The one thing that I want [my readers] to know; the more the church has been crushed beneath the cross, the more clearly has the power of God *shown itself* in raising it up again.'[84] Here is the center of Calvin's theology of the cross: the notion that no matter how much the church has been crushed in persecution, God will *repeatedly raise up the church* throughout human history so that God's power and providence is made known throughout the world.

Though it is beyond this study to give a thorough examination of Calvin's understanding of God's power and providence in the suffering church, this point is clear: Luther's insight that God and self become known in the experience of suffering is affirmed by Calvin. More specifically, Calvin teaches that a knowledge of God's power and providence, that is the power of Christ's resurrection, is made known in the raising up of the church from its suffering throughout human history. In fact, the faithfulness of the suffering church provides the whole world with this knowledge—'*a shining testimony of the divine power*'.[85] Hence a knowledge of God's power is broadcast when the church suffers because the source of the church's life in Christ is revealed. Therefore, Calvin's teaching may be summarized as follows: the greater the cross the church is called to bear, the greater the manifestation of God's power and providence.

---

ent from any worldly power; and indeed no one would doubt that it is ruled according to human standards if it had persisted to this very day in the accustomed manner. But when we see that its life has nevertheless endured for so many generations as if through innumerable deaths, we are bound to conclude that it was preserved by the providence of God'—*Concerning Scandals*, 30–31 (*OS* 2.180, 34-181, 3).

[82] It is important to note that Calvin thinks this long passage is actually in keeping with his commitment to brevity. He writes, 'Examples of God's providence in preserving the Church deserve to be distinguished by great brilliance of language, but so that I may not appear to be writing a history (because after all that is not our present purpose), it is enough for me to touch upon them lightly, as if in passing. However, the plan of this work does not allow me to mention even the tenth part'—*Concerning Scandals*, 39–40 (*OS* 2.186, 37-187, 1).

[83] Calvin emphasizes this conclusion in some form in the following passages: *OS* 2, 180, 37; 180, 41-42; 181, 42; 182, 1-5; 184, 27-30; 184, 34-35; 185, 4-9; 185, 29-31; 185, 36-186, 3; 186, 5-7; 186, 11-13; 186, 37-40; 187, 1-4; 187, 18-21; 187, 33-34; 188, 1-2; 188, 7-13; 188, 30-34; 189, 10-14; 189, 37-39; 190, 1-3; 190, 8-9; 190, 20-23; 190, 25-29; 191, 12-14; 192, 1-3; 192, 16-17; 192, 25-26; 193, 18-19; 193, 31-35; 194, 2-4.

[84] *Concerning Scandals*, 40 (*OS* 2.187, 1-4).

[85] *Concerning Scandals*, 47 (*OS* 2.191-92).

*5. Conclusion: a theology of the cross is a theology of revelation*

At the outset of this study I stated that Luther believed the cross not only provided God's gracious atonement for sin, but that it had an epistemological dimension as well; namely, the cross disclosed an understanding of the way God manifests God's knowledge to the world.[86] It should be noted that Luther's *theologia crucis* was a new way of understanding the significance of the cross in the history of Christian thought. Graham Tomlin demonstrates that Luther's conviction that the 'privatized speculative theology of late medieval scholasticism' and 'popular and monastic piety' were mutually incompatible, giving birth to his *theologia crucis.*[87] Luther stands out not only from his background but also from among his contemporaries. Even though Anabaptists suffered greatly for their faith, they never reflected upon the epistemological dimensions of the cross. They never articulated thoughts like Luther's, that *God's revelation is paradoxical, hidden under the sign of its opposite,* namely, the suffering, weakness, folly and ignominy of the cross, which is why *it must be discerned by faith, and not by reason.*[88]

This point is significant for this study. If Calvin resembles Luther on these ideas, even their broad outlines, there is only one field from which this constellation of ideas could be gleaned, and that field was Luther's writings. The conclusion of this study is in line with Selderhuis' work on Calvin and the Psalms; namely, Calvin was indeed 'Luther's student' on the point that God's knowledge is hidden under an opposite.[89]

In *Concerning Scandals* Calvin teaches that the church suffers because God wishes to display God's power and providence through them. As shown above, Calvin understands that the suffering of the church reveals a knowledge of God to the world and that this knowledge is displayed under its opposite; God's power under powerlessness, and God's providence under apparent defeat and chaos, and God's glory under ignominy. My purpose in this study was to lay-out the broader outlines of Luther's *theologia crucis* and demonstrate its echo in Calvin's ecclesiology of the suffering church as it is articulated in Calvin's pastoral treatise, *Concerning Scandals,* written to the persecuted church in

---

[86] Kadia, 'Luther's Theology of the Cross,' 177.

[87] Graham S. Tomlin, 'The Medieval Origins of Luther's Theology of the Cross,' *Archiv für Reformationsgeschichte* 89 (1988), 39.

[88] The Anabaptist movement lacked learned theologians like Calvin and Luther and was more biblicist than theological. Robert Friedmann sees 'the problem of Anabaptist theology' as an overall 'lack of documents of an explicit theological nature'. He explains that no clear central theological reflection ever developed even though 'we have untold creedal statements or formulations by the Anabaptists, we have confessions of faith, proceedings of trials, minutes of debates, and the like'—Robert Friedmann, *The Theology of Anabaptism* (Scottsdale: Herald Press, 1973), 21-22.

[89] Selderhuis, *Calvin's Theology of the Psalms,* 179-80, also makes this claim when speaking about Calvin's understanding of God's hiddenness.

France.[90] Yet, unlike Luther, Calvin *repeatedly* emphasizes the theme of God's power and providential care for the suffering church. I am unaware of any writing where Luther marches through biblical and church history for multiple pages to recount the way God's power and providence are made known in the sufferings of the people of God.

In his comments on Paul's 'abasement' in 2 Corinthians 12.10, Calvin provides a window into his thinking about the relationship between the cross of suffering and the revelation of God's knowledge in God's people.

> Now the point in question was Paul's outward abasement. He proceeded farther, for the purpose of showing, that the Lord humbled him in every way, that, in his defects, the glory of God might shine forth the more resplendently, which is, in a manner, concealed and buried, when a man is in an elevated position.[91]

Luther's gift to Calvin was the understanding that it takes a cross of suffering to reveal knowledge. In this text Calvin claims that without a cross, either Paul or the church is elevated, and whenever humanity is elevated the knowledge of God's glory and power remains buried and concealed. In other words, for Calvin as for Luther, there is no other way except through weakness and suffering to make manifest a knowledge of God in the lives of God's people.

---

[90] The evidence that *Concerning Scandals* was a pastoral treatise to the suffering church is demonstrated by the fact that it was written in both French (for the people) and in Latin (for the scholar) in 1550 and not only in Latin.

[91] *Comm 2 Cor.* 12.10, *CO* 50.142.

# CHAPTER 10

# John Calvin and Herman Bavinck on the doctrine of justification in relation to ethics

## Timothy Shaun Price

The role of justification has played an important role in the development of Protestant Reformed theology. From Calvin to the present, Reformed theologians have emphasized the importance of understanding why the manner in which one is justified before God effects how one interprets other areas of theology. In fact, the role of justification became one of the key points of contention in the Reformation. This chapter will first examine how this doctrine was understood by John Calvin, and then compare his understanding to the later Reformed theologian, Herman Bavinck. The purpose in doing so will be to provide a broad picture of how justification remained an important topic of discussion in Reformed theology from Calvin to Bavinck, writing approximately 350 years later.

Both Calvin and Bavinck took the doctrine of justification to have a significant place in their understanding of Christian theology. Although Martin Luther usually takes the center stage in conversations concerning justification and the Reformation, John Calvin also set an important trajectory in the history of the doctrine of justification. Calvin, a second generation reformer, saw the role that justification played in sparking the Reformation, and had much to write on the topic. Bavinck, an early twentieth century Dutch neo-Calvinist, also viewed the doctrine of justification as important to forming the practical implications of one's theology.

One may ask, 'What is the value of performing such a comparison between John Calvin and Herman Bavinck?' There are at least two reasons why such a comparison could prove beneficial. First, the comparison of two excellent theological minds allows the reader also to reflect on the topic. Since the Reformation, justification has taken the stage as a central doctrine of the Christian faith. Such a comparison could lead one to a better understanding of the nuances of the subject. Second, understanding their similarities and differences could allow the reader to see the practical implications of their differences of opinion on the issue. For instance, if one is justified by a combination of works and grace it will affect what one sees as the fruit of such works. Calvin and Bavinck both tried to walk a fine line between salvation by works and a salvation which called for sanctification being unnecessary, and this line of inquiry will be examined further throughout this chapter.

It is easy to take the doctrine of justification for granted, but understanding how a sinner is made right before a holy God can have far-reaching consequences for other parts of one's theology. Calvin well understood the importance of justification in theology, and as he developed as a theologian, his writing on justification was also expanded. Bavinck, too, viewed justification as one of the most important doctrines in one's theology. In Bavinck's introductory notes on the doctrine of justification he goes so far as to write, 'Justification is the doctrine on which the church stands or falls. Either we must do something to be saved, or our salvation is purely a gift of grace.'[1] The ramifications of this statement for both theologians will be examined throughout this paper. Bavinck views the Christian's understanding of the role of being justified as crucial to how one lives as a Christian. The question of the Philippian jailer in Acts 16.30 is crucially relevant to the doctrine of justification: 'What must I do to be saved?' As will be examined further, attempting to sort out such a statement as to whether one is saved by works or grace was one of Bavinck's major emphases in his work on justification.

## John Calvin

In this comparison John Calvin looms as a giant among giants in theology. Calvin's *Institutes of the Christian Religion* has proved to be an invaluable resource for the faith and teaching of laity and clergy alike. This section will begin by providing a brief glimpse into Calvin's work on justification in the *Institutes*, and then transition to his Commentary on Romans. As Calvin's *Institutes* developed from the early 1536 edition to the definitive 1559 edition, the place of justification within the book developed as well. Alister McGrath writes, 'The most significant contribution to the development of the early Reformed doctrine of justification was due to John Calvin. Although the 1536 edition of the *Christianae religionis institutio* contains a few scant lines on justification, that of 1539 and subsequent editions describe the doctrine of justification as the "main hinge upon which religion turns," and the "sum of all piety".'[2] In the 1559 edition of the *Institutes*, Calvin includes two chapters specifically on the subject of justification.[3] These chapters come in Book 3, and only after he provides a thorough discussion of sanctification. The title of Chapter 13 is 'Two Things to be Noted in Free Justification,' and the 'Two Things' which

---

[1]  Herman Bavinck, *Holy Spirit, Church, and New Creation* (ed. John Bolt, trans. John Vriend: Grand Rapids: Baker, 2008), 177.
[2]  Alister McGrath, *Justitia Dei* (Cambridge: Cambridge University Press, 1986), 2.36.
[3]  John Calvin, *Institutes of the Christian Religion*. Chapter 13 is entitled, 'Two Things to be Noted in Free Justification' and chapter 14 is entitled, 'The Beginning of Justification and Its Continual Progress'.

Calvin wishes to address are 'that the Lord's glory should stand undiminished and, so to speak, in good repair, and that our consciences in the presence of his judgment should have peaceful rest and serene tranquility'.[4] Calvin argues that the first component of the undiminished glory of God is unaccomplished when humanity attempts to claim a righteousness which derives in themselves. If one is righteous by his or her own account, there is no need for justification. As Calvin often does in his work, he therefore aims to exalt the glory and righteousness of Christ and to make people well aware of their own sinfulness and need of a savior. He writes, 'Paul accommodates those words to this use when he teaches that every part of our salvation rests with Christ that we may glory in the Lord alone [I Cor. 1.30-31]. His meaning is this: whoever thinks that he has anything at all of his own rises up against God and casts a shadow upon his glory.'[5]

Calvin believes that the starting point for understanding justification is understanding Christology and human depravity. Understanding Jesus as the holy God who died in the sinner's place leads to an understanding of the depths of one's own sin. He attempts to walk a fine line, as earlier in the *Institutes* he explains the need for sanctification and holiness in the life of the believer. He further writes, 'To sum up, man cannot without sacrilege claim for himself even a crumb of righteousness, for just so much is plucked and taken away from the glory of God's righteousness.'[6] In his understanding of this aspect of justification, Calvin refers to Paul (particularly Rom. 3), but he also refers to Prov. 20.9; Ezek. 20.44; Isa. 45; Jer. 9; 1 Cor. 1; and 1 Pet. 2. Most of these scriptural references serve to show the role of depravity in a person's inability to account for his or her sin in regards to justification. Most of these scriptural references are secondary, and Calvin focuses upon the book of Romans to form his doctrine of justification. Calvin's understanding of justification is firmly grounded in our first understanding our need to be justified. This sentiment is similar to how Calvin begins Book 1.1 of the *Institutes*: 'Without knowledge of self there is no knowledge of God.'[7] This knowledge leads to an understanding that a person cannot be justified by his or her own ability.

The second aspect which Calvin notes is that when relying upon the substitutionary atonement of Christ for salvation, we are unable to stand before Christ with what he terms 'peaceful rest and serene tranquility'.[8] Calvin sees a natural congruence between being justified by faith in Christ and a deep trust in the work of Christ. Because people are unable to save themselves, one can do nothing but trust Christ. This trust should not be out of fear of judgment, but rather a firm trust in God for salvation and provision. Elsewhere in the *Institutes* Cal-

---

[4]   *Inst* 3.13.1.
[5]   *Inst* 3.13.2.
[6]   *Inst* 3.13.2.
[7]   *Inst* 1.1.1.
[8]   *Inst* 3.13.1.

vin stresses the importance of sanctification and of pleasing God through one's actions, but such works have no place in his section on justification: 'Therefore, those who prate that we are justified by faith because, being reborn, we are righteous by living spiritually have never tasted the sweetness of grace, so as to consider that God will be favorable to them.'[9] The thrust of this statement is that even after one is justified through faith in Christ this justification is not upheld by what Calvin terms 'living spiritually'. Rather, he wishes to make clear that this justification is only through the imputation of Christ's righteousness and not through any person's good works. Anthony Lane writes, 'Justification and sanctification are inseparable, because they both flow from union with Christ, which Calvin describes as a "mystical union" (*Inst* 3.11.10).'[10] Calvin and Bavinck are in agreement on this. Bavinck succinctly makes this point: 'Christ does not justify anyone whom he does not also at the same time sanctify. We, accordingly, are not justified by works, but neither are we justified without works.'[11] Calvin and Bavinck both attempt to eliminate the idea that somehow justification is separated from the action of good works, but at the same time wish to affirm the necessity of good works as the fruit of a believer. Both of these thinkers strain to make this point very clear in their writings.

Calvin's *Commentaries* also reveal much of what Calvin thought concerning the doctrine of justification, particularly his commentary on Romans. Calvin was as much a pastor as he was a formal theologian, hence the value of such a set of commentaries. Calvin's commentary on Romans, as well as an edition of the *Institutes* that expanded its section on justification, were published in 1539. One commentator argues that it could have been because of Calvin's further reflections on the book of Romans at this stage that he chose to expand his thoughts on justification in the *Institutes*.[12] It is quite plausible that further reflection upon the epistle to the Romans formed a sense of the importance of the doctrine of justification in Calvin's theology.

Perhaps one of the most relevant passages concerning the doctrine of justification is Romans 3.20-26:

[20]For by works of the law no human being will be justified in his sight, since through the law comes knowledge of sin. [21]But now the righteousness of God has been manifested apart from the law, although the Law and the Prophets bear witness to it [22]the righteousness of God through faith in Jesus Christ for all who believe. For there is no distinction: [23]for all have sinned and fall short of the glory of

---

[9] *Inst* 3.13.5.
[10] Anthony Lane, *Justification by Faith in Catholic-Protestant Dialogue* (London: T. & T. Clark, 2002), 24.
[11] Herman Bavinck, *Reformed Dogmatics* (ed. John Bolt, trans. John Vriend: Grand Rapids: Baker Academic, 2008), 4.200.
[12] Karla Wubbenhorst, 'Calvin's Doctrine of Justification: Variations on a Lutheran Theme', in Bruce McCormack (ed.), *Justification in Perspective* (Grand Rapids: Baker, 2006), 105.

God, [24]and are justified by his grace as a gift, through the redemption that is in Christ Jesus, [25]whom God put forward as a propitiation by his blood, to be received by faith. This was to show God's righteousness, because in his divine forbearance he had passed over former sins. [26]It was to show his righteousness at the present time, so that he might be just and the justifier of the one who has faith in Jesus.

To understand justification, one must understand the need to be justified. Calvin views this as essential to the doctrine. This justification must also be grounded in no place other than the work of Christ. In his exposition of Romans 3 Calvin writes, 'There is not one method for justifying some, and a different one for others, but all alike must be justified by faith, because all are sinners, and have therefore no cause for glorifying before God. He takes it for granted that everyone is conscious of sin when he comes to the tribunal of God, and is discomfited and lost beneath a sense of his own shame, so that no sinner can bear the presence of God, as we see in the example of Adam.'[13] On Calvin's interpretation of Romans 3 Wubbenhorst writes, 'Faith, as Calvin sees it, is a wholly receptive faculty—it recumbs on the mercy of God, the promises attested in Christ.'[14] Faith is given to the believer, and is fully dependant upon God and his truth.

Calvin sets forth similar ideas of the centrality of Christology in justification in other instances in his Romans commentary. Romans 10.10 says, 'For with the heart one believes and is justified, and with the mouth one confesses and is saved.' On this verse, Calvin writes, 'This passage may assist us in understanding justification by faith. It shows that we obtain righteousness by embracing the goodness of God offered to us in the Gospel. We are, therefore, justified by our believing that God is gracious to us in Christ.'[15] Again, in this instance one is justified by believing in the Gospel and placing one's faith in Christ. Calvin's ideas in the *Commentaries* coincide well with what he writes in the *Institutes*.

### Distinctive aspects of Calvin's doctrine of justification

As Calvin matured as a theologian, his writing on justification became more distilled. One of the most interesting aspects of Calvin's development of this doctrine is its Trinitarian focus. It was mentioned earlier that Calvin's understanding of depravity led him to focus on Christ's righteousness in justification. The believer is justified before God by the imputed righteousness of Christ. Karla Wubbenhorst writes, 'One of the things that makes Calvin's mature doctrine of justification distinctive is this role he gives to the Spirit. Not only sanctification but also justification in the 1559 *Institutes* is unquestionably pneumatological. It is moved to the third book; it is dependent on the faith that the Holy

---

[13] Calvin, *Comm. Rom.* 3.23, CNTC 8.74.
[14] Wubbenhorst, 'Calvin's Doctrine of Justification,' 108.
[15] Calvin, *Comm. Rom.* 10.10, CNTC 8.227-28.

Spirit creates and on the fellowship of righteousness, the bond of mystical union that the Spirit establishes between the believer and Christ.'[16] G.C. Berkouwer also sees this pneumatological focus in Calvin. He writes, 'It is only through the Holy Spirit, he [Calvin] emphasizes, that the promise of salvation penetrates our hearts. . . . This attitude toward faith, as worked in us by the Holy Spirit, controls Calvin's entire treatment of the way of salvation.'[17]

Another distinctive aspect in Calvin is the sheer importance of the doctrine of justification in Christian theology. As mentioned earlier, both Calvin and Bavinck saw this magnitude of understanding justification in the overall picture of their theology. The doctrine of justification is crucial to Calvin's theology because it involves the ultimate question of how a human is made right before God.

## Herman Bavinck

Herman Bavinck (1854-1921) was a systematic theologian in the Dutch Reformed tradition. He began his teaching career at Kampen Theological Seminary, and later moved to the Free University of Amsterdam under the influence of Abraham Kuyper. He is most well-known for his four-volume *Reformed Dogmatics*, but later in his life wrote at length on issues such as psychology and pedagogy. He made it a point in his work to attempt to understand and address the culture of his time, while also being a thorough systematic theologian. As a young man Bavinck was trained in the theological liberalism of his day, but he eventually rebelled against his teachers to be a 'co-laborer in the attack upon ultra-liberalism'.[18]

Bavinck has a detailed chapter dealing with the concept of justice and what justification means in Christianity in volume 4 of his *Reformed Dogmatics*.[19] His chapter on justification falls between the chapters 'Faith and Conversion' and 'Sanctification and Perseverance'. It is contained in 'Part I: The Spirit Gives New Life to Believers'. With this structure in mind, he sets forth to examine how the Spirit works in justification, sanctification, and conversion.

One of the particularities of Bavinck's writings is the sheer amount of secondary literature he is able to integrate into his work. Calvin is often a dialogue partner whom Bavinck incorporates in his chapter on justification. Bavinck's work on Calvin is a natural result of his Dutch Reformed tradition. When think-

---

[16] Wubbenhorst, 'Calvin's Doctrine of Justification,' 110-111.

[17] G.C. Berkouwer, *Faith and Justification*, Studies in Dogmatics (Grand Rapids: Eerdmans, 1954), 28.

[18] Cornelius Jaarmsa, *The Educational Philosophy of Herman Bavinck* (Eerdmans: Grand Rapids, 1935), 23.

[19] As volume 4 of *Reformed Dogmatics* has just been translated for the English speaking world in 2008, it is doubtful that much contemporary English scholarship has been done on his subsection of justification unless one is familiar with the Dutch editions.

ing of who to engage on justification, Calvin would have certainly been one of the first thinkers to come to mind. Rather than quote Calvin verbatim, Bavinck chooses to complement Calvin in some places, and separate himself from Calvin in others. Bavinck was well versed in Calvin, and published articles specifically on Calvin such as 'Calvin and Common Grace'.[20] In his writing on justification in this volume Bavinck is mostly positive in his assessment of the work of Calvin. He speaks against having a caricature of Calvin. He writes, 'Men sometimes speak as if Calvin knew of nothing else to preach but the decree of predestination with its two parts of election and reprobation. The truth is that no preacher of the Gospel has ever surpassed Calvin in the free, generous proclamation of the grace and love of God.'[21] He rests this claim partly upon the fact that predestination is not dealt with in a systematic fashion until the third book of the *Institutes* occurring after his discussion on the life of faith. In the quotation one is able to discern a high degree of respect that Bavinck has for Calvin.

In Bavinck's section entitled 'Objective and Subjective: Active and Passive' it is primarily Calvin with whom Bavinck interacts. Bavinck relies on Calvin in this regard because he believes Calvin does a better job than Luther of linking the doctrines of election and justification. He sees this distinction as due to the fact that 'Luther ever-increasingly pushed predestination into the background. Calvin, on the other hand, increasingly made it the center of his theology and also viewed justification in its light.'[22] It is insightful that Bavinck here uses Calvin as his dialogue partner because Bavinck saw as important understanding the relation of predestination to justification. Bavinck places the connection between election and justification in a much more lucid light than does Calvin. In the midst of interpreting the *Institutes* 3.13 Bavinck writes, 'The elect are justified by God so that they would glory in him and in nothing else.'[23] Bavinck views the fact that people are elected to justification as a primary impetus for sanctification. Election frees people not to rely on their own good works to be justified, but rather to rely on the work of Christ.

Although Bavinck and Calvin have much in agreement, Bavinck was not completely in step with Calvin's understanding of justification. Bavinck writes, 'Yet, although Calvin proved his independence also in the doctrine of justification, he did not solve all the problems that present themselves in the study of this article of faith. This applies especially to the relationship of justification to election and sanctification, on one hand, and to sanctification and glorification, on the other.'[24] Because Calvin is one of the primary voices in the Reformed tradition regarding the doctrine of justification, Bavinck makes it a point to

---

[20] Emile Doumergue, August Lang, Herman Bavinck, and Benjamin B. Warfield, *Calvin and the Reformation* (New York: Fleming H. Revell, 1909).

[21] Doumergue, *Calvin and the Reformation*, 116.

[22] Bavinck, *Reformed Dogmatics*, 4.200.

[23] Bavinck, *Reformed Dogmatics*, 4.200.

[24] Bavinck, *Reformed Dogmatics*, 4.201.

show how he differs from Calvin. The point Bavinck is trying to push here is how justification finds a median between the traps of nomism and antinomianism. Bavinck did not believe that Calvin went far enough to make it clear how a Christian avoids the twin errors of being a strict law-keeper for no purpose and having no law at all. This returns to the relationship between justification and sanctification. One can understand the fear Bavinck has here. Working in the late nineteenth and early twentieth centuries, Bavinck was also attempting to counter the trends toward liberalism in his time. Bavinck is addressing an error in exegesis with which Calvin may not have needed to deal.

The first option of nomism becomes present when one believes that external law-keeping is what saves a person from sin. This tendency could lead to an unhealthy perfectionism. The opposite extreme to nomism is antinomianism. Antinomianism literally means 'no law'. Antinomism would occur in this regard when a person believes that because he or she is justified, there is no need for sanctification. In this strain one takes freedom in Christ to be a freedom to sin rather than a freedom to do good works. Perhaps these dangers were not things that were immediately in Calvin's perception in regards to justification. Whatever may be the case, Bavinck believes this is the primary area in which Calvin fell short in his exposition of justification.

Bavinck addresses these concerns a bit earlier in his section on justification where he examines how even in the early church one could be accused of being antinomian for holding to an incorrect doctrine of justification by faith (Rom. 3.8,31; 6.1,15). Therefore, one extreme in understanding justification by faith is to say that because one is justified there is no law by which one should live. Such a philosophy is countered by Paul in Romans 6.1-2, 'What shall we say then? Are we to continue in sin that grace may abound? By no means! How can we who died to sin still live in it?'[25] Bavinck sees a fall into antinomianism as a possible resulting problem from a misunderstanding of justification. This misunderstanding would involve the fact that one is justified as providing a license to sin.

On the opposite side of antinomianism are 'Others, acting out of reaction, [who] began to cultivate a nomistic and ascetic lifestyle (Rom. 14.1ff.; Gal. 4.10; Col. 2.16; 1 Tim. 4.3-4).' Bavinck believes the tendency towards nomism is most clearly seen in the Catholic sacrament of penance: 'In this sacrament, after the contrition (or attrition) of the heart and the confession of the mouth, believers were absolved from the guilt of sin and eternal punishment, but remained obligated to bear temporal punishments and to perform the good works imposed on them (the work of sanctification).'[26] He argues that the absolving of sin by any authority other than God is a form of works-based righteousness. Through the necessary confession of sin to a temporal authority, the Christian is forced to the impossibility of earning one's righteousness. Bavinck believed

---

[25] All biblical citations are taken from the English Standard Version.
[26] Bavinck, *Reformed Dogmatics*, 4.187.

that Catholic penance resulted from a misunderstanding of the purpose of baptism. He writes:

> The common view of baptism had a powerful influence. Since baptism related only to the forgiveness of past sins and since many Christians committed various—even grave—sins also after baptism, therefore, unless the church was prepared to exclude them from its fellowship and from eternal salvation forever, it had to find a second remedy. And this remedy consisted in penances and good works that, especially under the influence of Tertullian, took on a 'satisfactory' or 'meritorious' character, and that led, after a long development, to the Roman Catholic sacrament of penance.[27]

In other words, sin was divided into pre and post-baptism and needed separate types of remission. This view can become problematic in that the addition of 'good works' to justification brings into question by what means a person is justified.

Returning to Bavinck's interpretation of Calvin, he writes, 'If one's purpose is to maintain the objective forensic character of justification, it is natural to tie it closely with election and sanctification. It then becomes the imputation of the righteousness of Christ, which took place long before, in the gospel, in the resurrection of Christ, or even from eternity, and is then appropriated much later by the subject in faith.'[28] To say that there is an 'objective forensic character' to justification is simply to invoke law court imagery in which it is God who is both the objective judge and the one who justifies. R. C. Sproul writes, 'The doctrine of justification involves a legal matter of the highest magnitude. It involves a matter of judgment before the supreme tribunal of God. The most basic of all issues we face as fallen human beings is the issue of how we as unjust sinners can hope to survive a judgment before the court of an absolutely just God.'[29] Bavinck is working through the relationship of faith and justification in a reformed setting in which it is both God who grants faith and it is God who justifies. He is attempting to eliminate the possibility of good works being tied to justification as seen in the penances and good works cited above. In this paradigm justification is tied closely to election and sanctification because of the imputed righteousness of Christ to the believer. Bavinck argues that the Reformed perspective provides the balance between the dual concerns of antinomianism and nomism.

Bavinck argues that another imbalance he sees in Calvin's work is between 'election and satisfaction, on the one hand, and to sanctification and glorification, on the other. If justification has a place somewhere between the two, there is always a reason to connect it more with the preceding or more with the fol-

---

[27] Bavinck, *Reformed Dogmatics*, 4.187.
[28] Bavinck, *Reformed Dogmatics*, 4.201.
[29] R.C. Sproul, 'The Forensic Nature of Justification', in Don Kistler (ed.), *Justification by Faith Alone* (Morgan, PA: Soli Deo Gloria, 2003), 24.

lowing group of benefits, depending on the choice made, and justification itself acquires a different meaning.'[30] Bavinck well understands that drifting too far in one of these two directions, in neglect of the other, will lead to error in one's theology. Because the believer's justification is placed in the work of Christ, there is nothing a human can do to further add to that justification. In the same vein, because justification in this framework is not a works-based righteousness it frees the believer to fulfill the mandate of Ephesians 2.10, 'For we are his workmanship, created in Christ Jesus for good works, which God prepared beforehand, that we should walk in them.' The freedom found in Christ through justification is that the condemnation of God for sin has been removed in place of the righteousness of Christ.

Bavinck possesses a thorough understanding of Calvin and of justification. Bavinck writes, 'Calvin feels that he is in the presence of God, placed before his judgment seat; and looking up at the holiness and majesty of God, he no longer dares to speak, with reference to puny sinful humans, of works of their own, of merits, or of reason for boasting in themselves. On the contrary, nothing befits such a person other than humility and confidence in God's mercy. The elect are justified by God so that they would glory in him and in nothing else.'[31] Bavinck seems to appreciate the perspective Calvin has that it is in justification that the person is able properly to stand before the judgment seat of God.

To reiterate the point, the main separation between Calvin and Bavinck in their understanding of justification is that Bavinck believes that there is a theological need to draw a distinction between active and passive justification. Active justification is that which takes place 'from eternity, in the resurrection of Christ, in the gospel, before and after the gift of faith, but sums up everything in a single concept'.[32] Passive justification is said to take place by faith and hence follow in a temporal sense. Bavinck argues that the reformers did not use this terminology, but did speak of justification in a concrete sense. He writes that the need for the distinction between active and passive justification arose in Reformed theology to prevent the attacks of nomism and antinomianism. In fact, he argues that active eternal justification was often rejected when this distinction was not made because of the ease present to fall into antinomianism.

One of the few theologians to have dealt with the doctrine of justification in Calvin and Bavinck is the twentieth century Reformed theologian, G.C. Berkouwer. In his book *Faith and Justification*[33] Berkouwer grounds his position on justification (as he does many of his other doctrines) on the work of

[30] Bavinck, *Reformed Dogmatics*, 4.201.
[31] Bavinck, *Reformed Dogmatics*, 4.201.
[32] Bavinck, *Reformed Dogmatics*, 4.202.
[33] G.C. Berkouwer, *Faith and Justification* (Studies in Dogmatics: Grand Rapids: Eerdmans, 1954).

Calvin and Bavinck.[34] Naming a few of the distinctive aspects Berkouwer saw in Bavinck's theology may prove helpful in distinguishing between Calvin and Bavinck on justification.

One area that Berkouwer believed Bavinck differed from Abraham Kuyper and others was in his rejection of eternal justification. The question being asked here is whether justification proceeds *from eternity* rather than *in time*.[35] Bavinck's rejection of justification from eternity hinged on his belief that such a doctrine would lead to antinomianism, as discussed above.[36] Berkouwer writes that Bavinck rejects eternal justification, 'first, because the Scriptures nowhere speak of it. Furthermore, he said, if one speaks of justification as eternal he should consistently also speak of creation, incarnation, sacrifice, calling, and regeneration as eternal. He was grateful that Reformation theology generally, from fear of antinomianism, had shied away from the idea.'[37]

Berkouwer is also helpful in understanding Bavinck in that he clarifies the type of antinomianism to which Bavinck is referring. This is not a completely uncritical, licentious antinomianism. Berkouwer writes,

> This antinomianism is not simply a radical disavowal of the validity of the law in the life of believers. The antinomianism we are dealing with here has far reaching implications for the work of Christ and for the doctrine of justification. Antinomianism tirelessly preached the completely and perfectly finished work of Christ on the cross. Redemption was accomplished in this unrepeatable and definitive event, and from this it was concluded that there is really nothing for the believer to do, that every effort to ascribe an activity to the believer was a refined form of work-righteousness, and that this was an attempt to add self-righteousness to the work of Christ as though His work were insufficient.[38]

Bavinck recognized that there was an element of truth in this position, namely that one cannot add to Christ's righteousness, but also recognized the danger if this position is brought to fruition.[39] He therefore sought to counter the claim by further clarifying his doctrine of justification, and providing some criticism that this was not earlier done by Calvin.

---

[34] Berkouwer also references the work of Abraham Kuyper and Karl Barth in numerous places in this book, but Berkouwer himself is more in line with Calvin and Bavinck in his understanding of justification.

[35] It may be beneficial to note that the question here was not whether people remained justified *through* eternity, i.e. eternal security. The question is whether people are justified prior to the moment at which they come to faith in Christ.

[36] Berkouwer, *Faith and Justification*, 146.

[37] Berkouwer, *Faith and Justification*, 147.

[38] Berkouwer, *Faith and Justification*, 148-49.

[39] Berkouwer, *Faith and Justification*, 149.

## Practical implications

What has been the benefit of this brief comparison of these two theologians in a volume on justification and the Reformation? As stated above, the primary difference in their thinking about justification is that Bavinck did not think Calvin went far enough in stating the ethical principles involved with justification. As with other areas of the Christian life, one must find the balance contained in keeping God's law—but one must also realize that justification does not come through that law-keeping. Bavinck warned that when considering the doctrine of justification it is far too easy to stray too far towards election or sanctification to the neglect of the other.

Perhaps most importantly what one learns from Bavinck and Calvin's exposition is the assurance of faith which justification grants to the believer in Christ. Because justification is the fact that believers are in right relationship before God, it frees the believer to do good works in the knowledge of salvation and sanctification. These works are no longer done for penance or to justify oneself, but rather out of the freedom granted through justification. Calvin refers to this in the *Institutes* 3.13.5 which he entitles, 'Faith in God's free grace alone gives us peace of conscience and gladness in prayer.' Calvin says, 'Paul consistently denies that peace or quiet joy are retained in consciences unless we are convinced that we are "justified by faith" (Rom. 5.1).'

Bavinck states a similar idea at the very end of his chapter on justification. He says,

> For faith, by its very nature, is opposed to all doubt. Certainty is not added to it later from without, but is from the beginning implicit in faith and in due time produced by it, for it is a gift of God, a working of the Holy Spirit. . . . And this assurance of faith gives buoyancy and strength to the Christian life. . . . Among Catholics, justification is a process of equipping people for a moral purpose; among Protestants, it is the restoration of the religious relationship with God.[40]

It is perhaps best to end with Bavinck's closing words on justification:

> In justification we have been granting peace with God, sonship, free and certain access to the throne of grace, freedom from the law, and independence from the world, then from that faith will naturally flow a stream of good works. They do not serve to acquire eternal life but are the revelation, seal, and proof of the eternal life that every believer already possesses. Faith that includes the assurance that with God all things are possible, that he gives life to the dead, calls into existence the things that do not exist (Rom. 4.17), and always enables people to do great things. This faith says to a mountain: 'Be lifted up and thrown into the sea,' and it will be done (Matt. 21.21).

---

[40] Bavinck, *Reformed Dogmatics*, 4.229.

149

# CHAPTER 11

## Justification by obedience: faith and works in the royal theology of Henry VIII and his apologists

*André A. Gazal*

When the Reformation Parliament passed the Act of Supremacy in 1534 declaring the monarch 'the Supreme Head of the Church of England,' it did far more than merely confirm the transfer of ecclesiastical authority over the English Church from the papacy to the king; it fundamentally codified by statute a theology of kingship which underlay the ascription of spiritual power to the 'Imperial Crown' of England. At the heart of this theology of kingship was a doctrine of obedience. Richard Rex persuasively argues in his important article, 'The Crisis of Obedience,' that this doctrine of obedience was the definitive theological principle of the Henrician Reformation.[1] Since the theology of kingship, with its attendant doctrine of obedience, was the guiding first principle of the ecclesiastical reform undertaken by Henry VIII (1491-1547) and his government, it also determined the contents of other doctrines, especially the doctrine of justification. Because Henry VIII viewed the Lutheran doctrine of forensic justification as subversive to his biblical theology of kingship, and particularly its core doctrine of obedience, the king and his major apologists promoted a doctrine of justification that coincided with the government's royal theology. Specifically, within the overall framework of this theology of kingship, obedience to the law of God functioned as the necessary ground of justification. This understanding of justification is evidenced in the principal works of the period defending Royal Supremacy: Richard Sampson's *Oratio* (1533), Stephen Gardiner's *De Vera Obedentia* (1535), and Henry VIII's own corrections of *The Bishops' Book* (1538). Finally, this conception of justification finds full expression in *The King's Book* (1543), which served as the Henrician regime's official declaration of doctrine. The specific arguments in these works will be considered after a brief description of the theology of kingship in which this doctrine of justification occurs, as stated in Edward Foxe's *The True Difference Between Regal and Ecclesiastical Power* (1534).

---

[1] Richard Rex, 'The Crisis of Obedience: God's Word and Henry's Reformation,' *Historical Journal* 39 (December, 1996), 863-94.

## The Henrician biblical theology of kingship: Edward Foxe's *The True Difference Between Regal and Ecclesiastical Power*

Edward Foxe was Bishop of Hereford and one of the most prominent ambassadors who endeavored to solicit support for Henry's annulment abroad. He wrote the first significant work outlining and defending the basic theology of the Royal Supremacy, *Regiae et Ecclesiasticae Potestatis*, or *The True Difference Between Regal and Ecclesiastical Power* (1534).[2] In this work, Foxe argues that Scripture differentiates between two types of power established by God. Coercive authority belongs only to the royal power and purely spiritual or teaching authority belongs to ecclesiastical power. A definitive aspect of coercive royal power is the necessary prerogative to see that the ecclesiastical is functioning properly, which evidences the subordination of ecclesiastical authority to royal power by divine ordinance.[3] Foxe clearly points out that this is the scriptural teaching based on the literal sense of the biblical text.[4] He establishes royal ecclesiastical authority on the basis of the Old Testament historical narrative accounts recording the specific actions of the kings of Israel and Judah regarding religion, such as assigning the priests their tasks and initiating cultic reform.[5] Thus assignment of coercive power, which included authority over the church, to the office of kingship, provides the necessary warrant for obedience to the king by all persons of every order, including the clergy. This was the central theological framework in which the Henrician doctrine of justification functioned as first of all propagated in Richard Sampson's *Oratio*.

### Richard Sampson's *Oratio*

The central thesis of this short work composed by Richard Sampson, a royal diplomat and bishop of Chichester, is that the acceptance of the king's proposed title of Supreme Head was an extension of loving obedience to God.[6] He begins

---

2   Though originally published in Latin, this work was translated into English during the reign of Edward VI (r.1547-1553). This is the edition that will be referenced throughout this discussion. See Edward Fox[e], *Opus eximium. De Vera Differentia Regiae Postestatis et Ecclesiasticae, et quae sit ipsa veritas ac virtus utriusque* (London: Thomas Berthelet, 1534; STC (2nd ed.) / 11218 [Database online–subscription only]: Early English Books Online, http://eebo.chadwyck.com [accessed 24 July 2006]); Edward Fox[e], *The true dyfferens betwen ye regial power and the Ecclesiasticall power Translated out of latyn by Henry lord Stafforde* (London: 1548; STC (2nd ed.) / 11220 [Database online–subscription only]: Early English Books Online, http://eebo.chadwyck.com [accessed 24 July 2006]).
3   Foxe, *The true dyfferens*, 35v-36r.
4   Foxe, *The true dyfferens*, 6r-6v.
5   Foxe, *The true dyfferens*, 59r-59v, 60r-66v.
6   Richard Sampson, *Richardi Sampsonis, Regii Sacelli Decani Oratio, qua docet, hortatur, admonet omens potissimum Anglos regiae dignitati cum primis ut obediant, quia verbum dei precipit, episcopo Romano ne sint audientes, qui nullo iure divino, in eos quincq potestatis habet, postq ita iubet et rex, ut illi non obediant* (London:

his discussion by citing John 13.34: 'Love one another just as I have loved you.'[7] From this verse, Sampson infers three types of love: love of humans by God, love of God by humans, and love of human beings by human beings.[8] After discussing God's love for humanity in redemption, Sampson proceeds to the second type of love, which serves as the basis for his thesis.[9] Humanity expresses its love for God by keeping his commandments.[10] From this proposition, Sampson enters into his discussion of Romans 13.

Sampson argues that to obey the king is to obey God, thereby showing love for God. The power which the king possesses and exercises is from God, and for this reason he is called the 'Supreme Head'.[11] 'Whatever therefore the prince commands, it is necessary that you do it, for thus God commands it. The only exception is when the prince commands against God.'[12] 'For it is the word of God, from which we are taught, that we obey this power.'[13] It is thus commanded by God himself that all, including the bishops, obey the king who holds supreme power from God.[14] All are subject to him by divine mandate.

Sampson's *Oratio* contains the essential elements of a doctrine of justification shaped fundamentally by the theology of kingship that served as the basis for the subordination of the church to royal authority. Obedience to the divine commandments was the manifestation of faith working through love whereby one was justified. Subjection to royal authority served the ultimate end of justification. It is this obedience to the king which authenticates submission to all the other divine commandments, most fundamentally, the commandment to love under which all the commandments are subsumed. Because love for God principally shows itself in obedience to the king, Sampson summarily identifies this type of obedience to the Word itself when he declares, 'The Word of God is to obey the king.'[15] Evident in this short work is the appropriation into this royal theology of a late medieval conception of justification resulting from faith working through love which is more fully developed by Stephen Gardiner in his seminal work, *De Vera Obedientia*.

---

Thomas Berthelet, 1533; STC (2nd ed.) / 21681 [Database online–subscription only]: Early English Books Online, http://eebo.chadwyck.com [accessed 24 July 2006]). See, also, Andrew Chibi, 'Richard Sampson, his "Oratio," and Henry VIII's Royal Supremacy,' *Journal of Church and State* 39 (1997), 545.

7  Sampson, *Oratio*, A2r. The Latin is translated by the author.
8  Sampson, *Oratio*, A2r.
9  Sampson, *Oratio*, A3r.
10  Sampson, *Oratio*, A3v.
11  Sampson, *Oratio*, B1v.
12  Sampson, *Oratio*, A4r.
13  Sampson, *Oratio*, A4v.
14  Sampson, *Oratio*, B1r.
15  Sampson, *Oratio*, C7v.

## Stephen Gardiner's *De Vera Obedientia*

Considered 'the intellectual leader of English religious conservatism,'[16] Stephen Gardiner became bishop of Winchester in 1529. As one of Henry's ambassadors, he appeared frequently before the papal court in behalf of Henry's request for an annulment. Originally published in 1535, Gardiner's *De Vera Obedientia* (*On True Obedience*) received acclaim on the continent by no less a personage than Martin Bucer, the reformer in Strasbourg, where it underwent several printings.[17] A Protestant exile on the Continent translated *De Vera Obedientia*, along with the Preface by Edmund Bonner (1500-1569), into English during the reign of Mary Tudor (r.1553-1558) as an indictment of its author's later rejection of the Royal Supremacy.[18] By that time, Gardiner had become a figure most hated by Protestants. It has been capably argued by Richard Rex that *De Vera Obedientia* is not an evangelical work, but one in which the author sought to reinforce Catholic tradition by relating obedience to the monastic virtue of charity with reference to the king in an attempt to counter the influence of Luther's doctrine of justification by faith alone.[19]

Gardiner defines true obedience as obeying the truth.[20] To obey the truth is to obey God, for 'god is the truth as scripture recordeth, wherein he geveth his chefe light unto us'.[21] Moreover, obedience is a requirement of faith; we 'shoulde . . . both beleve in obeieng, and obeie in beleving'.[22] Gardiner then commends Christ who procured human redemption by perfect obedience to his Father's commandments as the definitive example of all Christian obedience.[23] Gardiner further defines true obedience as obeying God for God's sake.[24] Such obedience proceeds from divine truth and ends with it.[25] He confirms this un-

---

[16] Alec Ryrie, 'Divine Kingship and Royal Theology in Henry VIII's Reformation,' *Reformation* 7 (2002), 71.

[17] Diarmaid MacCulloch, *Thomas Cranmer* (New Haven: Yale University Press, 1996), 174. Bucer, Caspar Hedio (1494-1552), and Wolfgang Capito (1478-1541) together wrote a preface for one of the Strasbourg editions of the work.

[18] The edition referenced for this discussion will be Stephen Gardiner, *De Vera Obedientia AN ORAtion made in Latine by the ryghte Reverend father in God Stephan B. of Winchestre, nowe lord Chauncellour of England, . . . touchinge true Obedience . . . and nowe translated into english and printed by Michael Wood* (Roan: Michael Wood, 1553; STC (2nd ed.) / 11585 [Database online–subscription only]: Early English Books Online, http://eebo.chadwyck.com [accessed 24 July 2006]). For the Latin, see Stephani Winton. Episcopi *de Vera Obedientia Oratio* (Hamburg: In officina Francisci Rhodi, 1536; STC (2nd ed.) / 11584 [Database online–subscription only]: Early English Books Online, http://eebo.chadwyck.com [accessed 24 July 2006]).

[19] Rex, 'The Crisis of Obedience', 886-87.
[20] Gardiner, *De Vera Obedientia*, 13v.
[21] Gardiner, *De Vera Obedientia*, 13v
[22] Gardiner, *De Vera Obedientia*, 9v.
[23] Gardiner, *De Vera Obedientia*, 10r-12r.
[24] Gardiner, *De Vera Obedientia*, 12v.
[25] Gardiner, *De Vera Obedientia*, 12v

derstanding of obedience by appealing to Colossians 3 in which Paul admonishes servants to obey their masters for the Lord's sake.[26]

Gardiner proceeds to state that the chief intention of Scripture is to teach true obedience by way of commands.[27] Next, he distinguishes the commands given in the Old and New Testaments. Many of the commandments in the Old Testament were intended to maintain external order among the ancient Israelites; these are no longer useful.[28] Yet, the 'new law,' which is the Gospel, did not abolish the 'moral precepts' commanded by God which are universally binding on all nations.[29] Christ, in fact, 'enlarge[d] the limittes of holynesse and chastitie' prescribed by the moral law when he said 'that we shall not enter into the kyngedome of heaven, onles oure righteousnesse exceade the righteousnesse of the Scribes and Pharisies'.[30] The Gospel, as the 'newe lawe,' demands even greater inward spiritual obedience to the moral precepts of God.

In order 'to encrease aboundaunce of glory in us,' as well as 'to exercise our selfes godly and thank worthily,' God 'substituted men' for himself who would require obedience as his 'vicegerents'.[31] To obey them is to obey God himself.[32] Those occupying this place are princes who as 'representours of his image,' are to be regarded as 'suprem' among all human beings.[33] Gardiner then substantiates this identification of princes by citing Proverbs 7, 1 Peter 2 and Romans 13.[34] Gardiner's definition of obedience and his understanding of divine commands, together with his order of obedience to various authorities,[35] become the basis for the central concern of his work, Royal Supremacy over the church in the realm.

Gardiner's *De Vera Obedientia* thus represents a conservative espousal of the doctrine of Royal Supremacy. Rejecting Luther's teaching of justification by faith alone, the bishop of Winchester linked obedience to princes to the general obedience to God's commands which faith requires, thus presenting it as a meritorious work—a view shared also by Henry.

## Henry VIII's annotations of the *Bishops' Book*

The *Institution of the Christian Man*, otherwise known as the *Bishops' Book* (1537), was a collaborative work by Henry's bishops intended, as per the king's command, to set forth the rudiments of Christian doctrine to engender peace

---

[26] Gardiner, *De Vera Obedientia*, 13r.
[27] Gardiner, *De Vera Obedientia*, 14r.
[28] Gardiner, *De Vera Obedientia*, 14r-v.
[29] Gardiner, *De Vera Obedientia*, 14v-16r.
[30] Gardiner, *De Vera Obedientia*, 14v-15r.
[31] Gardiner, *De Vera Obedientia*, 16r.
[32] Gardiner, *De Vera Obedientia*, 16r.
[33] Gardiner, *De Vera Obedientia*, 16r.
[34] Gardiner, *De Vera Obedientia*, 16r.
[35] Gardiner, *De Vera Obedientia*, 16v-17v.

within the realm. Specifically, the *Bishops' Book* was an exposition of the Creed, the Seven Sacraments, the Ten Commandments, the Lord's Prayer, and the Ave Maria, followed by brief articles on justification and purgatory. In essence, it represented a compromise between the evangelical and conservative bishops who continued to be divided on a host of theological issues. While the *Bishops' Book* reflected the king's theological convictions for the most part, he did not find it entirely satisfactory. Henry particularly objected to the *Bishops' Book*'s affirmation of justification by grace alone.

In 1538, Henry made several corrections to the *Bishops' Book*. Most of these had to do with statements concerning justification. By means of marginal comments, Henry recast sentences clearly averring justification by divine grace alone to make justification dependent upon the cooperation of human effort. For instance, the *Bishops' Book* alleges the following concerning the unilateral role of the Holy Spirit in bringing human beings to Christ as the way to the Father:

> Like as Christ is the author, the mean, and the very highway to come unto God the Father, so is this Holy Spirit the very conductor, the guide, the director, and the governor, to bring us into the same highway, and to minister unto us not only alacrity and strength to walk and run therein, but also perseverance to continue in the same, until we shall come unto our journey's end.[36]

The king altered this statement by adding this conditional clause to the end: 'if we accept the same, and join our will to his godly motions'.[37] In other words, the Holy Spirit's work in the initiation and continuation of salvation is contingent upon the agreement of the subject's will in the process.

More significantly, Henry links justification to the conditional performance of duty. This occurs in at least five places throughout his corrections. The first instance has to do with the efficacy of Christ's death. Where the *Bishops' Book* states, 'And I believe that by this passion and death of our Saviour Jesu Christ, not only my corporeal death is so destroyed that it shall never have power to hurt me, but rather it is made wholesome and profitable unto me,'[38] Henry inserted the words 'I doing my duty' after 'Jesu Christ,' so as to make the efficacy of his death depend upon the faithful execution of duty.[39] Likewise, the king makes the Christian's adoption by the Father contingent upon perseverance 'in his precepts and laws,' which are the Ten Commandments.[40] Furthermore, Henry identifies the primary work of the Holy Spirit as his recalling to Christians their duty.[41] The king again specifies this duty in his corrections of the *Bishops'*

[36] Charles Lloyd (ed.), *Formularies of Faith* (Oxford: Clarendon Press, 1825), 74.
[37] Thomas Cranmer, *The Miscellaneous Writings and Letters of Thomas Cranmer* (ed. John Edmund Fox: Cambridge: The Parker Society, 1846), 93.
[38] Lloyd, *Formularies of Faith*, 40.
[39] Cranmer, *Miscellaneous Writings*, 89.
[40] Cranmer, *Miscellaneous Writings*, 84.
[41] Cranmer, *Miscellaneous Writings*, 90.

*Book*'s exposition of the fifth article of the Apostles' Creed. There he character-izes this duty as obeying God's 'precepts,' which Henry cites as the prerequi-site for participating in the resurrection which Christ secured by his death and own resurrection.[42] Finally, the king states explicitly that, as the condition for his ultimate justification, one principally obeys God's precepts by 'truly doing his office whereto he is called'.[43] A person primarily obeys God's command-ments by functioning rightfully in Christian society according to the position he has been divinely assigned, 'be he craftsman, be he labourer'.[44] Simply stated, one is justified by obedience to God's commandments according to the rightful fulfillment of one's 'calling,' or appointed function in Christian society.

When taken together, Henry VIII's proposed corrections of statements in the *Bishops' Book* comprise a doctrine which posits obedience to God's com-mandments principally by rightful discharge of one's assigned position in soci-ety as the requirement for justification. Fulfilling God's precepts by functioning in one's calling in Christian society comprehensively manifested itself as obe-dience to the king. This view of justification was later fully embodied in the 1543 doctrinal formula, *The Necessary Doctrine and Erudition for any Chris-tian Man*, otherwise known as the *King's Book*.

### Justification by obedience as official doctrine: *The King's Book*

After much negotiation involving Cranmer and three other bishops, Thomas Thirlby of Westminster, Nicholas Heath of Rochester, and John Salcot of Salis-bury,[45] the new declaration of official doctrine, *The Necessary Doctrine and Erudition for any Christian Man*, was published in 1543.[46] It was only apt that it also be called the *King's Book*, since Henry enthusiastically endorsed its con-tents.[47]

The *King's Book* begins with a declaration of faith followed by extensive expositions of the Apostles' Creed, Seven Sacraments, Decalogue, Pater Nos-ter, and Ave Maria. It concludes with articles on free will, justification, and good works, ending with a prayer for departed souls. These discussions occur within the framework of traditional late medieval soteriology similar to that espoused by Gardiner. Yet, the central theme occurring in all of these treat-ments is obedience to the prince as an essential feature of keeping the divine commandments as a means of justification.

---

[42]  Cranmer, *Miscellaneous Writings*, 92.
[43]  Cranmer, *Miscellaneous Writings*, 108.
[44]  Cranmer, *Miscellaneous Writings*, 108.
[45]  A.G. Dickens, *The English Reformation* (2nd edition; University Park, Pa: Pennsylva-nia State University Press, 1993), 207.
[46]  MacCulloch, *Thomas Cranmer*, 309.
[47]  MacCulloch, *Thomas Cranmer*, 309.

## The Preface

The Preface, authored by Henry himself, sets forth the agenda of the treatise. It specifically accentuates the function of the Ten Commandments as 'the high way' ordained by God 'wherein each man should walk in his life to finish his journey here, and after to rest eternally in joy with him'.[48] Clearly the Decalogue is portrayed as the prime means of salvation. Henry closely associates his prerogative to enjoin obedience to the Commandments with his royal authority. Specifically, the compulsion to obedience stems from the king's power to control popular access to biblical content. Only the clergy, who are charged with teaching, need to study the Holy Scripture. For the laity, it is fitting that they read only what 'the prince and policy of the realm shall think convenient . . . to be tolerated or taken from it'.[49] Henry then alludes to legislation which underscored the necessity of mediating biblical knowledge through officially sanctioned preachers to his lay subjects, with the view that they would receive only the scriptural instruction required of them to obey the Commandments inwardly and outwardly for the attainment of salvation.[50] Thus, the Bible functioned as a royal primer of divine precepts sorted through the agency of the church to inculcate obedience. However, in order to propagate a coherent doctrine of justification by obedience, it had to be maintained within a specific soteriological framework.

## The Declaration of Faith

The Declaration of Faith, following the preface, resembles late medieval soteriology by positing two kinds of faith. The first kind of faith, conferred by divine grace, constitutes belief in the truthfulness of God's Word.[51] However, this differs substantially from the second kind of faith, which

> is considered as it hath hope and charity annexed and joined unto it: and faith so taken signifieth not only the belief and persuasion before mentioned in the first acception, but also a sure confidence and hope to attain whatsoever God hath promised for Christ's sake, and an hearty love to God, and obedience to his commandments. And this faith is a lively faith, and worketh in man a ready submission of his will to God's will. And this is the effectual faith that worketh by chari-

---

[48] Lloyd, *Formularies of Faith*, 216.

[49] Lloyd, *Formularies of Faith*, 218.

[50] Lloyd, *Formularies of Faith*, 218. This was the 1543 Act for the Advancement of True Religion. See Gerald Bray (ed.), *Documents of the English Reformation* (Minneapolis: Fortress Press, 1994), 179-80; Ryrie, 'Divine Kingship and Royal Theology,' 68-69; Alec Ryrie, *The Gospel and Henry VIII: Evangelicals in the Early English Reformation* (Cambridge: Cambridge University Press, 2003), 220-21.

[51] Lloyd, *Formularies of Faith*, 220-21.

ty, which St. Paul unto the Galatians affirmeth to be of value and strength of Christ Jesu.[52]

The first type of faith, mere belief, cannot itself suffice for attaining salvation. Instead, the faith that is truly efficacious proceeds to work itself out in love. This Augustinian view of faith serves as the catalyst for obedience to the Decalogue.[53] The incorporation of this traditional understanding of faith into the royal theology of obedience propounded in this treatise will make submission to the king the ultimate manifestation of love, and therefore faith.

### The Apostles' Creed

The extended discussion on the Apostles' Creed construes obedience to the prince as an essential article of faith. The first article of the Creed, 'I believe in God the Father Almighty,' 'signifieth also that we must obey unto his will, as well as in all our inward thoughts and affections as also in our outward acts and deeds'.[54] To confess the articles of the faith assumes the internal disposition towards obedience. This functions as the basis for an implicit demand for submission to God's commandments throughout the remaining articles.

The article on Christ's resurrection confesses 'very God and man which was promised in scripture to come to save and to redeem all those that believing in him ordered themselves in obeying and following his precepts and commands accordingly'.[55] Furthermore, we will share in Christ's resurrection 'if we order and conform our will in this world to his precepts'.[56] The profession of the resurrection of Christ, then, like the other articles of faith preserved in the Creed, also contains an implied and inextricable commitment to obedience. The explanation of the seventh article concerning the Final Judgment further reinforces the necessity of conforming oneself to God's will, thereby exercising 'the works of right belief and charity'.[57]

The explanations of the individual articles up to this point are brought together in the discussion concerning 'the Holy Catholic Church'. Belief in the church entails acknowledgement of not only Christ's Headship of the universal church, but also Royal Supremacy, whereby all Christians, clerical and lay alike, are

> bound to honor and obey, next unto himself, Christian princes, which be the head governors under him in the particular churches, to whose office it appertaineth not only to provide for the tranquility and wealth of their subjects in temporal and worldly things, to the conservation of their bodies, but also to foresee that within

---

[52] Lloyd, *Formularies of Faith*, 222.
[53] Alister McGrath, *Iustitia Dei: A History of the Christian Doctrine of Justification* (Cambridge: Cambridge University Press, 1998), 145-54.
[54] Lloyd, *Formularies of Faith*, 229.
[55] Lloyd, *Formularies of Faith*, 235.
[56] Lloyd, *Formularies of Faith*, 235.
[57] Lloyd, *Formularies of Faith*, 239.

their dominions such ministers be ordained and appointed in their churches as can and will truly and purely set out the true doctrine of Christ, to teach the same, and to see the commandments of God well observed and kept, to the wealth and salvation of souls.[58]

The above statement is fundamentally a summary of the doctrine of Royal Supremacy, which was the heart of Henrician theology. Directly under Christ, the prince governs the national church within his realm. In so doing, he maintains the spiritual, as well as the physical, well-being of his subjects. Towards this end, he oversees the clergy's execution of their sacred duties, paramount of which is to teach 'the true doctrine of Christ,' and 'to see the commandments of God well observed and kept'. Because the prince's divinely mandated authority places him immediately under Christ, everyone is to submit to him. Furthermore, the prince's authority to oblige the clergy to teach the commandments makes him the ultimate human arbiter of revealed truth, since in the royal theology of the regime the purpose of this authority is to enjoin obedience to God. Thus, for one to confess belief in 'the Holy Catholic Church' meant subscription to Royal Supremacy, which required commitment to obey the king as its earthly head in England.

This exposition of the article concerning the church also established the Apostles' Creed as simultaneously a confession of faith and profession of obedience. Obedience as the justifying expression of faith receives primary emphasis in the commentary on the Ten Commandments that follows.

### The Ten Commandments

The exposition of the Ten Commandments is arguably the core of the *King's Book*. Like the commentary on the Apostles' Creed, this section closely associates God's laws with the prince's. Interpreting the Third Commandment, the commentary alleges the taking of God's name in vain to involve, among other things, taking an oath contrary to a previous one, to 'the laws of God, or to the due obedience to the princes and their laws'.[59] Conversely, to obey the king and his laws is to honor God's name. The explanation of the Fourth Commandment, 'Remember the Sabbath Day, to keep it holy,' identifies worshiping God rightly with obedience to the king. While a ceremony's inclusion in public worship required sanction of both antiquity and royal ecclesiastical authority, the comment suggests that even if a ceremony conformed to the custom of the ancient church, its usage in worship ultimately depended upon royal consent, which means that royal ecclesiastical authority superseded ancient tradition.[60] The basis for this is that kings and princes 'next to God be the chief head of the churches'.[61] Royal Supremacy assigned a liturgical authority to the monarch,

[58] Lloyd, *Formularies of Faith*, 248-49.
[59] Lloyd, *Formularies of Faith*, 304.
[60] Lloyd, *Formularies of Faith*, 310.
[61] Lloyd, *Formularies of Faith*, 310.

even to the point of altering traditional forms. In response to the divinely prescribed power of the king to regulate worship, subjects were not to opine concerning the forms he approved, but observe them in the public worship of God on whose authority the sovereign acts.[62] To honor the Sabbath Day was to worship in the way the king dictated. In short, this comment in the *King's Book* legitimizes the prince's authority over public worship as a central feature of Royal Supremacy.

The extensive discussion of the Fifth Commandment is the most emphatic one enjoining obedience to the King. It begins with an analysis of the words 'father' and 'mother'. These denote more than simply one's natural parents, 'but also princes and all other governors, rulers, and pastors, under whom we are nourished, and brought up, ordered, and guided'.[63] However, biblical honor requires more than simply respect towards one of higher societal rank; honor, in the biblical sense, fundamentally means obedience to their commands, stemming from a sincere love and reverence for them.[64] Such honor, in particular, is to be rendered to the king.[65] Scripture itself ascribes the names 'Father' and 'Mother' to rulers in such places as Isaiah 49, thereby corroborating obedience to them as fulfillment of this commandment.[66] Having justified the application of this commandment to obedience to the prince, the exposition proceeds to give a summary of the prince's paternal responsibility towards his subjects. According to Scripture, princes, as fathers to their subjects, maintain true religion, govern via equitable laws, see to the stability of the commonwealth, and defend it against foreign invasion.[67] Finally, they are to dispense justice impartially, with 'fatherly pity,' aiding the innocent, while punishing the guilty. For these reasons, subjects are

> bound by this commandment, not only to honor and obey the said princes, according as subjects be bound to do, and to owe their truth and fidelity to them as unto their natural lords; but they must also love them as children do love their fathers, yea, they must more tender the surety of their prince's person and his estate than their own or any other's: even like as the health of the head is more to be tendered than the health of any other member.[68]

The love that subjects should have for their rulers must exceed that for themselves or anyone else. This love and obedience for their sovereign is to persist even if he proves to be tyrannical.[69] Indeed, 'by this commandment they be bound to obey also all the laws, proclamations, precepts, and commandments,

---

[62] Lloyd, *Formularies of Faith*, 310.
[63] Lloyd, *Formularies of Faith*, 311.
[64] Lloyd, *Formularies of Faith*, 311-12.
[65] Lloyd, *Formularies of Faith*, 315.
[66] Lloyd, *Formularies of Faith*, 315.
[67] Lloyd, *Formularies of Faith*, 315.
[68] Lloyd, *Formularies of Faith*, 315-16.
[69] Lloyd, *Formularies of Faith*, 316.

made by their princes and governors, except they be against the commandments of God'.[70] Moreover, this same commandment compels subjects to aid the king in any public capacity should he require it.[71] The portion of the commentary applying the commandment to obedience to the prince lends further support by citing the two classic New Testament passages commanding obedience to earthly rulers, Romans 13.1-7 and 1 Peter 2.[72]

Much of the material comprising the exposition of the Fifth Commandment was not unique to the Henrician regime. This application which required obedience of subjects to secular princes was characteristic of a catechetical tradition in Europe dating to around the fourteenth century.[73] What makes this exposition of the Fifth Commandment significant, however, is the appropriation of it by the government and its theologians to promote a doctrine of justification in which obedience to the Ten Commandments, especially with reference to the king who exercises divinely prescribed authority over the national church, is the primary means of salvation. The government also made use of other doctrines in order to enhance its royal theology founded upon obedience. One of these was free will.

### Article of Free Will

The Article of Free Will has in view obedience of the Commandments: 'The commandments and threatenings of Almighty God in scripture, whereby man is called upon and put in remembrance what God would have him to do, most evidently do express and declare that man hath free will also now and after the fall of our first father Adam'.[74] The commandments as well as the threats for violating them imply human ability to keep them. This means that there 'should be some faculty or power left in man whereby he may, by the grace and help of God, (if he will receive it when it is offered unto him) understand his commandments, and freely consent and obey unto them: which thing of the catholic fathers is called freewill'.[75] Afterwards the article defines free will as 'a power of reason and will, by which good is chosen by the assistance of grace, or evil is chosen without the assistance of the same'.[76] Although, as attested here as well as later in the article, the ability to keep God's commandments depends upon divine grace,[77] it seems to make such enablement conditional upon the permission of the will. Thus, this discussion ascribes priority to the human will in the matter of obedience because it must first consent to receiving the grace

---

[70] Lloyd, *Formularies of Faith*, 316.
[71] Lloyd, *Formularies of Faith*, 316.
[72] Lloyd, *Formularies of Faith*, 317.
[73] Robert Bast, *Honor Your Fathers: Catechisms and the Emergence of a Patriarchal Ideology in Germany, 1400-1600* (Leiden: Brill, 1997), 146-234.
[74] Lloyd, *Formularies of Faith*, 359.
[75] Lloyd, *Formularies of Faith*, 359.
[76] Lloyd, *Formularies of Faith*, 359.
[77] Lloyd, *Formularies of Faith*, 361.

requisite for it. Obedience to the Commandments, then, depends chiefly upon the exercise of the will towards it.

## Article of Justification

The precedence of the will in obedience to the Commandments becomes even more apparent in the Article of Justification. The view of justification espoused in this article is more or less traditional.[78] Justification is described as the end result of conversion, ending in eventual salvation.[79] Moreover, the operation of grace whereby one is converted has a specific purpose: 'that by his grace we may walk so in his ways, that finally we may be reputed and taken as just and righteous in the day of judgment, and so receive the everlasting possession of the kingdom of heaven'.[80] In keeping with traditional soteriology, justification as the making of one righteous will occur on the Day of Judgment for having 'walked in his ways,' or having obeyed his commandments.

Because God's grace is prerequisite to doing any good, he is 'the principal cause and chief worker in our justification'.[81] However, one must receive this grace which will empower him so that he

> shall also be a worker by his free consent and obedience to the same, in the attaining of his own justification, and by God's grace and help shall walk in such works as be requisite to his justification, and so continuing, come to the perfect end thereof by such means and ways as God hath ordained.[82]

As in the Article of Free Will, the achievement of justification depends on obedience to what God has prescribed. Implicit in this article is a repudiation of Luther's doctrine of forensic justification, according to which God reckoned one righteous on the basis of Christ's imputed righteousness. What is affirmed instead is a justification which one had to earn by living obediently. This meant performing certain specific works discussed by the following article.

## The Article of Good Works

The article concerning good works begins with a declaration of the purpose towards which all preaching and teaching of the Word is to be directed:

> All preaching and learning of the word of God in Christ's church ought to tend to this end, that men may be induced, not only to know God, and to believe and trust in him, but also to honour and serve him with good works, wrought in faith and charity, and utterly to forsake the works of sin and the flesh, which whosoever do

---

[78] See Dickens, *The English Reformation*, 208; MacCulloch, *Thomas Cranmer*, 343-45; Ashley Null, *Cranmer's Doctrine of Repentance* (Oxford: Oxford University Press, 2000), 157-58; Bernard, *The King's Reformation*, 586-87.

[79] Lloyd, *Formularies of Faith*, 364.

[80] Lloyd, *Formularies of Faith*, 364.

[81] Lloyd, *Formularies of Faith*, 364.

[82] Lloyd, *Formularies of Faith*, 365.

commit (except they repent and amend by penance) they shall not (as St. Paul saith) inherit the kingdom of God.[83]

Although preaching of the Word should foster faith in God, its primary objective is to motivate the faithful to perform good works in service to him. As in the discussion about faith above, this article employs the Augustinian formula of faith working itself out in love in averring the necessity of good works. What is of particular significance is the manner in which the article subordinates faith to works. Faith is a means for the production of works, without which salvation cannot be realized. A description of the specific works meriting justification soon follows.

The explicit rejection of monastic piety represents a departure from traditional medieval soteriology.[84] Rather, 'we speak of such outward and inward works as God hath prepared for us to walk in, and be done in the faith of Christ, for love and respect to God, and cannot be brought forth only by man's power, but he must be prevented and holpen thereto by a special grace'.[85] Four things characterize those works to be performed for justification: God foreordained them; faith serves as the means for doing them; the honor of God is their purpose; one can perform them only with the aid of divine grace. Furthermore, these works are classified into two categories. The first, termed 'the works or fruits of righteousness,' are those bearing all four characteristics.[86] Although the deeds in and of themselves are imperfect, yet they are accepted because of Christ's passion, 'and [are] meritorious towards the attaining of everlasting life'.[87] The statements here emphasize God's gracious disposition towards such works and thus maintain justification while avoiding Luther's imputed righteousness. The second category of works consists of acts of penance, which, although they are inferior to the 'works of righteousness,' nevertheless are received by God since they are done by his grace 'in faith and good affection of heart'.[88] In both instances, grace and faith are devices for generating works as the actual means of justification. 'Wherefore as we continue and persevere in good works, so more and more we go forward and proceed in our justification, and in increasing in the same.'[89]

Finally, the article reveals the magistrate as a particular object of good works in a brief exposition of Titus 2.11. The explanation of the word 'justly' is the part of the overall exposition with special reference to the prince: '[I]n saying *justly*, he containeth all works of charity towards our neighbor, with due obedi-

[83] Lloyd, *Formularies of Faith*, 369.
[84] Lloyd, *Formularies of Faith*, 370; Bernard, *The King's Reformation*, 586-87.
[85] Lloyd, *Formularies of Faith*, 370.
[86] Lloyd, *Formularies of Faith*, 370.
[87] Lloyd, *Formularies of Faith*, 370-71.
[88] Lloyd, *Formularies of Faith*, 371.
[89] Lloyd, *Formularies of Faith*, 373.

ence to our princes, heads, and governors.'[90] While Christians are to perform general works of love to all, they demonstrate a particular kind of love to the prince, which is obedience. Obedience to the magistrate occurs in conjunction with spiritual devotion to God.[91] While these are distinguishable, they are inseparable.

## Conclusion

The theology of kingship which undergirded the official Reformation under Henry VIII encompassed a doctrine of justification whose ground was obedience to the commands of God. As indicated particularly in Sampson's *Oratio*, Gardiner's *De Vera Obedientia*, Henry's own comments on passages in the *Bishops' Book*, and the ideas of the *King's Book*, obedience to the divine commandments served as the necessary precondition for human justification. This in turn required a soteriology which began with the exertion of human effort via the exercise of the will with grace and faith serving as secondary supports. Hence the Henrician theology of kingship forthrightly repudiated the evangelical doctrine of justification by grace alone, and instead promulgated one in which grace made possible the duty of obedience which ultimately ensured salvation for the Christian subject. These works further show how the particular commandments of God were seen as culminating in the command to obey the king. Thus, during the Henrician period of the Reformation, justification was obedience to the king.

---

[90] Lloyd, *Formularies of Faith*, 374.
[91] Lloyd, *Formularies of Faith*, 375.

# CHAPTER 12

# Justification in the
# English reformers

## *H. Chris Ross*

Curators at the National Portrait Gallery in London were amazed when they discovered, through X-ray analysis, that a sixteenth-century painting of the Protestant archbishop and martyr, Thomas Cranmer, had originally depicted a Roman Catholic cardinal, whose identity is unknown.[1] For some reason, Cranmer's face had been painted over that of the original subject. Aside from being a curiosity of art history, this portrait presents a metaphor of the Church of England, as it appeared after emerging from the enormous changes of the sixteenth century: its body and its clothing—that is, its ecclesiological structure and its liturgy—still resembled in many ways the Catholic past; but its head—that is, its guiding theological mentality—had been radically transformed, or reformed, by Protestant ideas, one of the most important of which was, of course, justification by faith alone.

The pioneers of early English Protestantism featured in this chapter—John Wycliffe, William Tyndale, Thomas Cranmer, and Richard Hooker—all shared an appreciation for both new and old ways of thinking which this odd Cranmer portrait signifies. This appreciation was complemented by an intellectual cautiousness, which led all but one of them to adhere to Augustinian, moralistic emphases in their respective soteriologies, even as they accommodated the ideas of Luther, Calvin and other Protestants. In addition, because these English reformers were 'quick to hear' ancient, medieval, and modern witnesses on matters of doctrine, and 'slow to speak,' that is, to introduce new theological concepts themselves, one is hard-pressed to find a great deal of doctrinal innovation in their work. Nevertheless, their views are far from identical, and each one possesses nuances which distinguish it from other voices of the period.

---

[1]  This discovery is described in *The Work of Thomas Cranmer* (ed. G.E. Duffield; Philadelphia: Fortress Press, 1965), xiii, 275.

## John Wycliffe (1328–1384)

John Wycliffe lived almost two centuries before the Protestant Reformation swept through Europe, but his thoughts on justification are examined here because he has so often been portrayed as a forerunner of that historical phenomenon. John Bale, an English historian and contemporary of the sixteenth-century reformers, claimed that Wycliffe had 'shone like the morning star in the midst of a cloud,' and the fourteenth-century Oxford scholar has been called the 'Morning Star of the Reformation' ever since.[2] Wycliffe did share some important sentiments with the Protestants. He earned the name *Doctor Evangelicus* because he placed Scripture at the centre of his philosophy and theology.[3] He had strong predestinarian views and believed that God elected those who would be saved.[4] With a fervour that increased during the last years of his life, Wycliffe assailed the ungodliness of popes, cardinals, priests, and friars who lusted after temporal rather than heavenly rewards. He famously challenged the authority of the pope and transubstantiation, and denounced the veneration of saints, asserting that Christ is the sole mediator between God and humanity.[5] Yet, though he agreed with the reformers of the sixteenth century on several doctrines, justification *sola fide* was not one of them. The most basic components of Wycliffe's view of justification, in fact, seem to have been rather typical of the late medieval period.

In Wycliffe's day there were several different schools of opinion which divided over subtler elements of salvation doctrine, yet practically all of these used as their starting point the notion that *iustificare* (the Latin translation of the New Testament's *dikaiow*), means 'to make righteous,' as Augustine had concluded in the fifth century. 'What does "justified" mean,' he had written, 'other than "made righteous," just as "he justifies the ungodly" means "he makes a righteous person out of an ungodly person"?'[6] The influence which the Bishop of Hippo wielded upon the Middle Ages was enormous, in this matter as in many others. 'All medieval theology was Augustinian, to a greater or lesser extent,' Alister McGrath notes.[7] Within this Augustinian framework, which conceived of justification as encompassing a process of spiritual regeneration and sanctification, individuals were thought to gain acceptance before God by

2 John Bale, *Illustrium Maioris Britanniae Scriptorum . . . Summarium* (1548), fol. 154v; translated from Latin and cited by Margaret Aston in *Lollards and Reformers: Images and Literacy in Late Medieval Religion* (London: Hambledon, 1984), 245.
3 Stephen E. Lahey, *John Wyclif* (New York: Oxford University Press, 2009), 135.
4 Richard Rex, *The Lollards* (New York: Palgrave, 2002), 38.
5 Anne Hudson, *The Premature Reformation: Wycliffite Texts and Lollard History* (Oxford: Clarendon Press, 1988), 294, 311.
6 Augustine, *De Spiritu et Littera*, xxvi, 45; in *Corpus Scriptorum Ecclesiasticorum Latinorum* (Vienna: Verlag de österreichischen Akademie der Wissenschaften, 1886), 60.159.12-13; cited in Alister McGrath, *Iustitia Dei: A History of the Christian Doctrine of Justification* (Cambridge: Cambridge University Press, 2005), 47.
7 McGrath, *Iustitia Dei*, 38.

doing *quod in se est*, 'that which lies within them'.[8] Mercifully, God would reward those who, without the help of his grace, exercised contrition and took steps towards him, however meagre, by endowing them with a small deposit of grace. Such works, performed prior to the bestowal of grace, were thought to earn *congruous* merit. This term denoted that these works, though not inherently worthy of reward, nevertheless accurately manifested 'that which lay within' the individual before grace had come. After receiving the implantation of a germinal 'habit of grace,' the same individual was spiritually empowered to accomplish acts worthy of real or *condign* merit in increasing measure, as he or she cooperated with this infused grace. Ideally, a sufficiency of condign merit would bring them to final justification—actual spiritual renovation, in the Augustinian sense—and its concomitant reward, eternal life in glory.

Wycliffe subscribed to the common view that God mercifully infuses in contrite human beings a habit of grace, by which they are enabled to perform meritorious works and (eventually) to attain justification. Thus he affirmed the concept of congruous merit. The distinctiveness of Wycliffe's view lies in the fact that Wycliffe completely rejected the possibility of condign merit, reasoning that works performed with the assistance of grace cannot be justly credited to a person as worthy of reward, since these are not truly his or her own.[9] Inasmuch as humans need grace from start to finish in order to achieve justification, he concluded that all merit they earn is rightly considered congruous.

'Wyclif believed that God would recognize good works well done, not as a right, but because that was the only fair and reasonable thing to do,' writes John Stacey, who goes on to note that 'however pleasing this may appear it clearly took the sola from sola fide'.[10] Stacey's point is a crucial one: Wycliffe did not question the value of merit itself as a means to justification. In a passage which typifies his understanding of the doctrine, he expounds upon the keys Jesus said he would give to Peter (Matt. 16.19):

> Thes two keies ben sothli seid witt and power, to teche men the weie to Hevene and to opene hem the gatis. . . . Thes wordis weren not oonli seid unto Petre but comunli to the apostlis, as the Gospel tellith after, and, in persones of apostlis weren seid to prestis, and, as many men thenken to alle Cristen men. For if man have mercy on his soule, and unbinde it, or binde it, God bi his jugement in Hevene jugith the soule sich. For ech man that shal be dampned is dampned for his owne gilt, and ech man that shal be saved is saved bi his owne merit.[11]

Wycliffe believed that God predestines those who will be saved, but he reconciled this understanding with the medieval framework of merit by invoking the

---

8   See McGrath, *Iustitia Dei*, 107-16.
9   McGrath, *Iustitia Dei*, 148.
10  John Stacey, *John Wyclif and Reform* (Philadelphia: Westminster Press, 1964), 120.
11  *Sermons. The Gospel on the Chairinge of Seint Petre*, in *Select English Writings* (ed. Herbert E. Winn; New York: AMS, 1976), 95.

concept of 'hypothetical necessity,' claiming that God's election is contingent on the actions of individuals during their lives. 'According to Wyclif, God's will is to save all people,' explains J. Patrick Hornbeck,

> and accordingly God makes prevenient grace available to all. Those who accept God's offer receive merit as well as additional forms of grace, including the grace of predestination, whilst those who either reject prevenient grace, or accept it at one point but reject it later, are for that reason excluded from the congregation of the elect.[12]

Thus, Wycliffe can insist in his sermon that God judges souls according to their 'owne gilt' and their 'owne merit'. While God does predestine, salvation is granted on the basis of congruent effort, from the perspective of the believer.

Wycliffe's teaching on justification may have deviated slightly from the general medieval consensus, but he did not at any time envisage a reappraisal of the basic Augustinian interpretation of the term *iustificare*, as Luther, Calvin, and two of the other three English figures discussed here would. 'Wyclif's intent was far from that of the later Reformers,' Stephen Lahey writes, 'not least because he never seemed to imagine the doctrine of justification by faith.'[13] Luther's spokesman, Philip Melanchthon, concluded that Wycliffe 'neither understood nor believed the righteousness of faith'.[14] There were other traits of Wycliffe which were more typically medieval than reformist, as well. He regularly referred to the New Testament as the *lex Christi*, the 'law of Christ,' and he did not believe the elect could not know with certainty that they were such without being granted a special revelation from God.[15] The most that can be said about Wycliffe's soteriology, on behalf of the view which sees him as a precursor to Protestantism, is that he adopted a version of the received medieval consensus which placed more emphasis on divine sovereignty and grace than on human effort and in some doctrines peripheral to justification he anticipated the reformers. Given his high view of Scripture, it seems fair at least to speculate that if he had lived (and studied) longer, Wycliffe might have been compelled to challenge Rome's teaching on salvation at a more fundamental level, as his sixteenth-century admirers did.

---

[12] J. Patrick Hornbeck, *What is a Lollard?: Dissent and Belief in Late Medieval England* (Oxford: Oxford University Press, 2010), 34. In this observation Hornbeck follows Ian C. Levy, 'Grace and Freedom in the Soteriology of John Wyclif,' *Traditio* 60 (2005), 313.

[13] Lahey, *John Wyclif*, 189.

[14] Preface to *Sententiae veterum de Coena Domini*, cited in Stacey, *John Wyclif and Reform*, 120.

[15] Rex, *Lollards*, 41-42.

## William Tyndale (c.1494–1536)

With William Tyndale one reaches the age in which justification *sola fide* was understood and taught explicitly. Tyndale was likely an admirer of Wycliffe, and may have read his writings and those of his followers, but his interaction with Luther's ideas was much more consequential for his theology.[16] Even so, while Tyndale may have adopted the basic form of Luther's doctrine of justification *sola fide*, his articulation of it was unique in at least three notable ways.

First, Tyndale framed his soteriological ideas within the concept of a covenant made between the members of the Godhead: God the Son agreed to shed his blood to satisfy the justice of God the Father; those who trusted in the blood of Christ would be born again and brought into the covenant with the Father, as his children; and, God the Holy Spirit covenanted to apply the blood of Christ to those who had been chosen, and to regenerate and sanctify them. 'When we believe, and are come under the covenant of God, then are we sure of the Spirit by the promise of God, and then the Spirit accompanieth faith inseparably, and we begin to feel his working,' he explains in his *Prologue upon the Epistle to the Romans*, a paraphrase of Luther's Romans preface.[17]

For their part, as covenant participants, believers are expected to resolve to obey the Lord's commands: 'all the good promises which are made us throughout all the scripture, for Christ's sake, for his love, his passion or suffering, his blood-shedding or death, are all made us on this condition and covenant on our party,' he writes, 'that we henceforth love the law of God, to walk therein, and to do it, and fashion our lives thereafter'.[18] Tyndale's thought here diverges somewhat from that of Luther and other continental reformers in that he posits a set of relationships and transactions which are more familial than forensic.[19] 'The forensic covenant of the Lutheran and the Swiss Reformers gave a totally different and more formal approach to good works than we find in Tyndale,' writes Ralph Werrell. 'Tyndale's familial covenant showed that the Christian, as a child of God, does good works naturally because he has been born anew into God's family.'[20]

---

[16] Ralph S. Werrell mentions that Tyndale was involved in the publication of Lollard tracts at one time, and notes the similarity in rhetoric between Tyndale and the Lollards of his day, in *The Theology of William Tyndale* (Cambridge: James Clarke, 2006), 18; and Donald D. Smeeton makes a case for Lollard influence on the translator and martyr in *Lollard Themes in the Reformation Theology of William Tyndale* (Sixteenth Century Essays and Studies, no. 6: Kirksville, MO: Sixteenth Century Journal, 1986).

[17] *The Work of William Tyndale* (ed. G.E. Duffield: Philadelphia: Fortress Press, 1965), 125.

[18] *Exposition upon the Fifth, Sixth, and Seventh Chapters of Matthew, Work of Tyndale*, 185.

[19] Werrell portrays this covenant as the guiding motif of Tyndale's theology, in *Theology of William Tyndale*.

[20] Werrell, *Theology of William Tyndale*, 128.

Second, where Luther emphasised the contrast between law and grace, and often portrayed God's law in negative terms, Tyndale stressed the fact that the law, which accused and condemned the sinner before conversion, actually became a pleasing source of instruction for the born-again individual after conversion, through the work of the Holy Spirit.[21] MacCulloch observes Tyndale's fascination with the Old Testament law, which he thinks 'Luther would have found unhealthy.'[22] But for Tyndale it is the Spirit who makes the law appealing to believers. He explains: 'Hereof cometh it, that faith only justifieth, maketh righteous, and fulfilleth the law: for it bringeth the Spirit through Christ's deservings; the Spirit bringeth lust, looseth the heart, maketh him free, setteth him at liberty, and giveth him strength to work the deeds of the law with love, even as the law requireth.'[23]

A third, related feature of Tyndale's theology which distinguished it from Luther's was the strong link Tyndale posited between justification and sanctification. Some scholars, in fact, believe Tyndale blurred the boundary between these two, adhering stubbornly to an Augustinian notion of justification. Corneliu Simut claims that 'the line between being considered righteous and being made righteous is thin enough to be easily crossed' in his works. Carl Trueman says that Tyndale 'reworks Lutheran themes and categories to give them a meaning closer to the Augustinian-Reformed tradition than would have been acceptable in Wittenberg'. And Alister McGrath says that Tyndale 'tends to interpret justification as "making righteous",' especially in his early polemical works.[24] Nor was such a tendency unique to Tyndale, McGrath contends.

> The English Reformers seem to have understood that their continental colleagues developed a doctrine of justification *by fayth onely*, and that its leading feature was the total exclusion of human works from justification. Several of them also apparently understood this faith to be 'reputed' as righteousness. . . . They do not, however, appear to have realised precisely what was meant by the very different concept of imputation of righteousness, or its potential theological significance. In general, the English Reformers seem to have worked with a doctrine of justification in which humanity was understood to be *made* righteous *by fayth onely*, with good works being the natural consequence of justifying faith. This is clearly a

---

[21] Carl Trueman, 'Pathway to Reformation: William Tyndale and the Importance of the Scriptures', in P.E. Satterwhite and David F. Wright (eds), *A Pathway into the Scriptures* (Grand Rapids: Eerdmans, 1994), 22.

[22] Diarmaid MacCulloch, *The Later Reformation in England, 1547-1603* (New York: Palgrave, 2001), 57.

[23] *Romans, Work of Tyndale*, 125.

[24] McGrath, *Iustitia Dei*, 258; Corneliu C. Simut, *The Doctrine of Salvation in the Sermons of Richard Hooker* (New York: Walter de Gruyter, 2005), 68; Trueman, 'Pathway to Reformation,' 28.

possible interpretation of the Lutheran teaching . . . it is, however, not the most reliable such interpretation.[25]

Indeed, a small sampling of Tyndale's work reveals the ambiguity in his understanding of justification. A passage which could be interpreted as an Augustinian articulation of the doctrine is found toward the beginning of his *Prologue upon the Epistle to the Romans*, where the important terms Paul uses in his letter are addressed. As Werrell explains,

> For Luther our righteousness is not 'real' to us, 'It is called "the righteousness of God" because God gives it, and counts it as righteousness for the sake of Christ our Mediator, and makes a man to fulfil his obligation to everybody.' Whereas, for Tyndale, it [righteousness] is 'real', for 'Righteousness is even such a faith; and is called God's righteousness, or righteousness that is of value before God. For it is God's gift, and it altereth a man, and changeth him into a new spiritual nature, and maketh him free and liberal to pay every man his duty.'[26]

In the following excerpt from his *Exposition of Matthew*, Tyndale discusses the importance of justification and sanctification, portraying these as related but separate elements of 'the profession and religion of a christian man'.

> To believe in Christ for the remission of sins, and, of a thankfulness for that mercy, to love the law truly: that is to say, to love God that is the Father of all and giveth all; and Jesus Christ, that is Lord of us all . . . and our brethren for our Father's sake . . . and to long for the life to come, because this life cannot be led without sin. These three points (I say) are the profession and religion of a christian man, and the inward baptism of the heart, signified by the outer washing of the body. . . . The church of Christ, then, is the church of all them that believe in Christ for the remission of sin; and, of a thankfulness for that mercy, love the law of God purely and without glosses.[27]

Later in the same work, Tyndale answers the objections of those who would accuse him of joining good works (hope and love) to faith as requirements for justification. 'I answer,' he writes, 'though they be inseparable, yet they have separate and sundry offices. . . . Faith only, which is a sure and undoubted trust in Christ, and in the Father through him, certifieth the conscience that the sin is forgiven . . . and with such persuasions mollifieth the heart, and maketh her love God again and his law.'[28] In other words, a believer is justified by faith alone. Yet, later on in the same work, when Tyndale actually addresses the *na-*

---

[25] McGrath, *Iustitia Dei*, 262.

[26] Ralph S. Werrell, 'Tyndale's Disagreement with Luther in the Prologue to the Epistle to the Romans,' *Reformation and Renaissance Review* 7.1 (2005): 63. Werrell quotes *LW* 35.371; and Tyndale's *Prologue to Romans* (Parker Society), 1.494.

[27] *Work of Tyndale*, 189-90.

[28] *Work of Tyndale*, 192.

*ture* of justification, he seems to suggest that it involves the transformation of the believer—*making* him or her righteous.

> Now at the first covenant-making with God, and as oft as we be reconciled, after we have sinned, the righteousness cometh of God altogether. But after the atonement is made and we reconciled, then we be partly righteous in ourselves and unrighteous; righteous as far as we love, and unrighteous as far as the love is unperfect. And faith in the promise of God, that he doth reckon us for full righteous, doth ever supply that unrighteousness and imperfectness, as it is our whole righteousness at the beginning.[29]

Here, at least, Tyndale seems to articulate what could be interpreted as a proleptic, Augustinian understanding of justification, according to which God treats a person as righteous in view of the full righteousness he or she will one day possess, and in response to the person's present faith. It is unclear whether Tyndale failed to grasp fully the concept of imputed righteousness, as McGrath suggests, or whether he fully understood the Lutheran view of justification but chose to align more closely with Augustine. Considering that he lived during the nascent phase of the Reformation—he was executed before Lutheran ideas had made much headway in England—it is conceivable that he saw the espousal of Augustinian anti-Pelagianism, rather than full-blown Lutheranism, as the most prudent step forward on the path of reform.

## Thomas Cranmer (1489–1556)

It is somewhat difficult to trace the development of Thomas Cranmer's view of justification, since most of the documents attributed to him were actually drawn up in collaboration with other figures, both reformed and conservative. During his early career, Cranmer was tasked with accommodating the mercurial and reactionary sentiments of his master, Henry VIII, while proceeding with his own meticulous appraisal of the new theological ideas promulgated abroad. For these reasons, the writings he edited or authored later, during the reign of Edward VI—especially the *Homily of Salvation* and the *Forty-Two Articles*—are probably more reliable reflections of his mature, personal outlook on the doctrine. From a survey of the documents associated with his early and later life, one can make out in Cranmer's thought a progression from a more factitive, Augustinian understanding of justification to one very close to that of the continental reformers.

According to J.I. Packer, Cranmer made it his 'theological life's-work . . . first, to verify whether the upsurging of Luther and his followers . . . was the catholic faith or not, and second . . . to carry through in the English church a reordering of faith, worship, and discipline which would restore full catholicity

---

[29] *Work of Tyndale*, 268.

to it'.[30] Towards this end, he spent many hours poring over the words of Scripture and the works of the Fathers, the Scholastics, and modern reformers, with the goal of finding areas of doctrinal concord. Writes Packer,

> What Cranmer was looking for was a coincidence between the plain sense of Scripture, as he read it, and the teaching set forth as expository of Scripture, and in professed subjection to Scripture, by the leading divines of Christian history. He believed that where he perceived such a coincidence, there he could be sure that his own understanding of Scripture was not just a private eccentricity, but that he had found the true catholic faith.[31]

Given these habits, one should not be surprised to find that Cranmer was apparently slow to embrace the Lutheran conception of justification. The *Ten Articles*, drawn up in 1536 by Cranmer, along with a mixed group of reform-minded and conservative bishops, represents only a cautious step away from Roman Catholic doctrine, as one would expect. The article on justification borrowed from the 1530 Augsburg Confession, composed by Melanchthon, as well as his *Loci Communes*. 'This word justification signifieth remission of our sins,' it read, 'and our acceptation or reconciliation into the grace and favour of God, that is to say, our perfect renovation in Christ.'[32] One revision the committee made is telling. The Augsburg Confession read,

> Justification signifies the remission of sin and the reconciliation of acceptance of a person to eternal life. Now according to the Hebrew sense, 'to justify' is a forensic term; it is as if one were to say that the people of Rome justified Scipio when accused by the court, that is, absolved him, and pronounced him to be righteous.[33]

The *Ten Articles* omitted Melanchthon's exposition of forensic justification, and instead equated justification with 'perfect renovation in Christ'. To characterise the doctrine in this way, McGrath believes, 'eliminates any possibility of a distinction between *iustificatio* and *regeneratio*'.[34] The same article went on to underscore the importance of good works, affirming that 'sinners attain this justification by contrition and faith joined with charity'.[35]

Interestingly, two years later, when Cranmer revised these articles in collaboration with a group of Lutheran divines visiting England, he did not change this statement significantly. The *Thirteen Articles* of 1538, which were never approved as official statements of the English church, read, 'On justification, we teach that its proper meaning is remission of sins and acceptance or recon-

---

[30] *Work of Cranmer*, x-xxxvii.
[31] *Work of Cranmer*, xix.
[32] *The Church History of Britain* (ed. Thomas Fuller: Oxford: Oxford University Press, 1845), 3.153.
[33] Philipp Melanchthon, *CR* 21.421; in McGrath, *Iustitia Dei*, 260.
[34] McGrath, *Iustitia Dei*, 261.
[35] *Church History*, 153.

ciliation of us into the grace and favour of God; that is, true renewal in Christ.'[36] 'Perfect renovation in Christ' had become 'true renewal in Christ,' a phrase which still suggests a factitive justification, but the article went on to mention that sinners 'are not justified in virtue of the worth or merit of their repentance, or of any of their works or merits; but they are justified freely for Christ's sake through faith. . . . This faith God imputes for righteousness in his sight.'[37] It was during the same year, as Cranmer began to read and critique the king's theological contributions to what had been the 'Bishops' Book,' that MacCulloch says he 'for the first time gives extended unambiguous statements of the heart of his evangelical thought'.[38] All of this suggests that though the archbishop remained cautious, Lutheran ideas were beginning to have a greater influence on his teaching. In spite of this internal shift, during the last decade of Henry's life, Cranmer found it difficult to advance any reformation in the English church, as first the king and then a band of conservative adversaries challenged his efforts.

Under the regency of Edward Seymour, Cranmer enjoyed more liberty as a reformer and shaper of the church, and he also began to entertain Reformed doctrines more than Lutheran ones. He eschewed the Lutheran view of the Eucharist during the 1540s, and welcomed a handful of leading figures from Zurich and Strasbourg to England to assist the reformation there. The *First Book of Homilies* was published in 1547, and contained twelve sermons on key doctrines. Four were written by Cranmer, including the third, *Of the Salvation of Mankind by Only Christ Our Saviour from Sin and Death Everlasting*. This work 'displays the settled judgment at which Cranmer had arrived on this important issue,' Philip E. Hughes observes.[39] It is likely Cranmer would have agreed, since the eleventh of the *Forty-Two Articles*, composed under his leadership in 1552, refers readers back to this homily for a full explanation of the doctrine, proclaiming simply, 'Justification by only faith in Jesus Christ, in the sense as is declared in the Homily of Justification, is a most certain and wholesome doctrine for Christian men.'[40]

McGrath calls attention to the fact that 'the crucial concept of imputed righteousness is still not explicitly stated' in Cranmer's *Homily of Salvation*, which he says, 'simultaneously develops an Augustinian concept of justification and a Melanchthonian doctrine of justification *per solam fidem*'. But McGrath may be exaggerating Cranmer's deference to Augustine in the work. Though he does not present an extended discussion of imputation *per se*, Cranmer does

[36] *Work of Cranmer*, 3.
[37] *Work of Cranmer*, 4.
[38] Diarmaid MacCulloch, *Thomas Cranmer: A Life* (New Haven: Yale University Press, 1996), 209.
[39] Thomas Cranmer and Richard Hooker, *Faith and Works: Cranmer and Hooker on Justification* (ed. Philip E. Hughes: Wilton, CT: Morehouse-Barlow, 1982), 31.
[40] Cranmer and Hooker, *Faith and Works*, 33.

touch on the concept of imputation repeatedly in the *Homily*. He highlights three ways that Christ accomplishes the salvation of believers: by satisfying divine justice and taking God's wrath upon himself, by paying their ransom, and by fulfilling the law for them.

> [I]t pleased our heavenly Father of his infinite mercy, without any our desert or deserving, to prepare for us the most precious jewels of Christ's body and blood, whereby our ransom might be fully paid, the law fulfilled, and his justice fully satisfied. So that Christ is now the righteousness of all them that truly do believe in him. . . . So that now in him, and by him, every true Christian man may be called a fulfiller of the law, forasmuch as that which their infirmity lacked Christ's justice hath satisfied.[41]

There is no mention of an 'alien righteousness' in passages like this, but Cranmer describes something very close. Moreover, when he does use the phrase 'made righteous' in the work, Cranmer consistently qualifies it with the phrase 'before God,' so that he seems to imply, rather plainly, that he is speaking of forensic and not factitive justification. The opening lines of the *Homily* read, 'Because all men be sinners and offenders against God, and breakers of his law and commandments, therefore can no man by his own acts, works, and deeds . . . be justified and made righteous before God.'[42] Later in the work, he affirms that 'our own works do not justify us, to speak properly of our justification; that is to say, our works do not merit or deserve remission of our sins and make us, of unjust, just before God'.[43] In light of statements such as these, which are typical of the *Homily* from beginning to end, it seems more reasonable to conclude that Cranmer's mature understanding of justification represented a recognisable departure from 'an Augustinian concept of justification,' and was much closer to the forensic view held by continental Protestants.

### Richard Hooker (1554–1600)

Richard Hooker is best known for his treatise *Of the Lawes of Ecclesiastical Politie*, in which he laid down his vision of an English church established on the triple foundation of Scripture, human law, and natural reason. Ever since Hooker's own lifetime, there has been disagreement over the degree to which his theological positions were consistent with or deviated from the main tenets of the Reformation. Hooker's puritan colleague and outspoken critic, Walter Travers, was perhaps the first to question his views on nature, grace, and faith, and the hope of salvation he postulated for ignorant Catholics living in previous

---

41  Cranmer and Hooker, *Faith and Works*, 51-52.
42  Cranmer and Hooker, *Faith and Works*, 49.
43  Cranmer and Hooker, *Faith and Works*, 56.

centuries; but there have been many others.[44] In spite of the suspicion that has surrounded Hooker, in the work he composed that touches upon the doctrine of justification most directly—*A Learned Discourse of Justification, Works, and how the Foundation of Faith is Overthrown*—he seems to articulate a position that terminates near the centre of Protestant, and especially Reformed, belief, on nearly every important point.

Hooker's *Learned Discourse* was a written version of a sermon or set of sermons he delivered in 1586 at London's Temple Church, where he had been appointed master. These sermons were delivered in response to a controversy Hooker had entered into with Walter Travers. Travers had complained to the Privy Council concerning a previous sermon Hooker had preached, which was eventually published as *A Learned and Comfortable Sermon of the Certaintie and Perpetuitie of Faith in the Elect*. In it Hooker had challenged the conventional Protestant view which equated faith with full assurance of one's salvation, claiming that Habakkuk was a biblical example of a believer who struggled with weak faith and doubts about the goodness of God, but who was not cast off by God on that account. Travers had been alarmed by Hooker's claim 'that the assurance of that we believe by the word, is not so certeyne as of that we perceive by sense'.[45]

While Travers was correct that Hooker's stated position on faith diverged from the view taken by most reformed figures, it had nevertheless been common for most of these other writers to speak of faltering faith, as Debora K. Shuger notes.

> [T]he same Reformed theologians who define faith as 'a full and fixed assurednes' also (and often on the same page) grapple with the spiritual cost of this definition along lines very close to Hooker's: acknowledging that faith is always imperfect . . . Hooker's [sermon on] *Certaintie* seems to be the first serious attempt to resolve the contradiction entailed by holding that justifying faith cannot be and yet is always mingled with doubt.[46]

Instead of placing emphasis on the strength of the believer's faith, Hooker insisted, in both the *Learned Sermon* and his *Learned Discourse*, that it is the character and faithfulness of God himself which is most crucial in salvation. 'I know in whom I have beleved,' he wrote in the former, 'I am not ignorant of whose precious blood haith bene sheed for me, I have a sheperd full of kindness

---

[44] Ranall Ingalls provides a thorough historiographical review of studies on Hooker in 'Sin and Grace', in Torrance Kirby (ed.), *A Companion to Richard Hooker* (Brill's Companions to the Christian Tradition, vol. 8: Leiden: Brill, 2008), 152-60.

[45] Walter Travers, *A Supplication to the Privy Council* (The Folger Library Edition of the Works of Richard Hooker, vol. 5: ed. W. Speed Hill: Cambridge, MA: Belknap Press of Harvard University Press, 1977-1998), 200.

[46] Debora K. Shuger, 'Faith and Assurance', in Torrance Kirby (ed.), *A Companion to Richard Hooker* (Leiden: Brill, 2008), 232-33.

full of care and full of power: unto him I committ my self.'[47] As a corollary to this emphasis on God's reliability, Hooker consistently affirmed the doctrine of the saints' perseverance, though it was not yet called by that name. 'Hooker's sermons,' notes Shuger, '. . . repeatedly hinge on the promise that "the fayth wherby ye are sanctified cannot faile," for although "we are apte prone and redy to forsake god," yet he will not "forsake us".'[48]

In his *Learned Discourse*, Hooker was very clear in identifying justification as a forensic declaration of righteousness, separate from sanctification, which affects the believer inherently. 'The righteousness wherein we muste be found if we wilbe justified,' he wrote, 'is not our owne, therefore we cannott be justefied by any inherent qualitie. Christe hath merited rightuousnes for asmany as are found in hym.'[49] In his *Lawes* Hooker affirmed, 'We are partakers of Jesus Christ by imputation.'[50] He also underscored the importance of good works, while maintaining that they were a result of and not a means to justification. The fault of the Roman church, he said, was 'not that she requireth workes att theire handes that wilbe saved but that she attributeth unto workes a power of satisfying god for syn and a virtue to merite both grace here and in heaven glorye'.[51]

Somewhat uniquely, Hooker employed the concept of the union of divine and human natures in Christ, and Christ's union with his church, to show how Christ both justified and sanctified the church.

> [T]he participation of Christ importeth . . . a true actuall influence of grace where-by the life which wee live accordinge to godlines is his, and from him wee receave those perfections wherein our eternall happines consisteth. Thus wee participate Christ partelie by imputation, as when those things which he did and suffered for us are imputed unto us for righteousnes; partlie by habituall and reall infusion, as when grace is inwardlie bestowed while wee are on earth and after-wardes more fullie both our soules and bodies made like unto his in glorie.[52]

---

[47] *A Learned and Comfortable Sermon of the Certaintie and Perpetuitie of Faith in the Elect* (The Folger Library Edition of the Works of Richard Hooker, vol. 5: ed. W. Speed Hill. Cambridge, MA: Belknap Press of Harvard University Press, 1977–1998), 82.

[48] Shuger, 'Faith and Assurance'. She cites Hooker's *Sermon*, 73, and his *Discourse*, 140.

[49] Richard Hooker, *A Learned Discourse of Justification* (The Folger Library Edition of the Works of Richard Hooker, vol. 5: ed. W. Speed Hill: Cambridge, MA: Belknap Press of Harvard University Press, 1977–1998), 112.

[50] Richard Hooker, *Of The Lawes of Ecclesiastical Politie* (The Folger Library Edition of the Works of Richard Hooker, vol. 1: ed. W. Speed Hill: Cambridge, MA: Belknap Press of Harvard University Press, 1977–1998), 5.56.12; cited in Grislis, 'Hooker Among the Giants,' 6.

[51] Hooker, *Learned Discourse*, 153.

[52] *Lawes*, V.56.10; 2:242.26–243.9.

The most controversial aspect of Hooker's *Learned Discourse* was the theological tolerance he extended to Catholics whose only fault lay in their ignorant, misplaced belief in meritorious justification. Even though people in such a position might not believe in or understand the doctrine of justification by faith, Hooker insisted, they might still be saved by a merciful God.

> Gyve me a man what estate or condicion soever, yea a cardynall or a pope whome att thextreame pointe of his life afliction hath made to knowe him self, whose harte god hath towched with trewe sorowe for all his synnes and filled with love toward the gospell of Christe, whose eyes are opened to see the truth and his mouth to renounce all heresie and errour any waie opposite there unto, this one opynion of merites excepted which he thincketh God will require at his handes, and because he wanteth, therfore trembleth and is discouraged . . . and shall I thincke because of this one onlie error, that such a man toucheth not so much as the hem of Christes garment?[53]

This openness towards the errant was a logical development of Hooker's understanding of salvation: since faith is prone to falter, and it is God, the object of the believer's faith, who ultimately accomplishes the salvation of the faltering believer, it was not inconceivable that he would save one whose faith was adorned with some false elements, through no fault of his or her own.

## Conclusion

Three summary points may be drawn from this brief survey of key figures in England's Reformation. First, the claim of McGrath and others, that Augustine continued to influence reformers in England while Protestants elsewhere were formulating a more radical, forensic doctrine of justification, would appear to have some validity, especially as it pertains to the English reformers' understanding of the *nature* of justification. It is not certain that Tyndale ever adopted anything other than a factitive view of the doctrine, and it would seem Cranmer did so only during the last decade of his life.

Second, in all four of these figures' teaching one may observe an enthusiastic coupling of faith and works. Wycliffe, of course, understood works to be an actual component of justification, but his assertion that the elect will necessarily walk in meritorious righteousness is very similar to the refrain heard repeatedly from Tyndale, Cranmer and Hooker, that the same faith which lays hold of Christ for justification necessarily produces good works in the life of the justified.

And, third, the cautious approach to theological reflection which characterised these four figures did not prevent them from fashioning doctrinal expressions that were genuinely unique; in fact, their cautiousness may have facilitated their creativity. Wycliffe was exceptional in anticipating many of the new

---

[53] Hooker, *Learned Discourse*, 162.

sentiments of the sixteenth century, but one could argue it was the prolonged, honest attention he gave to Scripture, more than anything else, which provided the impetus for his reform efforts. One might also observe Tyndale's use of the covenant as an organising motif, Cranmer's emphasis on the three-fold work of Christ in satisfying justice, paying the sinner's ransom and fulfilling the law, and Hooker's honest appraisal of the weakness of faith and recourse to the faithfulness of God, and conclude that these distinctive ideas were, for the most part, products of each reformer's sincere deliberation—in other words, original—and not borrowed hastily or heedlessly from others. It would seem this same cautiousness has continued to guide the course of the Anglican Church, which has always negotiated an original *via media* between extremes.

# BIBLIOGRAPHY

PRIMARY WORKS

Bavinck, Herman, *Reformed Dogmatics*, volume 4 (ed. John Bolt; trans. John Vriend: Grand Rapids: Baker, 2008).

Bernard of Clairvaux. *De gratia et libero arbitrio* (Paris: Cerf, 1993).

—. *Sermons on the Song of Songs* (4 vols; trans. Kilian Walsh; Collegeville, MN: Cistercian Publications, 2005).

Beza, Theodore, *The Life of John Calvin.* In H. Beveridge and J. Bonnet (eds), *Selected Works of John Calvin*, vol. 1 (Grand Rapids, MI: Baker, 1983).

Calvin, John. *A Harmony of the Gospels Matthew, Mark, and Luke and the Epistles of James and Jude* (trans. A. W. Morrison: eds. D. W. Torrance and T. F. Torrance; Grand Rapids, MI: Eerdmans, 1972).

—. *Commentaries on the Catholic Epistles* (Edinburgh: Calvin Translation Society, 1855).

—. *Commentaries on the Epistle of Paul the Apostle to the Hebrews* (Grand Rapids, Mich.: Eerdmans, 1948).

—. *Commentaries on the First Twenty Chapters of the Book of the Prophet Ezekiel*, vol. 1 (trans. Thomas Myers; Grand Rapids, MI: Eerdmans, 1963).

—. *Commentaries on the Twelve Minor Prophets*, vol. 1, Hosea (trans. John Owen; Grand Rapids, MI: Eerdmans, 1963).

—. *Commentaries on the Twelve Minor Prophets*, vol. 5, Zechariah and Malachi (trans. John Owen; Grand Rapids, MI: Eerdmans, 1963).

—. *Commentary on the Book of Psalms*, vols. 1-4 (trans. James Anderson; Grand Rapids, MI: Eerdmans, 1963).

—. *Concerning Scandals* (trans. John W. Fraser; Grand Rapids: Eerdmans, 1978).

—. *Ioannis Calvini opera quae supersunt omnia* (ed. William Baum, Edward Cunitz and Edward Reuss: 59 vols: Brunsvigae: C.A. Schwetschke and Son (M. Bruhn), 1863-1990).

—. *Ioannis Calvini opera, selecta* (ed. Peter Barth, Wilhelm Niesel and Dora Scheuner: 5 vols: Munich: Kaiser, 1926-1952).

—. *Sermons on the Book of Micah* (trans. B.W. Farley; Phillipsburg: Presbyterian & Reformed, 2003).

—. *The Epistles of Paul the Apostle to the Romans and to the Thessalonians* (trans. Ross MacKenzie; eds. D. W. Torrance and T. F. Torrance; Grand Rapids, MI: Eerdmans, 1958).

—. *The Institutes of the Christian Religion* (The Library of Christian Classics, vols xx and xxi; trans. F.L. Battles; ed. John T. McNeill; London: SCM Press, 1960).

—. *Theological Treatises* (Philadelphia: Westminster Press, 1954).

Cranmer, Thomas, *The Miscellaneous Writings and Letters of Thomas Cranmer* (ed. John Edmund Cox; Cambridge: The Parker Society, 1846).

# Bibliography

—. *The Work of Thomas Cranmer* (ed. G.E. Duffield; Philadelphia: Fortress, 1965).

—. and Richard Hooker, *Faith and Works: Cranmer and Hooker on Justification* (ed. Philip E. Hughes, C.T. Wilton; Morehouse-Barlow, 1982).

Dillenberger, John, *John Calvin, Selections from His Writings* (Atlanta: Scholars Press, 1975).

Erasmus, Desiderius, *De Libero Arbitrio*. In *Desiderii Erasmi Opera Omnia* (New York: Georg Olms Verlag, 2001), 9.1215-1247.

—. *The Free Will*. In Ernst F. Winter (ed. and trans.) *Discourse on Free Will* (New York: Ungar, 1961), 1-94.

Fox[e], Edward, *Opus eximium. De Vera Differentia Regiae Postestatis et Ecclesiasticae, et quae sit ipsa veritas ac virtus utriusque.* London: Thomas Berthelet, 1534; STC (2nd ed.) / 11218 [Database online–subscription only]: Early English Books Online, http://eebo.chadwyck.com [24 July 2006].

—. *The true dyfferens betwen ye regial power and the Ecclesiasticall power Translated out of latyn by Henry lord Stafforde* London: 1548; STC (2nd ed.) / 11220 [Database online–subscription only]: Early English Books Online, http://eebo.chadwyck.com [24 July 2006].

Gardiner, Stephen, *De Vera Obedientia AN ORAtion made in Latine by the ryghte Reverend father in God Stephan B. of Winchestre, nowe lord Chauncellour of England, ... touchinge true Obedience ... and nowe translated into english and printed by Michael wood* Roan: Michael Wood, 1553; STC (2nd ed.) / 11585. [Database online–subscription only]: Early English Books Online, http://eebo.chadwyck.com [24 July 2006].

Hilary of Poitiers, *On the Trinity,* 1.4 and 18. In Henry Wace (ed.), *Nicene and Post Nicene Fathers of the Christian Church*, 2d series (New York: Christian Literature Publishing, 1899), 9.41-45.

Hooker, Richard, *Tractates and Sermons* (The Folger Library Edition of the Works of Richard Hooker, volume 5: ed. W. Speed Hill: Cambridge, Massachusetts. Belknap Press of Harvard University Press, 1990).

Luther, Martin. *De servo arbitrio*. In *D. Martin Luthers Werke: Kritische Gesamtausgabe* (Weimar: Hermann Böhlaus Nachfolger, 1908), 18.600-787.

—. *Dictata super Psalterium: Ps LXXXIV-CL.* In *D. Martin Luthers Werke: Kritische Gesamtausgabe* (Weimar: Hermann Böhlaus Nachfolger, 1885), 4.1-462.

—. *Divi Pauli apostoli ad Romanos Epistola.* In *D. Martin Luthers Werke: Kritische Gesamtausgabe*, vol. 56 (Weimar: Hermann Böhlaus Nachfolger, 1938).

—. *D. Martin Luthers Werke: Kritische Gesamtausgabe* (Weimar: Hermann Böhlaus Nachfolger, 1883–87).

—. *First Lectures on the Psalms II: Psalms 76-126* (trans. Herbert J. A. Bouman). In Hilton C. Oswald (ed.), *Luther's Works*, vol. 11 (St. Louis: Concordia, 1976).

—. *In epistolam Pauli ad Galatas commentarius* (1519). In *D. Martin Luthers Werke: Kritische Gesamtausgabe* (Weimar: Hermann Böhlaus Nachfolger, 1884), 2.436–618.

—. *In epistolam Pauli ad Galatas Commentarius* (1535). *D. Martin Luthers Werke: Kritische Gesamtausgabe*, vol. 40/1 (Weimar: Hermann Böhlaus Nachfolger, 1911).

—. *Lectures on Galatians* (1519). (trans. Richard Jungkuntz). In Walter A. Hansen (ed.), *Luther's Works* (St. Louis: Concordia, 1964), 27.151-410.

—. *Lectures on Galatians* (1535): *Chapters 1-4* (trans. Jaroslav Pelikan). In Walter A. Hansen (ed.), *Luther's Works*, vol. 26 (St. Louis: Concordia, 1963).

—. *Lectures on Romans: Glosses and Scholia.* (trans. Walter G. Tillmanns and Jacob A. O. Preus). In Hilton C. Oswald (ed.), *Luther's Works*, vol. 25 (St. Louis: Concordia, 1972).

—. *Luthers Vorlesung über den Römerbrief*, 1515/1516 (Leipzig: Dieterich, 1908).

—. *Luthers Werke.* In Emanuel Hirsch (ed.), *Auswahl*, vol. 7: *Predigten* (3rd ed. Berlin: Walter de Gruyter, 1962).

—. *Luther's Works* (American edition: ed. Jaroslav Pelikan and Helmut T. Lehman, 54 vols: St. Louis: Concordia Publishing House / Philadelphia: Fortress Press, 1955-1957).

—. 'Preface to the New Testament'. In Theodore Bachmann (ed.), *Luther's Works* (trans. Charles M. Jacobs; St. Louis: Concordia, 1960), 35.357-362.

—. *Select Works of Martin Luther* (ed. Henry Cole: London: T. Bensley, 1826).

—. *Sermons on the Gospels* (2 vols; Rock Island, IL: Augustana Book Concern, 1871).

—. *Table Talk.* In Jaroslav Pelikan (ed.), *Luther's Works*, vol. 54 (ed. and trans. Theodore G. Tappert; St. Louis: Concordia, 1967).

—. *The Bondage of the Will.* In Philip S. Watson and Helmut T. Lehmann (eds), *Luther's Works*, vol. 33. (trans. Philip S. Watson and Benjamin Drewery; St. Louis: Concordia, 1972).

—. *The Book of Concord* (St Louis: Concordia Publishing House, 1950).

—. *The Freedom of a Christian.* In Harold J. Grimm and Helmut T. Lehmann (eds), *Luther's Works* (trans. W. A. Lambert and Harold J. Grimm; St. Louis: Concordia, 1957), 31.327-377.

—. 'Two Kinds of Righteousness'. In Harold J. Grimm (ed.), *Luther's Works* (trans. Lowell J. Satre; St. Louis: Concordia, 1957), 31.293-306.

Marbeck, Pilgram. *Pilgram Marbecks Antwort auf Kaspar Schwenckfeld's Beurteilung des Buches der Bundesbezeugung von 1542* (ed. Johann P. Loserth; Vienna: Carl Fromme, 1929).

*The Writings of Pilgram Marpeck* (trans. William Klassen and Walter Klaassen; Kitchener, ON: Herald, 1978).

Melanchthon, Philip. *Loci Communes 1543* (trans. J. A. O. Preus; St. Louis: Concordia, 1992).

—. *Loci communes theologici*. In the Library of Christian Classics (trans. Lowell J. Sartre; revised Wilhelm Pauck; Philadelphia: Westminster, 1969), 19.18-152.

—. *Melanchthon on Christian Doctrine. Loci Communes (1555)* (ed. Clyde Manschrenk: Grand Rapids: Baker, 1983).

—. *Paul's Letter to the Colossians* (trans. D. C. Parker; Sheffield: Almond, 1989).

—. *Prima Aetas Locorum Theologicorum ab Ipso Melanthone Editorum*. In Henry Ernest Bindseil (ed.), *Philippi Melanthonis Opera quae supersunt omnia* (Corpus Reformatorum, vol. 21; Brunswick, NJ: C. A. Schwetschke and Son, 1854; reprint, Johnston Reprint., 1964), 59-228.

—. *Secunda Aetas Locorum Theologicorum ab Ipso Melanthone Editorum*. In Henry Ernest Bindseil (ed.), *Philippi Melanthonis Opera quae supersunt omnia* (Corpus Reformatorum, vol. 21; Brunswick, NJ: C. A. Schwetschke and Son, 1854; reprint, Johnston Reprint., 1964), 230-559.

—. *Tertia Aetas Locorum Theologicorum ab Ipso Melanthone Editorum*. In Henry Ernest Bindseil (ed.), *Philippi Melanthonis Opera quae supersunt omnia*, (Corpus Reformatorum, vol. 21; Brunswick, NJ: C. A. Schwetschke and Son, 1854; reprint, Johnston Reprint., 1964), 560-1106.

Oecolampadius, Johann. *In Epistolam ad Hebraeos Ioannis Oecolampadii, Explanationes* (Strassburg: Mathiam Apiarium, 1534).

—. *In Epistolam B. Pauli Apost. ad Rhomanos Adnotationes à Ioanne Oecolampadio Basileae Praelectae* (Basel: Andream Cratandrum, 1525).

—. *In Epistolam Ioannis Apostoli Catholicam Primam, Ioannis Oecolampadii Demegoriae, Hoc Est, Homiliae Una & Viginti* (Nuremburg: Iohann Petreium, 1524).

—. *In Librum Iob Exegemata. Opus Admodum Eruditum, ac Omnibus Divinae Scripturae Studiosis Utile* (Geneva: Ioannis Crispini, 1554).

Origen, 'Against Celsus,' 6.65. In Alexander Roberts and James Donaldson (eds), *The Ante-Nicene Fathers* (Grand Rapids, MI: Eerdmans, 1956), 4.603.

Sampson, Richard. *Richardi Sampsonis, Regii Sacelli Decani Oratio, qua docet, hortatur, admonet omens potissimum Anglos regiae dignitati cum primis ut obediant, quia verbum dei precipit, episcopo Romano ne sint audientes, qui nullo iure divino, in eos quincq potestatis habet, postq ita iubet et rex, ut illi non obediant...* London: Thomas Berthelet, 1533; STC (2nd ed.) / 21681. [Database online–subscription only]: Early English Books Online, http://eebo.chadwyck.com [24 July 2006].

Tyndale, William. *The Work of William Tyndale* (ed. G.E. Duffield: Philadelphia: Fortress Press, 1965).

Winton, Stephani. Episcopi *de Vera Obedientia Oratio.* Hamburg: In officina Francisci Rhodi, 1536; STC (2nd ed.) / 11584. [Database online–subscription only]: Early English Books Online, http://eebo.chadwyck.com [24 July 2006].

# Bibliography

Wyclif, John. *The English Works of Wyclif, Hitherto Unprinted* (ed. F.D. Matthew. London: Trübner & Co., 1880).
—. *Wyclif: Select English Writings* (ed. Herbert E. Winn: New York: AMS Press, 1976).


## SECONDARY WORKS

Allen, R. Michael, *The Christ's Faith: A Dogmatic Account* (London: T. & T. Clark, 2009).

Althaus, Paul, *The Ethics of Martin Luther* (Philadelphia: Fortress Press, 1972).

—. *The Theology of Martin Luther* (Philadelphia: Fortress Press, 1966).

Asendorf, Ulrich, *Die Theologie Martin Luthers nach seinen Predigten* (Göttingen: Vandenhoeck & Ruprecht, 1988).

Aulén, Gustaf, *Christus Victor: An Historical Study of the Three Main Types of the Idea of the Atonement* (New York: Macmillan, 1986).

—. *Die Bekenntnisschriften der evangelisch-lutherischen Kirche, herausgegeben im Gedenkjahr der Augsburgischen Konfession 1930* (4th ed.; Göttingen: Vandenhoeck & Ruprecht, 1959).

Barnhouse, Ruth Tiffany and Urban T. Holmes, III (eds), *Male and Female: Christian Approaches to Sexuality* (New York: Seabury Press, 1976).

Bast, Robert, *Honor Your Fathers: Catechisms and the Emergence of a Patriarchal Ideology in Germany, 1400-1600* (Leiden: Brill, 1997).

Bayer, Oswald, 'Martin Luther.' In Carter Lindberg (ed.) *The Reformation Theologians. An Introduction to Theology in the Early Modern Period* (Oxford: Blackwell, 2002), 51-66.

Bernard, G.W., *The King's Reformation: Henry VIII and the Remaking of the English Church* (New Haven: Yale University Press, 2005).

Billings, J. Todd, *Calvin, Participation and the Gift: the Activity of Believers in Union with Christ.* Changing Paradigms in Historical and Systematic Theology (New York: Oxford University Press, 2007).

—. 'John Calvin: United to God through Christ.' In Michael Christensen and Jeffery A. Wittung (eds), *Partakers of the Divine Nature: the History and Development of Deification in the Christian Tradition* (Grand Rapids: Baker Academic, 2008), 200-218.

Blough, Neal, *Christ in our Midst: Incarnation, Church, and Discipleship in the Theology of Pilgram Marpeck* (Kitchener, ON: Pandora, 2007).

Bouwsma, William J., *John Calvin: A Sixteenth Century Portrait* (Oxford: Oxford University Press, 1988).

Boersma, Hans, *Violence, Hospitality and the Cross. Reappropriating the Atonement Tradition* (Grand Rapids: Baker, 2004).

Boyd, Stephen B., *Pilgram Marpeck: His Life and Social Theology* (Durham: Duke University Press, 1992).

Braaten, Carl E. and Robert W. Jenson (eds), *Union with Christ: The New Finnish Interpretation of Luther* (Grand Rapids: Eerdmans, 1998).

Bibliography

Bray, Gerald (ed.), *Documents of the English Reformation* (Minneapolis: Fortress Press, 1994).

Brecht, Martin, *Martin Luther* (3 vols; Philadelphia: Fortress Press, 1985, 1990, 1993).

Briggs, John H.Y. (ed), *A Dictionary of European Baptist Life and Thought* (Milton Keynes: Paternoster, 2009).

Bromiley, G.W., *Zwingli and Bullinger* (Philadelphia: Westminster Press, 1953).

Brown, Peter, *Augustine of Hippo* (Berkley, CA: University of California Press, 2000).

Buchwald, Georg, '*Einleitung.*' In WA 52.vii-xxxv.

Burnett, Amy Nelson, *Teaching the Reformation: Ministers and Their Message in Basel, 1529-1629* (Oxford: Oxford University Press, 2006).

Canlis, Julie, *Calvin's Ladder: A Spiritual Theology of Ascent and Ascension* (Grand Rapids: Eerdmans, 2010).

Châtillon, Jean, 'L'influence de S. Bernard,' *Analecta sacri ordinis cisterciensis* IX (1953), 280-81.

Chibi, Andrew, 'Richard Sampson, His "Oratio," and Henry VIII's Royal Supremacy,' *Journal of Church and State* 39 (1997), 543-560.

Christ, Carol and Judith Plaskow (eds), *Womanspirit Rising: A Feminist Reader in Religion* (San Francisco: Harper & Row, 1979).

Clark, R. Scott, '*Iustitia Imputata Christi*: Alien or Proper to Luther's Doctrine of Justification?' *Concordia Theological Quarterly* 70 (2007), 269-310.

Codling, James L., *Calvin: Ethics, Eschatology, and Education* (Cambridge Scholars Publishing, 2010).

Cornick, D., 'The Reformation Crisis in Pastoral Care.' In G.R. Evans (ed.), *A History of Pastoral Care* (London: Cassell, 2000), 223-251.

Cottret, Bernard, *Calvin A Biography* (Grand Rapids: Eerdmans, 1995).

Daly, Mary, 'After the Death of God the Father: Women's Liberation and the Transformation of Christian Consciousness.' In Carol Christ and Judith Plaskow (eds), *Womanspirit Rising: A Feminist Reader in Religion* (San Francisco: Harper & Row, 1979), 53-62.

—. *Beyond God the Father: Towards a Philosophy of Women's Liberation* (Boston: Beacon Press, 1973).

Davie, Martin, 'Calvin's Influence on the Theology of the English Reformation,' *Ecclesiology* 6 (2010), 315-341.

Davis, Thomas J., *The Clearest Promises of God: The Development of Calvin's Eucharistic Teaching* (New York: AMS Press, 1995).

Demura, Akira. 'Two Commentaries on the Epistle to the Romans: Calvin and Oecolampadius.' In Wilhelm H. Neuser, and Brian G. Armstrong (eds). *Calvinus Sincerioris Religionis Vindex* (Kirksville, Mo.: Sixteenth Century Journal Publishers, 1997), 165-188.

Dickens, A.G., *The English Reformation* (2nd ed. University Park, Pa.: Pennsylvania State University Press, 1993).

# Bibliography

Dieter, Theodor, 'Why Does Luther's Doctrine of Justification Matter Today?' In C. Helmer (ed.), *The Global Luther* (Minneapolis: Fortress Press, 2009), 189-209.

Doberstein, John W. 'Introduction.' In *Sermons* I, LW 51.xi-xxi.

Doumergue, Emile, August Lane, Herman Bavinck, and Benjamin B. Warfield, *Calvin and the Reformation* (New York: Fleming H. Revell, 1909).

Dinfried, Karl P., 'Paul and the Revisionists: Did Luther Really Get it all Wrong?' *Dialog* 46.1 (2007), 31-39.

Dunn, James D. G., *Jesus, Paul, and the Law: Studies in Mark and Galatians* (Louisville: Westminster John Knox Press, 1990).

—. 'The New Perspective on Paul,' *Bulletin of the John Rylands University Library of Manchester* 65 (1983), 95-122.

Ebeling, Gerhard. *Evangelische Evangelienauslegung: Eine Untersuchung zu Luthers Hermeneutik* (Darmstadt: Wissenschaftliche Buchgesellschaft, 1962).

Elwood, Christopher, *The Body Broken: The Calvinist Doctrine of the Eucharist and the Symbolization of Power in Sixteenth-Century France* (New York: Oxford, 1999).

Eppley, Daniel F., 'Richard Hooker.' In Carter Lindberg (ed.), (ed.) *The Reformation Theologians. An Introduction to Theology in the Early Modern Period* (Oxford: Blackwell, 2002), 253-266.

Evans, G. R., 'Calvin on Signs: An Augustinian Dilemma,' *Renaissance Studies* 3 (1989), 35-45.

—. *John Wyclif: Myth and Reality* (Downers Grove: InterVarsity Press Academic, 2005).

Ferguson, Sinclair, 'Calvin on the Lord's Supper and Communion with Christ.' In David F. Wright and David Stay (eds), *Serving the Word of God: Celebrating the Life and Ministry of James Philip* (Edinburgh: Rutherford House, 2002), 203-17.

Ferguson, W.K., *The Renaissance in Historical Thought. Five Centuries of Interpretation* (Cambridge, MA: Houghton Mifflin, 1948).

Finger, Thomas N., *A Contemporary Anabaptist Theology: Biblical, Historical, Constructive* (Downers Grove, IL: InterVarsity Press, 2004).

Fink, David C., 'Divided by Faith: The Protestant Doctrine of Justification and the Confessionalization of Biblical Exegesis' (unpublished doctoral dissertation; Duke Divinity School, 2010).

Fitzer, Joseph, 'The Augustinian Roots of Calvin's Eucharistic Thought.' In Richard Gamble (ed.), *Calvin's Ecclesiology: Sacraments and Deacons Articles on Calvin and Calvinism* (New York: Garland, 1992), 165-196.

Ford, James Thomas, 'Preaching in the Reformed Tradition.' In Larissa Taylor (ed.), *Preachers and People in the Reformations and Early Modern Period* (Boston: Brill, 2003), 65-88.

Forell, George W., 'Justification and Eschatology in Luther's Thought,' *Church History* 38.2 (1969), 164-174.

Bibliography

Friedmann, Robert, *The Theology of Anabaptism* (Scottdale, PA: Herald Press, 1973).

Frymire, John M., *The Primacy of the Postils: Catholics, Protestants, and the Dissemination of Ideas in Early Modern Germany* (Leiden: Brill, 2010).

Gaffin, Richard, 'Justification and Union with Christ.' In David W. Hall and Peter A. Lillback (eds), *A Theological Guide to Calvin's Institutes* (Phillipsburg, NJ, Presbyterian &Reformed, 2008).

Gamble, Richard, 'Sacramental Continuity Among Reformed Refugees.' In Frank A. James (ed.), *Peter Martyr Vermigli and the European Reformations: semper reformanda* (Leiden: Brill, 2004), 97-112.

Garcia, Mark, *Life in Christ: Union with Christ and Twofold Grace in Calvin's Theology* (Milton Keynes: Paternoster, 2008).

Gathercole, Simon, 'The Doctrine of Justification in Paul and Beyond: Some Proposals.' In Bruce L. McCormack (ed.), *Justification in Perspective. Historical Developments and Contemporary Challenges* (Grand Rapids: Baker Academic / Edinburgh: Rutherford House, 2006), 219-241.

George, Timothy, 'Martin Luther.' In Jeffrey P. Greenman and Timothy Larsen (eds), *Reading Romans Through the Centuries* (Grand Rapids: Brazos, 2005), 101-119.

—. *Reading the Scripture with the Reformers* (Downers Grove: InterVarsity Academic, 2011).

Gerrish, Brian A. (ed.), 'Calvin's Eucharistic Piety.' In David Foxgrover (ed.), *Calvin and Spirituality* (Grand Rapids: CRC, 1998), 52-65.

—. *Grace and Gratitude: The Eucharistic Theology of John Calvin* (Minneapolis: Fortress Press, 1993).

—. *Reformers in Profile* (Philadelphia: Fortress Press, 1967).

—. 'Sovereign Grace. Is Reformed Theology Obsolete?' *Interpretation* 57 (2003), 45-57.

—. 'The Chief Article—Then and *Now*,' *Journal of Religion* 63 (1983), 355-375.

—. '"To the Unknown God" Luther and Calvin on the Hiddenness of God.' In *The Old Protestantism and the New: Essays on the Reformation Heritage* (Chicago: University of Chicago Press, 1982), 131-159, 334-351.

Green, Joel B. and Mark D. Baker, *Recovering the Scandal of the Cross* (Carlisle: Paternoster, 2000).

Grosse, Christian, *Les Rituels de La Cene: le Culte Eucharistique Reforme a Geneve (XVIe - XVIIe siecles)* (Geneva: Droz, 2008).

Hall, David W. (ed.), *Tributes to John Calvin: A Celebration of his Quincentenary* (Phillipsburg, NJ: Presbyterian &Reformed, 2010).

Härle, Wilfred, 'Luthers reformatorische Entdeckung—damals und heute,' *Zeitschrift für Theologie und Kirche* 99 (2002), 278-295.

Heintze, Gerhard. *Luthers Predigt von Gesetz und Evangelium* (München: Chr. Kaiser Verlag, 1958).

Heinze, Rudolph W., *Reform and Conflict* (Grand Rapids: Baker, 2005).

Hendrix, Scott, 'Rerooting the Faith: The Reformation as Re-Christianization,' *Church History* 69.3 (2000), 558-577.

Hesselink, I. John, 'Calvin, the Holy Spirit, and Mystical Union,' *Perspectives* 13.1 (January 1998), 15-18.

Holm, Bo K., Zur Funktion der Lehre bei Luther. Die Lehre als rettendes Gedankenbild gegen Sünde, Tod und Teufel,' *Kerygma und Dogma* 51.1 (2005), 17-32.

Hornbeck, J. Patrick, 'Lollard Sermons?: Soteriology and Late Medieval Dissent,' *Notes and Queries* 53.1 (2006), 26-30.

—. *What is a Lollard?: Dissent and Belief in Late Medieval England* (Oxford: Oxford University Press, 2010).

Horton, Michael, *Covenant and Salvation: Union with Christ* (Louisville, KY: Westminster/John Knox, 2007).

Hudson, Anne, *The Premature Reformation: Wycliffite Texts and Lollard History* (Oxford: Clarendon Press, 1988).

Hughes, Philip E., *Theology of the English Reformers* (Grand Rapids: Eerdmans, 1966).

Huijgen, Arnold, 'Divine Accommodation and Divine Transcendence in John Calvin's Theology.' In H. J. Selderhuis (ed.), *Calvinus sacrarum literarum interpres: Papers of the International Congress on Calvin Research.* Reformed Historical Theology (Gottingen: Vandenhoeck & Ruprecht, 2008), 119-130.

Hunsinger, George, 'A Tale of Two Simultaneities: Justification and Sanctification in Calvin and Barth.' In C. Raynal (ed.), *John Calvin and the Interpretation of Scripture* (Grand Rapids: Calvin Studies Society, 2006), 223-245.

Ingalls, Ranall, 'Sin and Grace.' In Torrance Kirby (ed.), *A Companion to Richard Hooker* (Brill's Companions to the Christian Tradition, vol. 8: Leiden: Brill, 2008), 151-183.

Jaarmsa, Cornelius, *The Educational Philosophy of Herman Bavinck* (Grand Rapids: Eerdmans, 1935).

James, Frank A. III., 'Peter Martyr Vermigli.' In Carter Lindberg (ed.), *The Reformation Theologians. An Introduction to Theology in the Early Modern Period* (Oxford: Blackwell, 2002), 198-212.

Janetzki, Elvin W., 'The Place of the Historic Confessions in Christendom Today.' In H.P. Hamann (ed.), *Theologia Crucis. Studies in Honour of Hermann Sasse* (Adelaide: Lutheran Publishing House, 1975), 89-105.

Janse, Wim, 'Calvin's Eucharistic Theology: Three Dogma-Historical Observations.' In H. J. Selderhuis (ed.), *Calvinus sacrarum literarum interpres: Papers of the International Congress on Calvin Research.* (Gottingen: Vandenhoeck & Ruprecht, 2008), 37-69.

Johnson, Marcus P., 'Eating by Believing: Union with Christ in the Soteriology of John Calvin' (unpublished doctoral dissertation; Toronto School of Theology, 2006).

—. 'New or Nuanced Perspective on Calvin? A Reply to Thomas Wenger,' *Journal of the Evangelical Theological Society* 51. 3 (2008), 543-558.

—. 'The Genius of Luther's Theology. A Wittenberg Way of Thinking for the Contemporary Church,' *Calvin Theological Journal* 44.1 (2009), 189-191.

Kadia, Heino O., 'Luther's Theology of the Cross,' *Concordia Theological Quarterly* 63 (1999), 169-204.

Kärkkäinen, Veli-Matti, 'Theology of the Cross: A Stumbling Block to Pentecostal/Charismatic Spirituality.' In Wonsuk Ma and Robert P. Menzies (eds), *Essays in Honour of Russell P. Spittler* (New York: T. & T. Clark, 2004), 150–63.

Kelly, Robert A., 'The Suffering Church: A Study of Luther's *Theologia Crucis*,' *Concordia Theological Quarterly* 50 (1986), 3-17.

Kim, Jae Sung, 'Prayer in Calvin's Soteriology.' In David W. Hall (ed.), *Tributes to John Calvin: A Celebration of his Quincentenary* (Phillipsburg, NJ: Presbyterian & Reformed, 2010).

Kirby, W. and J. Torrance. *The Zurich Connection and Tudor Political Theology* (Studies in the History of the Christian Tradition, vol 131: Leiden: Brill, 2007).

Klaassen, Walter and William Klassen. *Marpeck: A Life of Dissent and Conformity* (Kitchener, ON: Herald Press, 2008).

Klassen, William. *Covenant and Community: The Life, Writings, and Hermeneutics of Pilgram Marpeck* (Grand Rapids: Eerdmans, 1968).

Köhler, W. '*Einleitung zur Wartburgpostille.*' In WA $10^{1,2}$.xli-lxxix.

Kolb, Robert, 'God's Gift of Martyrdom: The Early Reformation Understanding of Dying for the Faith,' *Church History* 64 (1995), 399-411.

—. 'Luther on the Theology of the Cross,' *Lutheran Quarterly* 16 (2002), 443-466.

—'Luther's Theology of the Cross: Fifteen Years after Heidelberg: Lectures on the Psalms of Ascent,' *Journal of Ecclesiastical History* 61 (2010), 69-85.

—. 'Martin Chemnitz.' In Carter Lindberg (ed.), *The Reformation Theologians. An Introduction to Theology in the Early Modern Period* (Oxford: Blackwell, 2002), 140-153.

Kreitzer , Beth. 'The Lutheran Sermon.' In Larissa Taylor (ed.), *Preachers and People in the Reformations and Early Modern Period* (Boston: Brill, 2003), 35-63.

Küng, Hans, *Justification* (London: Thomas Nelson, 1964).

Lahey, Stephen E., *John Wyclif* (New York: Oxford University Press, 2009).

Lane, A.N.S., *Justification by Faith in Catholic-Protestant Dialogue* (London: T. & T. Clark, 2002).

—. 'The Role of Scripture in Calvin's Doctrine of Justification.' In C. Raynal (ed.), *John Calvin and the Interpretation of Scripture* (Grand Rapids: Calvin Studies Society, 2006), 368-384.

Lawrence, J. David, 'Medieval Refinements in Augustinian Theology. Scholastic Foundations for the reformation,' *Fides et Historia* 33.2 (2001), 53-62.

Bibliography

Lecerf, Auguste, 'The Liturgy of the Holy Supper at Geneva in 1542.' In
Richard Gamble (ed.), Floyd D. Shafer (trans), *Calvin's Ecclesiology:
Sacraments and Deacons. Articles on Calvin and Calvinism* (New York:
Garland, 1992), 207-214.

Lehmann, Detlef, 'Luther als Prediger.' In *Oberurseler Hefte*, Heft 17
(Oberursel: Fakultät der Luth. Theol. Hochschule Oberursel, 1983), 5-23.

Levy, Ian C., 'Wyclif and the Christian Life.' In Ian C. Levy (ed.), *A
Companion to John Wyclif: Late Medieval Theologian* (Brill's Companions
to the Christian Tradition, vol. 4: Leiden: Brill, 2006), 293-363.

Lewis, Peter, *The Glory of Christ* (Chicago: Moody Press, 1997).

Lidgett, J. Scott, *The Fatherhood of God in Christian Truth and Life* (London:
Epworth, 1903).

Lindberg, Carter, *The European Reformations* (Oxford: Blackwell, 1996).

—. (ed.) *The Reformation Theologians. An Introduction to Theology in the
Early Modern Period* (Oxford: Blackwell, 2002).

Lloyd, C. (ed.), *Formularies of Faith* (Oxford: Clarendon Press, 1825).

Loewenich, Walther Von, *Luther's Theology of the Cross* (trans. Herbert J. A.
Bouman: Minneapolis: Augsburg, 1976).

Lohse, Bernhard, *Martin Luther's Theology: Its Historical and Systematic
Development* (Minneapolis: Fortress Press, 1999).

MacArthur, John, R.C. Sproul, Joel Beeke, John Gerstner, and Don Kistler,
*Justification by Faith Alone* (Morgan, PA: Soli Deo Gloria, 2003).

MacCulloch, Diarmaid, *The Later Reformation in England, 1547-1603* (2nd ed.
New York: Palgrave, 2001).

—. *Thomas Cranmer: A Life* (New Haven: Yale University Press, 1996).

MacGregor, Kirk R., *A Central European Synthesis of Radical and Magisterial
Reform* (Lanham, MD: University Press of America, 2006).

Madsen, Anna M., *The Theology of the Cross in Historical Perspective*
(Eugene, OR: Pickwick, 2007).

Mannermaa, Tuomo. *Christ Present in Faith: Luther's View of Justification*
(ed. Kirsi Stjerna; Minneapolis: Fortress Press, 2005).

Martin, Ralph P., 'Justification.' In Bruce M. Metzger and Michael D. Coogan
(eds), *The Oxford Companion to the Bible* (Oxford: Oxford University Press,
1993).

Matheson, Peter, *Argula von Grumbach. A Woman's Voice in the Reformation*
(Edinburgh: T. & T. Clark, 1995)

—. *The Imaginative World of the Reformation* (Edinburgh: T. & T. Clark,
2000).

McClendon, James W. Jr., *Systematic Theology: Doctrine* (Nashville, TN:
Abingdon Press, 1994).

McCormack, Bruce L., 'Union with Christ in Calvin's Theology: Grounds for a
Divinization Theory?' In David W. Hall (ed.), *Tributes to John Calvin: A
Celebration of his Quincentenary* (Phillipsburg, NJ: Presbyterian &
Reformed, 2010).

—. 'What's at Stake in Current Debates over Justification: The Crisis of Protestantism in the West.' In Mark Husbands and Daniel J. Treier (eds), *Justification: What's at Stake in the Current Debates* (Leicester: IVP, 2004).

McKee, Elsie Anne, 'Context, Contours, Contents: Towards a Description of the Classical Reformed Teaching on Worship,' *Princeton Seminary Bulletin* 16. 2 (January 1, 1995), 172-201.

—. (ed.), *John Calvin: Writings on Pastoral Piety*. The Classics of Western Spirituality (New York: Paulist Press, 2001).

McGrath, Alister E., *Christian Theology. An Introduction* (Oxford: Blackwell, 1994).

—. 'Forerunners of the Reformation? A Critical Examination of the Evidence for Precursors of the Reformation Doctrine of Justification,' *Harvard Theological Review* 75.2 (1982), 219-242.

—. 'Humanist Elements in the Early Reformed Doctrine of Justification,' *Archiv für Reformationsgeschichte* 73 (1 January 1982), 5-20.

—. *Iustitia Dei: A History of the Christian Doctrine of Justification* (Cambridge: Cambridge University Press, 1986).

—. *Iustitia Dei: A History of the Christian Doctrine of Justification* (3rd ed.; New York: Cambridge University Press, 2003).

—. 'Justification.' In Gerald F. Hawthorne, Ralph P. Martin and Daniel G. Reid (eds), *Dictionary of Paul and his Letters* (Leicester: InterVarsity Press, 1993), 517b-523b.

—. *Luther's Theology of the Cross: Martin Luther's Theological Breakthrough* (Grand Rapids: Baker, 1990).

—. *Reformation Thought. An Introduction* (Oxford: Blackwell, 1993).

—. *The Christian Theology Reader* (3rd ed. Malden, Mass.: Blackwell, 2007).

—. *The Intellectual Origins of the European Reformation* (Oxford: Blackwell, 1987).

McLaughlin, Eleanor L., 'Male and Female in Christian Tradition: Was there a Reformation in the Sixteenth Century?' In Ruth Tiffany Barnhouse and Urban T. Holmes III (eds), *Male and Female: Christian Approaches to Sexuality* (NY: Seabury Press, 1976).

McLelland, Joseph, 'Lutheran-Reformed Debate on the Eucharist and Christology.' In Paul McCord and Paul C. Empie (eds), *Marburg Revisited; A Re-examination of Lutheran and Reformed Traditions* (Minneapolis: Augsburg Press, 1966), 39-54.

Meuser, Fred W., 'Luther as Preacher of the Word of God.' In Donald K. McKim (ed.), *The Cambridge Companion to Martin Luther* (Cambridge: Cambridge University Press, 2003), 136-148.

—. *Luther the Preacher* (Minneapolis: Augsburg, 1983).

Moeller, Bernd, 'What Was Preached in German Towns in the Early Reformation?' In C. Scott Dixon (ed.), *The German Reformation: The Essential Readings* (Oxford: Blackwell, 1999), 36-55.

Bibliography

Montgomery, John Warwick, *Christ Our Advocate: Studies in Polemical Theology, Jurisprudence and Canon Law* (Bonn: Verl. für Kultur und Wiss., 2002).

Mosser, Carl, 'The Greatest Possible Blessing: Calvin and Deification,' *Scottish Journal of Theology* 55 (2002), 36-57.

Naphy, William, *Calvin and the Consolidation of the Genevan Reformation* (Louisville: Westminster John Knox Press, 2003).

Needham, Nick, 'Justification in the Early Church Fathers.' In Bruce L. McCormack (ed.), *Justification in Perspective. Historical Developments and Contemporary Challenges* (Grand Rapids: Baker Academic / Edinburgh: Rutherford House, 2006), 25-53.

Nestingen, James, A., 'Challenges and Responses in the Reformation,' *Interpretation* 46.3 (1992), 250-260.

Nichols, James H., 'The Intent of the Calvinistic Liturgy.' In John H. Bratt (ed.), *The Heritage of John Calvin.* Heritage Hall Lectures, 1960-1970 (Grand Rapids: Eerdmans, 1973), 87-109.

Noland, Martin R., 'Luther's Reformation and Its Ongoing Relevance Today,' *Logia* 13.4 (2004), 19-26.

Null, Ashley, *Cranmer's Doctrine of Repentance* (Oxford: Oxford University Press, 2000).

Oberman, Heiko Augustinus, 'Subita Conversion.' In Heiko Oberman (ed.), *Reformiertes Erbe: Festschrift Für Gottfried W. Locher* (Zürich: Theologischer Verlag, 1992), 279-295.

—. *The Dawn of the Reformation* (Edinburgh: T. & T. Clark, 1992).

—. 'The 'Extra'-Dimension in the Theology of Calvin,' *Journal of Ecclesiastical History* 21 (January 1970), 43-64.

Oey, Thomas G., 'Wyclif's Doctrine of Scripture Within the Context of His Doctrinal and Social Ideas' (unpublished doctoral dissertation; Vanderbilt University, 1991).

Parker, T.H.L., *Calvin. An Introduction to His Thought* (London: Geoffrey Chapman, 1995).

—. *John Calvin: A Biography* (Philadelphia: Westminster Press, 1975).

Parsons, Michael, 'Being Precedes Act: Indicative and Imperative in Paul's Writing.' In Brian S. Rosner (ed.), *Understanding Paul's Ethics: Twentieth Century Approaches* (Grand Rapids: Eerdmans / Carlisle: Paternoster, 1995), 217–247.

—. *Calvin's Preaching on the Prophet Micah. The 1550-1551 Sermons in Geneva* (Lewiston: Edwin Mellen, 2006).

—. *Martin Luther's Interpretation of the Royal Psalms: The Spiritual Kingdom in a Pastoral Context* (Lewiston: Edwin Mellen, 2009).

Pattison Bonnie L., *Poverty in the Theology of John Calvin* (Eugene OR: Pickwick, 2006).

Bibliography

Perdersen, Else M.W., 'Justification and Grace. Did Luther Discover a New
Theology or Did he Discover Anew Theology of Justification and Grace?'
*Studia Theologica* 57 (2003), 143-161.

Pelikan, Jaroslav, *Luther the Expositor: Introduction to the Reformer's
Exegetical Writings* (St. Louis: Concordia, 1959).

—. *Reformation of Church and Dogma (1300-1700)*. The Christian Tradition:
A History of the Development of Doctrine, vol. 4 (Chicago: University of
Chicago Press, 1984).

Pettegree, Andrew, *Reformation and the Culture of Persuasion* (Cambridge:
Cambridge University Press, 2005).

Pinnock, Clark H., and Robert C. Brow, *Unbounded Love* (Downers Grove:
InterVarsity Press, 1994).

Poythress, Diane Marie, 'Johannes Oecolampadius' Exposition of Isaiah,
Chapters 36-37' (unpublished doctoral dissertation; Westminster
Theological Seminary, 1992).

Quistorp, Heinrich, *Calvin's Doctrine of Last Things* (Eugene, OR: Wipf and
Stock, 2009).

Rainbow, Jonathan H., 'Double Grace: John Calvin's View of the Relationship
of Justification and Sanctification,' *Ex Auditu* 5 (1989), 99-105.

Raitt, Jill, 'Calvin's Use of Persona.' In *Calvinus Ecclesiae Genevensis Custos*
(Frankfurt -am Main, 1984), 273-287.

Rex, Richard, 'The Crisis of Obedience: God's Word and Henry's
Reformation,' *Historical Journal* 39 (December, 1996), 863-894.

—. *The Lollards* (New York: Palgrave, 2002).

Ridderbos, Herman, *Paul. An Outline of his Theology* (London: SPCK, 1977).

Roberts, Alexander and James Donaldson (eds), *The Ante-Nicene Fathers*, vol.
4 (Grand Rapids, MI: Eerdmans, 1956).

Rupp, E. Gordon, *Patterns of Reformation* (London: Epworth Press, 1969).

—. *Studies in the Making of the English Protestant Tradition* (Cambridge:
Cambridge University Press, 1949).

Russell, William R., *Luther's Theological Testament: The Schmalkald Articles*
(Minneapolis: Fortress Press, 1995).

Ryrie, Alec, 'Divine Kingship and Royal Theology in Henry VIII's
Reformation,' *Reformation* 7 (2002), 49-77.

—. *The Gospel and Henry VIII: Evangelicals in the Early English Reformation*
(Cambridge: Cambridge University Press, 2003).

Sanders, E. P., *Paul and Palestinian Judaism: A Comparison in Patterns of
Religion* (London: SCM, 1977).

—. *Paul, the Law, and the Jewish People* (Philadelphia: Fortress Press, 1983).

Sasse, Hermann, *This is My Body* (Adelaide: Open Book Publishers, 1977
[Augsburg, 1959]).

Scheible, Heinz, 'Philip Melanchthon.' In Carter Lindberg (ed.), *The
Reformation Theologians. An Introduction to Theology in the Early Modern
Period* (Oxford: Blackwell, 2002), 67-82.

Bibliography

Schreiner, Susan E., 'Calvin's Concern with Certainty in the Context of the Sixteenth Century.' In David Foxgrover (ed.), *Calvin, Beza and Later Calvinism* (Grand Rapids: Calvin Studies Society, 2006), 113-131.

Seifrid, Mark A., *Christ, Our Righteousness. Paul's Theology of Justification* (Downers Grove: InterVarsity Press, 2000).

—. 'Luther, Melanchthon and Paul on the Question of Imputation: Recommendations on a Current Debate.' In Mark Husbands and Daniel J. Treier (eds), *Justification: What's at Stake in the Current Debate* (Downers Grove, IL: InterVarsity Press, 2004), 137-152.

—. 'Paul, Luther, and Justification in Gal 2.15-21,' *Westminster Theological Journal* 65.2 (2003), 215-230.

Selbie, W.B. *The Fatherhood of God* (London: Duckworth Press, 1936).

Selderhuis, Herman J., *Calvin's Theology of the Psalms* (Grand Rapids: Baker Academic. 2007).

—. *John Calvin: A Pilgrim's Life* (Downers Grove, IL: InterVarsity Press, 2009).

Shuger, Debora K., 'Faith and Assurance.' In Torrance Kirby (ed.), *A Companion to Richard Hooker* (Leiden: Brill, 2008), 221-249.

Simut, Corneliu C., *The Doctrine of Salvation in the Sermons of Richard Hooker* (New York: Walter de Gruyter, 2005).

Slater, Jonathan, 'Salvation as Participation in the Humanity of the Mediator in Calvin's *Institutes of the Christian Religion*: a Reply to Carl Mosser,' *Scottish Journal of Theology* 58.1 (2005), 39-58.

Smeeton, Donald D., *Lollard Themes in the Reformation Theology of William Tyndale*. Sixteenth Century Essays and Studies, no. 6 (Kirksville, MO: Sixteenth Century Journal Publishers, 1986).

Spijker, Willem van't, '"*Extra nos*" and "*in nobis*" by Calvin in a Pneumatological Light.' In Peter De Klerk (ed.), *Calvin and the Holy Spirit*, (Grand Rapids: Calvin Studies Society, 1989), 39-62.

Spykman, Gordon J., *Reformational Theology. A New Paradigm for Doing Dogmatics* (Grand Rapids: Eerdmans, 1992).

Stacey, John, *John Wyclif and Reform* (Philadelphia: Westminster Press, 1964).

Staehelin, Ernst, *Das Theologische Lebenswerk Johannes Oekolampads*. Quellen und Forschungen zur Reformationsgeschichte 21 (New York: Johnson, 1939).

Starbuck, Margot, *The Girl in the Orange Dress: Searching for a Father Who Does Not Fail* (Downers Grove, InterVarsity Press, 2009).

Steinmetz, David C., 'The Intellectual Appeal of the reformation,' *Theology Today* 57.4 (2001), 459-472.

Stendahl, K., *Paul Among Jews and Gentiles* (Philadelphia: Fortress Press, 1976).

Stephens, W. Peter, 'The Soteriological Motive in the Eucharistic Controversy.' In Willem van't Spijker (ed.), *Calvin: Erbe and Auftrag, Festschrift for W. H. Neuser* (Kampen: Kok Pharos, 1991), 203-213.

# Bibliography

Strehle, Stephen, *The Catholic Roots of the Protestant Gospel: Encounter between the Middle Ages and the Reformation* (New York: Brill, 1995).

Strohl, Henri, *La pensée de la Réforme* (Neuchâtel: Delachaux et Niestlé, 1951).

Tamburello, Dennis E., *Union with Christ: John Calvin and the Mysticism of St. Bernard* (Louisville, KY: Westminster/John Knox, 1996).

Tappert, Theodore G. (ed.), *The Book of Concord: The Confessions of the Evangelical Lutheran Church* (Philadelphia: Fortress Press, 1959).

Thayer, Anne T., *Penitence, Preaching and the Coming of the Reformation* (Aldershot: Ashgate, 2002).

Tidball, Derek J., *Who are the Evangelicals?* (London: Marshall Pickering, 1994).

Tinker, Melvin, 'Language, Symbols and Sacraments: Was Calvin's View of the Lord's Supper Right?' *Churchman* 112.2 (1998), 131-149.

Tomlin, Graham S., 'The Medieval Origins of Luther's Theology of the Cross,' *Archiv für Reformationsgeschichte* 89 (1988), 22–40.

Torvend, Samuel, *Luther and the Hungry Poor. Gathered Fragments* (Minneapolis: Fortress Press, 2008).

Trumper, Tim J.R., 'A Fresh Exposition of Adoption, II: Some Implications,' *Scottish Bulletin of Evangelical Theology* 23.2 (2005), 194-215.

Trueman, Carl R., 'Is the Finnish Line a New Beginning? A Critical Assessment of the Reading of Luther Offered by the Helsinki Circle,' *Westminster Theological Journal* 65.2 (2003), 231-244.

—. 'Justification' in David M. Whitford (ed.), *T&T Clark Companion to Reformation Theology* (London: T. & T. Clark, 2012), 57-71.

—. 'Pathway to Reformation: William Tyndale and the Importance of the Scriptures.' In P.E. Satterthwaite and David F. Wright (eds), *A Pathway into the Holy Scripture* (Grand Rapids: Eerdmans, 1994), 11-29.

Tylenda, Joseph N., 'Calvin's Understanding of the Communication of Properties,' *Westminster Theological Journal* 38.1 (1975), 54-65.

—. 'The Ecumenical Intention of Calvin's Early Eucharistic Teaching.' In Dikran Y. Hadidian (ed.), *Reformatio Perennis. Essays on Calvin and the Reformation in Honor of Ford Lewis Battles* (Pittsburgh: Pickwick Press, 1981), 27-47.

Venema, Cornelis P., 'Union with Christ, the "Twofold Grace of God," and the "Order of Salvation" in Calvin's Theology.' In Joel Beeke (ed.), *Calvin for Today* (Grand Rapids, MI: Reformation Heritage Press, 2010).

Wace, Henry (ed.), *Nicene and Post Nicene Fathers of the Christian Church,* vol. 9 (2nd. Series; New York: Christian Literature Publishing, 1899).

Wainwright, Geoffrey, *Doxology. A Systematic Theology* (London: Epworth Press, 1980).

Wallace, Ronald S., *Calvin's Doctrine of the Christian Life* (Grand Rapids: Eerdmans, 1959).

—. *Calvin's Doctrine of the Word and Sacrament* (Grand Rapids: Eerdmans, 1957).

Wandel, Lee Palmer, *The Eucharist in the Reformation: Incarnation and Liturgy* (New York: Cambridge University Press, 2006).

Werrell, Ralph S., *Theology of William Tyndale* (Cambridge: J. Clarke, 2006).

—. 'Tyndale's Disagreement with Luther in the Prologue to the Epistle to the Romans,' *Reformation and Renaissance Review* 7.1 (2005), 57-68.

Wenger, Thomas L., 'The New Perspective on Calvin: Responding to Recent Calvin Interpretations,' *Journal of the Evangelical Theological Society* 50.2 (2007), 311-328.

Wengert, Timothy J., *Law and Gospel: Philip Melanchthon's Debate with John Agricola of Eisleben over* Poenitentia (Grand Rapids: Baker, 1997).

—. Review of Carl E. Braaten and Robert W. Jenson (eds), *Union with Christ: The New Finnish Interpretation of Luther*, *Theology Today* 56 (1999), 432-434.

Willis, E. David, *Calvin's Catholic Christology: The Function of the So-Called Extra Calvinisticum in Calvin's Theology* (Leiden: Brill, 1966).

—. 'Calvin's Use of Substantia.' In *Calvinus Ecclesiae Genevensis Custos* (Frankfurt -am Main, 1984), 289-301.

—. 'The *Unio Mystica* and the Assurance of Faith According to Calvin.' In Willem van't Spijker (ed.), *Calvin: Erbe and Auftrag, Festschrift for W. H. Neuser* (Kampen: Kok Pharos, 1991).

Wilterdink, Garret A. 'The Fatherhood of God in Calvin's Thought,' *Reformed Review* 30 (1976), 9-22.

Wright, David F., 'Justification in Augustine.' In Bruce L. McCormack (ed.), *Justification in Perspective* (Grand Rapids: Baker Academic / Edinburgh: Rutherford House, 2006), 55-72.

Wright, N.T., *Justification: God's Plan and Paul's Vision* (Downers Grove, IL: InterVarsity Press Academic, 2009).

—. 'New Perspectives on Paul.' In Bruce L. McCormack (ed.), *Justification in Perspective. Historical Developments and Contemporary Challenges* (Grand Rapids: Baker Academic / Edinburgh: Rutherford House, 2006), 243-264.

—. *The Climax of the Covenant: Christ and the Law in Pauline Theology* (Minneapolis: Fortress Press, 1991).

—. 'The Paul of History and the Apostle of Faith,' *Tyndale Bulletin* 29 (1978), 61-88.

Yarnell, Malcolm B., III., *The Formation of Christian Doctrine* (Nashville: Broadman and Holman, 2007).

Zachman, Randall C., *John Calvin as Teacher, Pastor, and Theologian: The Shape of His Writings and Thought* (Grand Rapids: Baker Academic. 2006).

—. *The Assurance of Faith: Conscience in the Theology of Martin Luther and John Calvin* (Louisville, KY: Westminster/John Knox Press, 1993).

Zahl, Paul F.M., 'Mistakes of the New Perspective on Paul,' *Themelios* 27.1 (2001), 5-11.

# Author Index

# Author index

Janetzki, E.W.,    11 fn.45
Jenson, R.W.,    31 fn.3
Johnson, M.P.,    14 fn.66

Kadia, H.O.,    119 fn.10
Kärkkäinen, V.-M.,    118 fn.7, 126 fn.44
Kelley, R.A.,    120 fn.14, 123-24, 129
Kim, J.S.,    109, 109 fn.36, 110
Klassen, Walter,    58 fn.1
Klassen, William,    58 fn.1
Köhler, W.,    21 fn.27
Kolb, R,    118 fn.7, 119 fn.9, 122 fn.29, 129-30, 134
Kreitzer, B.,    17 fn.8
Küng, H.,    xi

Lahey, S.E.,    166 fn.3, 168
Lane, A.N.S.,    1 fn.2, 101 fn.4, 141
Lawrence, J.D.,    1 fn.2
LeCerf, A.,    97 fn.52
Lehmann, D.,    17 fn.5
Levy, I.C.,    168 fn.12
Lewis, P.,    2 fn.4
Lidgett, S.J.,    78 fn.21
Lindberg, C.,    14, 14 fn.65
Lloyd, C.,    155 fn.36
Loewenich, W. von,    119 fn.9
Lohse, B.,    17 fn.4

MacCulloch, D.,    170, 174
MacGregor, K.R.,    59 fn.4, 58-71
MacKenzie, C.A.,    16-29
Madsen, A.M.,    118 fn.7
Mannermaa, T.,    31 fn.3
Martin, Ralph, P.,    x
Matheson, P.,    8 fn.31, 10, 10 fn.42
McClendon, J.W.,    x
McCormack, B.,    103-104, 103 fn.15

McGrath, A.E.,    x, 4, 4 fn.9, 5 fn.14, 13, 13 fn.57, 14, 14 fn.67, 32, 32 fn.5, 36 fn.31, 44, 45, 46, 47-48, 49, 52, 54, 56, 119 fn.9, 121, 121 fn.18, 139, 158 fn.53, 166, 170-71, 172, 173, 174-75, 178
McLaughlin, E.,    73, 75
McLelland, J.,    86 fn.2
Meuser, F.W.,    17 fn.5, 17 fn.6
Miller, E.,    47 fn.18
Miller, L.,    46 fn.7
Moeller, B.,    17 fn.8
Montgomery, J.W.,    45 fn.4

Nestingen, J.A.,    7 fn.23
Nichols, J.H.,    97 fn.51
Noland, M.R.,    14 fn.66
Null, A.,    162 fn.78

Oberman, H.,    6 fn.19
O'Kelley, A.,    30-43

Packer, J.I.,    172-73
Parker, T.H.L.,    9, 9 fn.41, 74 fn.5, 75 fn.8, 117
Parsons, M.,    1-15, 4 fn.10, 12 fn.54, 125 fn.37, 126 fn.45, 127 fn.49
Pattison, B.,    117-137, 127 fn.48, 133 fn.71
Pedersen, E.M.W.,    1 fn.2
Pelikan, J.,    18 fn.13, 71 fn.76
Pettegree, A.,    17 fn.7
Pinnock, C.,    6, 6 fn.16
Price, T.S.,    138-149
Poythress, D.,    48

Quistorp, H.,    113 fn.63

Rainbow, J.H.,    88 fn.13
Rex, R.,    150, 153, 166 fn.4
Ridderbos, H.,    3 fn.6
Ross, H.C.,    165-79

198

## Scripture Index

9.3    123 fn.30
10.9    65 fn.47
10.10    142
12.1    55
13    152, 154
13.1-7    161
14.1f.    145

*1 Corinthians*
1    140
1.17-2.8    120, 122
1.30    33, 88
1.30-31    140
6.11    2
14    18

*2 Corinthians*
5.21    72
12.10    131-32,
   137

*Galatians*
2.16    4, 38
3.10    35
3.13    4
4.4-5    4
4.6    72
4.10    145
5.5    4

*Ephesians*
2.10    147

*Colossians*
2.16    145

*1 Timothy*
2.4    62 fn.32
4.3-4    145
4.6    11

*2 Timothy*
2.11    127 fn.49
2.13    82

*Titus*
2.11    163
3.7    2

*Hebrews*
6.4-8    68
8    63 fn.34
10.24    47, 56

*1 Peter*
2    140, 154, 161
3.9    62 fn.32
3.20    67

*2 Peter*
2.20-22    68

*1 John*
2.19    69
3.1    82
3.10    50

## General Index

# General index

Royal Supremacy, 151, 154, 158-59, 159-60

Salcot, John, 156
Sampson, Richard, 150, 151-52, 164
sanctification, 4, 4 fn.10, 46 fn.11, 87, 93-94, 101, 105, 105 fn.24, 108, 149, 170
Satan, 60, 62, 65, 67
Saul, 41
scandals, 122-37
Scripture, 1, 10, 12, 35, 36, 39, 73, 77, 108, 112, 157, 166, 168, 173
self-righteousness, 7
Seymour, Edward, 174
sin(s), 3, 7, 11, 15, 18, 21, 26, 33, 35, 36, 38, 40, 42, 53-54, 60 fn.16, 61, 67, 68, 97, 114, 119, 123, 133, 140, 145, 175
Spalatin, Georg, 133 fn.73
suffering, 63, 63 fn.34, 66, 74, 117-37

Tertullian, 146
*theologia crucis*, 117-37
*theologia gloriae*, 120, 128, 129, 130, 131

Thirlby, Thomas, 156
Travers, Walter, 175, 176
Turretin, François, 46 fn.7
Tyndale, William, 165, 169-72, 178, 179

union with Christ, 87-91

*via moderna*, the, 31, 32
von Grumbach, Argula, 8 fn.31

Wartburg, the, 20
will, the, 40-41
Wolmar, Melchior, 74
works, 7, 16, 21, 24, 25 fn.4, 31-32, 34, 35, 37-38, 40, 46, 50, 51, 52, 53 fn.46, 54, 55, 56, 141, 144, 145, 146, 149, 162-64, 167, 177, 178
Wycliffe, John, 165, 166-68, 169, 178

Zell, Katharina, 8 fn.31
Zwingli, Ulrich, 8 fn.31, 45, 46, 46 fn.7, 47, 86, 91, 92, 93-94, 99

ND - #0095 - 090625 - C0 - 229/152/12 - PB - 9781842277775 - Gloss Lamination